NADIA RAGOZHINA was born in Moscow and moved to the UK in 2000. She is a senior journalist at BBC World News and has also worked for BBC World Service Radio and France 24 in Paris. Nadia writes and blogs about sustainability and zero waste living, which, other than books and her family, is her passion in life. She lives in London with her husband and two daughters. *Worlds Apart* is her first book.

GW00673380

WORLDS APART

The Journeys of My Jewish Family
in Twentieth-Century Europe

Nadia Ragozhina

SilverWood

Published in 2020 by SilverWood Books

SilverWood Books Ltd
14 Small Street, Bristol, BS1 1DE, United Kingdom
www.silverwoodbooks.co.uk

Quote by Gordon Craig (p.198) published with permission
from the Edward Gordon Craig estate

ISBN 978-1-78132-978-8 (paperback)
ISBN 978-1-80042-053-3 (ebook)

British Library Cataloguing in Publication Data
A CIP catalogue record for this book is available from
the British Library

Page design and typesetting by SilverWood Books

To my mother

Contents

Worlds Apart

THE NEYMAN - NEUMAN FAMILY

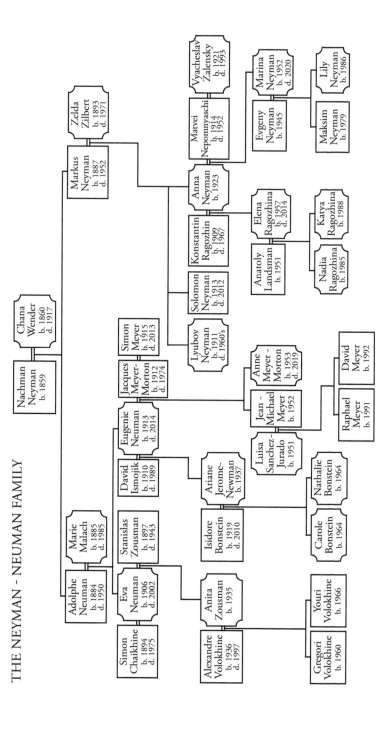

Prologue

When I was growing up, I would spend hours staring at my grandmother's photographs. Kept in an old yellow plastic file, the faded black-and-white images with their vintage scalloped edges had a barely legible scrawl on the back. My grandmother would carefully take them out one by one, trying not to damage her precious archive further. Her wrinkled hands holding onto the prints, her voice strong and powerful, she would talk me through the family neither she nor I had ever met. The backs of the photographs were signed in French and in German, and they were addressed to her father.

I thought that the people in the photographs looked terribly old-fashioned. The ladies with their elegantly feminine dresses and immaculately styled short hair looked like poster girls for the 1930s. The men were dapper in appearance and confident in their posture. I learnt that the glamorous women were my grandmother's cousins Eva and Eugenia, and the men their husbands. They lived in Switzerland, and the pictures had been taken in Geneva many decades ago. The mystery of their lives, the mystery of all that my grandmother didn't know about them and the questions that she couldn't answer haunted me. I was fascinated by their unsmiling faces and tried to imagine the lives they led, the dances the sisters attended and the presents their husbands gave them on their birthdays. I begged for more details. I wanted to know their ages and where they had been born, but I had to settle for very little.

I was also struck by the admiration with which my grandmother talked about her cousins' father – her uncle, Adolphe. He was an intelligent man who made the right choices in life, I was told, and his family lived a happy life in Switzerland. In the photo of Adolphe, I could see a stern-looking gentleman in an expensive white suit, but his eyes betrayed a kindness that I recognised from the photos of his brother Marcus – my grandmother's father and my great-grandfather. The two brothers shared a heavy build and looked alike.

Adolphe had gone to Switzerland in search of work. There, he found a trade and started a family, and eventually became a wealthy man. In Russia, which my great-grandfather Marcus set as his destination a decade later, the unpredictability of the Soviet system ultimately ruined him and his family. The two brothers left Warsaw, escaping poverty, a lack of jobs and the uncertainty of being Jewish in Russian Poland at the turn of the twentieth century.

Sitting in our Moscow apartment with the photos spread out on the bed in front of me, I tried to imagine Adolphe and Marcus. I pictured them as young boys growing up on the streets of Warsaw almost a century earlier. I had little to go by but I already knew that the decisions they made in their youth changed the course of their lives. And those choices were the reason why my grandmother had never met her cousins, and why I had to learn about my extended family through an old bundle of family mementos.

Many years later we were living in London, and I decided that it was time to find our Swiss family. I wanted to know if Eva and Eugenia's descendants still lived in Geneva, and connect the dots. One afternoon in late spring, as my mother and I attempted to retrace Adolphe's steps, we stumbled upon a genealogy website. The sun was setting and the living room of our Greenwich home was getting dark as we scrolled through hundreds of entries of people with similar surnames.

When we found Adolphe's name, and those of his daughters, we couldn't believe our eyes. It was an utterly surreal moment – the names my mother had heard as a little girl, the names she learnt never to utter outside the house, were in front of her in black and white.

When the two brothers said goodbye they could not have imagined that they would never see each other again, and that it would be another hundred years until their granddaughters would meet and start piecing together their family history.

And this is the story of this book. It is the story of two brothers who grew up and went searching for a better life. It is also the story of their daughters, and their granddaughters, and what happened to them as they lived through the political upheavals of the twentieth century.

Part One

1

Like a fairy tale

Geneva, 2010

'It's like a fairy tale!' Anna exclaimed to her cousin Eugenia, as they sat together one Sunday afternoon.

The autumn light seeping through the partially draped rectangular windows gave Eugenia's daughter's living room a cosy and relaxing glow, creating a perfect mood for the occasion. Sitting up straight on the modern white sofa in the middle of the room, Anna was too distracted to appreciate her surroundings. She was overwhelmed by the moment. Seeing her cousin for the very first time, my grandmother thought of her favourite poem by Heinrich Heine, and she recited the German words she had treasured since she first learnt them as a schoolgirl in Moscow nearly seven decades ago:

Ich weiß nicht, was soll es bedeuten
Daß ich so traurig bin,
Ein Märchen aus alten Zeiten,
Das kommt mir nicht aus dem Sinn.[1]

Suddenly, Eugenia started singing the same words, the lyricism of the writing reinforced by the melody of the song. Her now fragile voice added to the sadness of the poem. Anna's eyes glistened with tears as she clasped her hands, laughing.

Neither Anna nor Eugenia ever expected to meet in person. When they finally came face to face, they just looked at each other, searching for physical signs of resemblance, signs that would tell everyone that they were first cousins, almost sisters. Anna's miniature frame paled in comparison to her older cousin, who had a more imposing presence. Together they gave away a family trait that until then I had considered to be a beauty myth – an astonishing lack of wrinkles on their faces despite their age. As they sat together on the sofa, clasping hands and trying to find the right words for the occasion, it was the old German ballad that finally brought the tears and the sadness that both had felt since their meeting had become a possibility.

They thought back to their childhoods, and of the years gone by. They talked of what could have been had life not taken their fathers on such divergent paths, and they dreamt of having had a lifetime together. On the wall, overlooking the living room, a portrait of Adolphe hung in a beautiful frame of light brown oak, observing his daughter and his niece. He could not have foreseen that in the end the two families would be reunited, and as you looked at his portrait, you could almost imagine his face breaking into a smile.

Anna and Eugenia tried to make up for years of lost time. How do you get to know somebody you've known about your whole life but have

---

1   I do not know what it might bode
    That I should be so sad,
    A fairy tale from long ago
    Now will not leave my head. *(Translated by Anna Leader)*

never met? Do you start with their marriage, or their best years? Do you talk about the children and the grandchildren, and share the little details about your current life? You could also talk about the Second World War – some of the worst years you have both experienced – in the hope that sharing those moments might bring you closer. There is no right or wrong, no obvious solution. For Anna and Genia, as she is known in the family, there were whole decades to talk through. For a while the conversation lingered in the air, as the cousins were unable to take the plunge and settle on the most important, the most interesting or the most urgent.

At eighty-six years old, Anna didn't want to talk about herself. Again and again, she repeated that she had had a difficult time when she was married, but it was even worse when she was on her own, and the Soviet Union was a terrible place to live. She was much more comfortable interrogating her cousin, trying to get the answers to as many questions as she could think of, and Genia, who at almost ninety-seven was still as happy to talk and tell stories as she had ever been, happily obliged.

Anna and Genia might have felt that time around them stood still, but they were not alone. Their children, grandchildren and great-grandchildren, we were all there as well, curiously watching the two old ladies and eagerly listening to their conversation. One by one, people came closer to the white sofa in the middle of the room, where the two matriarchs, with their short bobbed hair styled to perfection and their best outfits on display to mark the occasion, were lost in conversation and a bubble of memories. A minute later one of Genia's granddaughters was sitting on the sofa next to her; Anna moved a little closer to her cousin to allow her daughter Elena to sit down on the other side of her.

There were too many people to name everyone, too many names to throw into the story at once, but as I looked around the room, I was overwhelmed by the sense that we were one family. I felt the link to Adolphe, no doubt helped by his likeness to his brother, my great-grandfather, Marcus. I wanted to know more about my cousins, their reaction to our sudden appearance in their lives, and what they knew about our side of the family from their father and grandfather.

Over the following years we would get to know one another better, exchanging stories from our lives and frequently travelling between London and Geneva for long weekends and each other's birthdays. That day, we were all spellbound by Genia and the stories she told about her life. Despite her age and poor mobility, her presence in the room was striking. Speaking a mix of French (to her family), English (to my mother) and German (to my grandmother, who had learnt the language as a schoolgirl in Moscow and taught it for many years), Genia entertained us with stories of her life and reminisced about the past.

Genia's first marriage took her to Palestine in the mid-1930s, when thousands of Jews were fleeing the anti-Semitic laws of Nazi Germany. She witnessed the development and construction of Tel Aviv in its early days,

Two branches of the family meet for the first time in Geneva, October 2010

Top row (from left to right): Raphael Meyer, Youri Volokhine, Delphine Volokhine, Michal Yaron, Luisa Meyer, Jean-Michel Meyer, Nathalie Bonstein, Nadia Ragozhina, Katya Ragozhina

Middle row (from left to right): Carole Bonstein, Elena Ragozhina, Anita Volokhine, Ariane Bonstein

Bottom row: Anna Nepomnyaschaya, Eugenia Meyer-Neuman

but didn't stay long enough to see it prosper and turn into the modern city that it is today. Her life took her back to Europe where she partied in Paris and broke hearts in Geneva, making her way through life with a confidence and panache that would have been unthinkable to my grandmother in the Soviet Union. As I listened to Genia, I could see the emotion in my grandmother's eyes – a rare sight that gave so much away. She couldn't help but compare Genia's story to her own life, lived in what she felt was a parallel universe. Unlike Anna, Genia didn't dwell on the past. She didn't immediately bring back the worries of the war years spent far away from her family, or the challenges that she faced later in life.

As I observed Anna and Eugenia, I couldn't help but think about life, and the twists and turns it throws to those who are simply trying to live it. The turns of fate. My mother, Elena, often said that you were the master of your fate, and that the decisions you made defined your future. It was her philosophy in life, and she often thought of the choices her grandfather Marcus had made and the reasons that took him to Russia. With the gift of hindsight it was clear to both my mother and my grandmother that they would have had an easier life had he followed his brother Adolphe to Switzerland. Listening to Genia's stories of holidays in the South of France and Venice, or looking at the photos of family trips skiing in the Alps, they couldn't shake off the feeling that Marcus had drawn the short straw, and that the lives of their Swiss relatives had been happier, freer and more fortunate.

Back home in London, as I listened to my mother and grandmother compare the Soviet repressions they had lived through to the calm post-war years of Switzerland, or their holidays in Odessa and Crimea to the luxury and glamour of Monaco and Biarritz, I was shocked to see how my mother, the most confident and positive person I had ever known, was suddenly overcome by pity towards herself and her former life. My mother always taught me that the glass was half full rather than half empty, but the visit to Geneva brought back memories of her childhood, and the comparison was difficult to resist.

The family visit to Geneva had a lasting effect, but it wasn't long until my mother's usual spirit and candour prevailed and she found her own way of recounting our family story. With that familiar spark in her eyes, she would tell friends and acquaintances that one of the brothers was clever, and the other one – an idiot. And that she was a descendant of the idiot. She was, of course, only jokingly referring to her grandfather Marcus, whom she had never met, as the foolish one, but most listeners found it difficult to believe that she, a successful career woman running a business in London, would be so disparaging of her grandfather.

That was my mother's way of dealing with life, but the strength of her belief that we were on the side of the stupid brother made me want to know more about the life of the so-called clever brother, Adolphe, and his family. Not only to see the contrast of their lives, but also to see how their experiences could relate to what my mother and grandmother went through.

What I learnt after only a few months of research became the foundation of this book. I felt as if I was rediscovering European history all over again. I found myself on the pages of the history books I had always loved, but this time it was the history of my own family that I was reading. I could see how some of the most significant political events of the last century influenced the lives of Adolphe's and Marcus' children, separating their destinies further than they could have ever imagined. I was fascinated by how alive history suddenly felt, and I became determined to bring those stories to life.

Very quickly, I also learnt that life is never as simple as we are led to believe. As I discovered some of the terrifying episodes in the lives of Adolphe and his daughters, I asked myself whether it is ever possible to compare people's experiences in different circumstances. Whether it is ever appropriate to say to those who lived through the horrors of the Nazi occupation that their lives had been better or worse, easier or more difficult than the lives of those who had lived under Stalin's rule of terror in the Soviet Union. Or could the experience of the Second World War in Russia be described using the same words applied to the tragic scenes witnessed in Western Europe? When viewed through the prism of one family, with the stories and experiences of my relatives competing for my attention, I realised that it is, of course, never possible to compare individual suffering. The lives of Eva and Eugenia might have seemed easy and carefree to my mother and grandmother, but each family has its own history, with the tragedies and successes that define it. Without diminishing the hardships of my family during the years of the Soviet Union, seeing what the other side went through in Western Europe gave me a valuable perspective with which to tell both their stories.

And as with any family history, there were many gaps to fill. In trying to piece together what happened to Adolphe and Marcus, I scoured archives and databases, and used all the letters from the past that I could find. I pored over the thick yellowing notebooks of the diaries that Adolphe's elder daughter, Eva, kept for many years and tried to visit all the places where my relatives had ever lived to be able to better imagine the lives they led. But I have very much had to rely on the memories of my grandmother and my family in Geneva, nagging them all with endless questions, asking them to imagine things they could have never known and begging them to remember just a little bit more. And it is strange, the things we remember. And the things we choose to forget. As Marcel Proust famously wrote, 'Remembrance of things past is not necessarily the remembrance of things as they were.' And even though this is certainly true of this story, who am I to say what is remembered correctly and what is misremembered by any one of my characters?

2

Nalewki Street

Warsaw, early 1900s

Nalewki Street was the centre of their life. Adolphe and Marcus would
run there from their home in the neighbourhood whenever they had a
chance. The heart of Jewish life in Warsaw, Nalewki Street was unlike
any other street in the city, and the boys were both fascinated by it and
terrified of it in equal measure. Throngs of men of all ages could be seen
rushing back and forth selling their wares, gesticulating wildly as they
tried to navigate the human sea in front of them. Trams ran at full speed,
laden with people and heavy goods, announcing their approach with loud
bells. The street was a beehive of tension and energy. And everywhere
you looked, there were tall four-storey houses adorned with signboards.

You could come back to the street every single day and discover a new sign advertising another shop or business, selling leather, soap, fabrics and fresh produce. There might be a shop on the ground floor, and a workshop or a factory on the first floor and at the very top in the attic. These buildings were also densely populated by the men on the street and their families – but the women were hidden away, looking after the house and the younger children, or busy in the workshop, tailoring, cutting and sewing fabrics that would later be taken to one of the shops to be sold.

Adolphe and Marcus came here to watch in fascination, trying not to get knocked over by a grumpy tradesman or his tired horse as they approached the warehouse after a long journey to the Polish capital. The noise and the smell were overpowering – there was no hiding the thousands of people who came to this street trying to make a living.

In the courtyards and in the backyards, away from the cobbles of the main street, there were also shops, shops and more shops. The houses were dirty from all the people they held, from all the activity that only stopped with the setting of the Friday sun. The Yeshiva boys, learning the Torah and ignoring the goings-on of this world were tucked away in the far corner of some of the buildings. Only occasionally one of them looked out of the window to the chaos below.

Over the years, Nalewki Street had not only provided the best entertainment for Adolphe and Marcus, but it was also the best distraction from their family life. Since their father, Nachman, abandoned his family and went in search of a better life in America, never to be heard from again, the two brothers sought every opportunity to escape their tiny apartment. Nachman had had big dreams and promised his sons that they would travel to join him in the United States, where life would be less hectic and more prosperous. But instead, they were forced to watch their mother frantically take odd jobs to support her growing boys and provide a roof over their heads.

The family was not used to living in need. Just several years before Nachman's departure they walked the few blocks to Nalewki Street together to pose for a photograph. Adolphe, a serious-looking boy of eight, protectively held Marcus' hand. His younger brother, at five years old, hadn't shed the cuteness of a toddler, but was already trying to imitate the serious faces of his father and brother. The Neyman family were posing together for the last time, oblivious of the impact their imminent separation would have on their lives.

I discover this photo by chance over a year into the writing of this book in one of the long-forgotten family albums in Geneva, and it leaves me speechless. I can finally see the whole family together. It is a snapshot of history, an extra piece of the puzzle, further evidence that this story started in Warsaw, just as I had been told. But for the two brothers, it was the last family memento before their father abandoned them for a better life across the Atlantic.

The boys' mother, Chana, had to make tough choices. Adolphe, as the eldest, was chosen to continue his studies and get an education. He made sure that his brother, only three years younger, wasn't far behind by bringing his classmates back home with him after school to help Marcus keep up with at least some of the disciplines. The boys still snuck out to Nalewki and other neighbourhood streets, where they were free to roam around, but Adolphe took his education seriously. Even on the street, he explained the realities of life to his brother, and together they took odd jobs where they could. The money was helpful, but it was the interaction with the people that Adolphe treasured the most. The melting pot of Jews from all walks of life fascinated him, and as a local boy fluent in Yiddish and Polish, as well as Russian, he understood the mechanics of business and trade that made this small world go round. Marcus wasn't far behind, but already he was finding himself more detached from the Jews he came across in the neighbourhood.

Soon a young man of sixteen years old, Marcus was drawn towards the newspaper sellers and publishers advertising their latest tracts and essays in the shop windows. Between the Zionist publications propagating the restoration of the Jewish homeland in Palestine, and the Bundist writings of the secular Jewish labour movement, as well as the tsarist, communist and religious literature available on the streets, Marcus was

Marcus and Adolphe with their parents Nachman and Chana Neyman.
Warsaw c 1891

quickly learning about the world he inhabited. Some of the ideas that he picked up through his debates with the street sellers, and his brother at home, would eventually come to define his life.

Adolphe's future was the first to be decided. At the age of twenty-one and while studying pharmacy at the University of Warsaw, he met the girl who would change the course of his life. Marie Malach, a dark-haired beauty with pale skin, came from a religious family. Soon after they were married, they decided to join Marie's older sister in Switzerland. It was not an easy choice to make, but the promise of jobs and stability in a small central European country influenced their decision. It was certainly the right time to be heading West, away from the increasingly anti-Semitic moods of the Pale of Settlement, the territory where Eastern Europe's Jews had been allowed to live since Catherine the Great's decree at the end of the eighteenth century, and towards new opportunities.

Marcus was devastated at his brother's departure. He promised to consider joining him in the near future, but it was more of a reassurance; both brothers knew that Marcus was unlikely to make the journey. His life was still firmly set in Warsaw and he would stay behind to look after their elderly mother.

Adolphe and Marcus. Warsaw, 1905

Before Adolphe left, as had become the family tradition, the two young men returned one last time to Nalewki Street, the scene of their childhood exploits, to pose for a final photograph. Adolphe, standing slightly forward from his younger brother on the left of the photo, and Marcus, slightly behind him on the right, stare ahead. In their faces, I try to glimpse the courage and determination that I know they would have had to rely on in the coming years. As they posed for the camera, they were undoubtedly contemplating how much their lives were about to change and hoping that they would see each other again.

3

A new life

Grenchen, Switzerland, 1905

At the foot of the Jura Mountains in Switzerland lies the town of Grenchen. Those living here over one hundred years ago would not recognise it today. It has been transformed by the watchmaking industry, as it was here that some of the first factories were created, based on specialised workshops that were more common in the previous century. Moving to this Swiss-German town would tie Adolphe's life with a trade that is seen as fundamentally Swiss.

Grenchen was also a new experience for Marie. Growing up with two brothers, Adash and Hillel, and three sisters, Paula, Berthe and Mania, crowded together in a small living space all her life, Marie had experienced hardship and poverty. As a girl she had been lucky to survive the typhus epidemic that killed her father, leaving her mother and five siblings almost destitute. The children would often go without shoes and Marie, as one of the oldest, would help her mother look after the younger children and cook for the family. The noise and smell of the family apartment would stay with Marie for the rest of her life, but her tough upbringing had also given her the strength and determination to embrace life and make necessary adjustments to improve it for herself and her loved ones.

The busy streets of Warsaw's Jewish neighbourhoods now seemed far away. Grenchen was heavenly in its peace and tranquillity. The population was barely 5,000 people and the air was still. Marie was often startled when she was woken by birdsong in the morning. She walked the streets to explore her surroundings and tried to take in the serenity of this almost village-like town. The quiet cobbled streets eventually gave way to unpaved roads leading to farms further out in the fields. The town was dominated by the tall spires of the Town Hall and the St Eusebius Church. The elaborate windows and masonry work of the Town Hall were reminiscent of some of the older Polish buildings Marie had seen in Warsaw's richer neighbourhoods, but she decided that she much preferred the local *Gemeindehaus*,[2] for its picturesque setting amid the greenery of the valley with the rolling hills in the distance.

The town lived its life in a measured and organised way. The local school, the church and the post office functioned in a quiet, dignified manner, and to Marie's foreign eye, it was perfect. But the pace of life was almost too quiet for the newly arrived couple.

Marie's sister Paula was there to welcome them to Grenchen. Family legend has it that Adolphe's first question was about the nearest university. He would have liked to continue his studies. But, with only twenty roubles in his pocket, enough to live on for a week or two, he was quickly disillusioned. With what money Adolphe and Marie had, they found a tiny room to rent, bought linen and cutlery, and tried to settle into their new lives.

---

2 Community hall (German)

31

At the turn of the twentieth century, Switzerland was not the beacon of economic stability we have come to see it as today. However, Adolphe and Marie arrived in Grenchen at one of the most exciting times for the country's watchmakers. In the previous twenty years the Swiss had realised that they would have to up their game if they wanted to beat the American manufacturers in the ever-competitive battle to dominate the watchmaking industry. The US factories had been the first to adopt mass production of watches, but the Swiss were learning fast. They knew their big advantage was their reputation for superior quality and that they needed to find a way to achieve mass production while maintaining that integrity. The solution was a system they called *etablissage*. The Swiss embraced mass production. Large centralised factories were now producing high quality standardised parts. In addition, traditional artisans who had previously been working in small workshops were now brought on to the factory floor and incorporated into the bigger picture. Lower-skilled workers were hired to operate the in-house parts assembly, increasing the speed and volume to match American-style production. By creating these hybrid factories, the Swiss revolutionised the industry.

For Adolphe and Marie, the timing was perfect. People were needed to work in the growing trade, and very soon they were learning their new craft in a factory specialised in making pocket watches. Each worker had to buy his own tools, lamp and a stool to sit on. It was an expensive investment for the young newlyweds, but after the initial training was complete Marie was earning five francs a day. Adolphe, who was considered to be less skilful, only earned three francs, but with their combined earning of eight francs, they were able to maintain a simple home.

The factory was the centre of Marie and Adolphe's new life. In several large rooms with tall windows to let in as much light as possible, nearly a hundred workers put together pieces of a complicated mechanism that would eventually make a watch. Despite the technical advances, skilful artisans were still needed to ensure the quality and the alignment of the timepiece. The assembly required meticulous cleanliness, and the oiling process was an art in itself. The timing, the main prerequisite of any good watch, was certainly made easier by the new instruments, but it was the theoretical knowledge of the engineer combined with his skill that would help produce a watch worthy of the Swiss name and reputation.

From morning till night, ten hours a day, every day of the week, the husband-and-wife team worked to build the foundation of their lives together. It was tiring, back-breaking work, and the level of concentration required made their eyes hurt when they came home, but they persevered. They set aside all the money they earned and made plans for the future. Adolphe was an intelligent man and very adaptable to new cultures and possibilities. He didn't dwell on the changes in his life, and he didn't let his thoughts wander back to the busy streets of Warsaw, for it was the company of his friends and their evening discussions that he missed the most. He appreciated that in this new place he could find stability and an income, which would allow him to start the family he had always wanted.

The first decade of the twentieth century saw the arrival of other Jews in the village. Among others, Jacob Grünberg and the Stroun brothers, who would later become Adolphe's business partners, were settling in Grenchen, forming a strong core of young Jews and the foundation of a future Jewish community in the area. They had all escaped the borders of the Pale of Settlement and were now talking politics among themselves. There was a lot to discuss. 1906 was a turbulent year for Russia. After the unsuccessful Revolution of the previous year, a constitution had been agreed, which stated that the tsar would share his absolute power with a parliament – a significant new development in Russian politics that would eventually pave the way for the abolition of the monarchy more than a decade later. Adolphe was closely following the developments in Russia, and his thoughts often turned to his brother.

As Adolphe and Marie made more acquaintances and familiarised themselves with life in a foreign country, Adolphe was noticed on the factory floor for his leadership skills and efficiency in organising people. He might not have been the best craftsman due to his relatively late

33

Marie Neuman. Grenchen, 1905

introduction to the trade, but as the process became more automated, and more supervision was required, he was promoted to head the atelier and ensure its smooth operation.

On 5 November 1906, Adolphe became a father. The birth of his daughter, Eva, was a proud moment in his life. Marie and Adolphe both continued working, and Marie walked to work with Eva strapped to her chest. It wasn't until Eva was old enough to start walking herself that doctors noticed that she had been born with a congenital dislocation of the hip – a devastating diagnosis. There are many treatments available for the condition today, but at that time, there was little the doctors could do. At one appointment after another, taking their daughter around the country seeking help, Adolphe and Marie were repeatedly told that Eva would struggle to walk properly. The doctors thought that the little girl would be in too much pain to learn to use her legs, which in the best-case scenario would leave her on crutches or in a wheelchair for the rest of her life. Adolphe didn't take the news well. For the rest of his life he would be embarrassed to have a disabled daughter.

Eva would grow up with a strong sense of shame of her condition and the effect it had had on her father. But as a little girl, she was a determined toddler, and she overcame the pain. She waddled along as she learnt to walk, her mother's protective hands guiding her from chair to table and onwards to the bed. It was a daily struggle and Marie gave up work to be able to support her daughter at home. Eva's task should have been almost impossible given her disability, but she walked. With one leg seven centimetres shorter than the other by the time she would finish growing, she would nevertheless learn to play tennis and go hiking, sometimes feeling that she had to prove to herself and to those around her that she was capable of a normal life. She used all her strength and resolve to fight the pain and walk, but she would limp for the rest of her life.

4

The Swiss dream

1910s–1920s

I didn't get a chance to meet Eva. By the time I rediscovered our Swiss family she would have been over a hundred years old, had she lived. So it was her younger sister who had to fill in the missing details.

Named after the Austrian Empress, Eugenia was born in the dying days of the Austro-Hungarian Empire on 19 June 1913. Her birth in the Austrian town of Bludenz came during one of Adolphe's many relocations around the region, where he had been busy setting up factories and ateliers for his employers. Soon after the birth of his second daughter, he moved the family back to Switzerland, this time to the small town of Biel. Later came another move, to the capital of the canton, the slightly bigger town of Solothurn. All these beautiful places with their red-tiled roofs and Swiss houses with square windows were just names on the map for Eva and her little sister, and when I ask Genia to tell me about her childhood, she tells me honestly that she feels like all of them have merged into one.

Solothurn was much bigger than the towns that Marie and Adolphe had made their home since they left Warsaw. The old town was a jewel of the region, made magnificent by the baroque architecture influenced by Italian grandeur, French charm and Swiss-German tradition. Its eleven churches with their green copper domes and tall gothic spires preserved the city's splendour, while the immaculately constructed buildings and the narrow cobblestone streets of the old city gave the place a distinctly medieval feel.

In their small apartment above a watch factory on the outskirts of the city, Adolphe and Marie created an idyllic environment for their daughters. They were sheltered from the world outside, and, at first, the raging Great War went unnoticed.

When Genia was three years old, she suddenly became aware of a world she had been protected from. Solothurn was on a rail route being used to evacuate wounded soldiers from the front line, and from the windows of the family apartment, where she would usually look out to admire the green hills of the Jura, Genia saw a railway carriage full of wounded men with bandages on their heads – soldiers being transported to hospitals by the Red Cross. As she watched the train move slowly past her window, she noticed that the men averted their eyes, almost embarrassed to be seen in their condition, or too weak to make eye contact with the little girl. Genia was shocked by what she saw; she could feel the fear and the pain of the young men, many of whom were destined to die in a hospital bed, never to return home.

Genia was still a little girl, and very soon she was back to playing outside and enjoying her childhood. She took great pleasure in waking up early to see the local farmer dragging his cow through the streets every morning. She could hear them from inside the apartment, the cow moodily resisting the farmer's efforts to get her to the right spot so he could milk her in front of the amused children whose mothers had sent them out to get fresh milk. Genia waited impatiently for her bucket to be filled with the warm liquid, and when the farmer was finished, Marie came outside to help her carry it back.

This was the beginning of a normal day in the family. Having had her milk for breakfast, Eva would prepare to walk to the nearby school. She was jealous of her little sister, who got to stay at home and play. Seven years old by the time Genia was born, Eva had found the past few years hard, and the two girls often fought for their parents' attention. Eva had distant memories of the day her life changed with Genia's arrival – for a long time she had been expecting a stork to appear and bring them her baby sister. When her parents told her that her sister had arrived and she could come and meet her, she was terrified of the huge white bird she imagined would be there with her. *They had to drag me by force, screaming from the fear of finding a gigantic bird by the crib*, she later recorded in her diary.

Genia didn't keep a diary, but if she had, she would have certainly described one of her favourite memories from her childhood – her friend, the parrot. The parrot lived across the street, she tells me, her eyes half closed. One day it simply appeared and took up a permanent position in the window of the elegant white brick house of the neighbours, watching the goings-on of the quiet road and looking at the children playing outside. The children were so curious to see this creature staring at them, watching their every move. But because the parrot didn't seem interested in interacting with Genia and her friends, eventually they forgot about it. Every day Genia's mother would open the window of their second-floor apartment and call out to her daughter to get back inside – '*Genia, khumm! Genia, khumm!*'[3] she would shout. After a few weeks of watching the girl's every move, the parrot learnt to imitate Marie, shouting out of the neighbour's window, imitating her accent: '*Genia, khumm! Genia, khumm!*' My cousin laughs as she recounts the events of more than nine decades ago.

---

3 'Genia, come! Genia, come!' (Swiss German)

38

In a faded black-and-white studio photograph of Genia that dates back to around that time, she is four years old. The little girl looks straight at the camera, so serious, with no hint of a smile. Would she rather be holding her favourite toy instead of the freshly picked bunch of daisies? Maybe she doesn't like her beautiful all-white outfit? Or is it possible that she is already so grown-up that she has adopted the fashion of the time? After all, it was not the done thing to smile for a photograph. I know that's not true, because Genia wasn't that grown-up when she was four years old. She once told me that she was a naughty child, always running around and climbing outside. Every time her mother put a new dress on her it would inevitably get torn by yet another tree branch. In this photo, in a simple outfit of all white, she looks like a little princess. Her hair falls long and loose behind her shoulders.

The second daughter born to my great-grandfather's brother, Eugenia didn't realise how hard her parents had worked to be able to dress her in the beautiful clothes in the photos. What did she think when she later looked at this picture of herself as she was growing up? Four years later she would send a copy to her uncle and aunt in Moscow. She was a lot more grown-up by then, as she proudly wrote on the back of the photo. *Voilà ma photo sur laquelle j'ai seulement 4 an, maintenant j'ai 8 an* [sic]. I was only four years old on the photo, now I am eight, she wrote in the uncertain lettering of a child, struggling with the spelling of a language that was new to her and foreign to both her parents. By then she was living in Geneva, where she had to learn to speak French. There was so much ahead of this girl, who was privileged and would eventually find happiness. That was still to come, and as I gaze at the photograph, I just want her to show me her beautiful smile.

By the time Adolphe relocated the family to Geneva, the war was drawing to its end. It was November 1918, and when the clock towers rang in the armistice, both of his daughters were old enough to remember it. The first family home was on Boulevard de la Cluse. A large cobbled street lined with trees and houses, today it is in one of the central neighbourhoods of

Genia Neuman. 1917

Geneva. Adolphe and Marie found it quiet and almost provincial. The building, constructed in the late nineteenth century, marked a big change from the family living arrangements in the countryside. The apartment was on the ground floor and had a large garden at the back.

The main attraction of Boulevard de la Cluse, as far as Eva and Genia were concerned at least, was the tram line that ran along the road to the nearby tram depot. Two trams operated on their street, and both girls were fascinated by the mechanics and the elaborate design of the metal box that went around the city taking people to their destination. Trams were not a new thing for the city of Geneva, but for the children arriving in the regional capital from the nearby towns and villages, it felt like an adventure.

Adolphe moved to Geneva to be at the heart of the watchmaking industry. Over the past ten years he had trained himself in most of the jobs at his employer's factory. The desire to move to the big city and set up on his own motivated him to understand the most intricate details of the watchmaking process and even take several trips across the Atlantic to learn from the American producers. When Adolphe told his boss in Solothurn that the time had come for him to stand on his own two feet, he was sent on his way with a generous loan of 5,000 Swiss francs – around a hundred thousand US dollars in today's value, by some estimates.

The investment was a huge sign of trust that had been put in Adolphe. In the post-war years of economic uncertainty he was taking an enormous risk by starting a new company. Yet he was a thorough and diligent man, certain of his success.

He went into business with his Grenchen acquaintances, the Stroun brothers. He had known Naum and Samuel since their first humble steps in the new country, and their knowledge would be valuable in the new endeavour. Most importantly, the brothers had made a significant fortune in the last few years and were able to add another 5,000 francs to the project. Adolphe pooled together all his savings and had just enough to begin his adventure.

He called his factory Etna Watch. The agreement was that Adolphe would run the factory without any outside interference from his investors, but at the end of the year he would give the Stroun brothers half the profit, as well as paying off the interest on his boss' share. Adolphe was an entrepreneur in the most classic sense of the word. He had learnt everything there was to learn about the industry, and now that he was starting on his own he had to implement his leadership and management skills to make it work. As in many first-time businesses, once the facilities and equipment were in place and the core workers had been hired, Adolphe was left to do everything else himself. He was now not only running the factory, overseeing the several men who were making the watches, but he was also selling them, making investments and betting on new markets.

Adolphe entered the market at the worst possible time for Swiss watchmakers. The post-war years were volatile, and the industry was struggling. Having finally managed to overtake their US competitors in the years before the First World War, by the time the hostilities were over Swiss watchmakers found that their reputation had suffered a huge blow. During the war Swiss manufacturers had been encouraged to contribute to the war effort, but they ended up selling optic instruments to the British and fuses to the Germans, seeing this as a means of maintaining their neutrality. But the Allies didn't see it that way. The growth of the industry was associated with the sales to the enemy, and Swiss exports to the United States plunged. Unemployment rates went up, meaning that the newly adopted factory-based assembly approach was once again put into question, and the old family-run workshops gained ground.

Adolphe was risking not only his own savings, but also his reputation and the finances entrusted to him by his partners. The stakes couldn't have been higher. Was he hoping that the increased popularity of wristwatches, based on their strong-man, can-do image associated with the battles in the trenches would help the industry get back on its feet?

Wristwatches had indeed entered the public's imagination during the First World War, but I doubt that this trend alone would have been enough for a man as pragmatic and careful as Adolphe. Using his knowledge of the industry on both sides of the Atlantic, he would have noticed that despite the damaged reputation and the volatility over the best practices in the industry, trade with the US was slowly beginning to pick up. The US industry was lagging behind after diverting its attention to helping the war effort, whereas the Swiss maintained their know-how and expertise by simply diversifying their production. While domestic watches were still being produced in America, their movements and parts were imported almost exclusively from Switzerland. Adolphe saw that as an opportunity and decided to make a bet on the US industry: he would concentrate on producing watch parts for export, hoping to capitalise on the Swiss name and renown for the quality of its product. In New York, it was Marie's sister Paula who was now supporting the family enterprise, and at Adolphe's request, she helped him find buyers for his merchandise.

Adolphe's gamble paid off, and in 1925 the family moved to Champel – a quiet residential neighbourhood that was still being built, to the south of the centre of Geneva. This was where the family would live for many years to come – and where Adolphe's granddaughters still reside today. The new family apartment was on the elegant Avenue Peschier. Today, the window shutters on the outside of the building are painted green, blending in gently with the green leaves of the trees in Park Bertrand across the road. The park is so close it is almost a front garden for the building. I imagine Eva and Genia happily exploring its grounds after school, reminiscing about the days they lived in the countryside.

Adolphe also found better premises for Etna Watch. He relocated to Quai du Seujet, on the banks of the river Rhône, where he joined other business owners who were renting sites for factories and storage areas. The densely built-up industrial neighbourhood hid many cobblestoned cul-de-sacs and alleyways, criss-crossing between the main streets. Tucked away were residential balconies with linen hanging out to dry, small ateliers belonging to local tinsmiths, locksmiths and milliners, and many cafes where working men gathered in the evenings.

It was here that Adolphe was able to find a bigger factory space, where he now employed eighty workers. With high ceilings and big windows looking over the river, Adolphe felt very much the factory boss he had always aspired to be. The noisy and at times dirty conditions in this working-class neighbourhood meant that rents were cheaper and labour was easier to find, and when the school day was over the streets teemed with boys and girls looking for food and entertainment. It was in stark contrast to the calm streets of Champel where Adolphe was living with his family, but he felt at home.

He was suddenly transported back to the clatter of Warsaw's Nalewki Street, where as a young boy he first learnt about trade and opportunity. In his new workshop, Adolphe didn't need to sweep the floors himself at the end of the day or look after the heating of the premises; he now had people hired to perform the maintenance tasks. The partnership with the Stroun brothers had paid off, at least so far, and he was looking forward to seeing his returns grow further.

Geneva was a bustling place for a young industrialist like Adolphe. Many of his friends, who, like him, had settled in the small villages of the Jura when they first arrived from Eastern Europe, were now beginning to arrive in the city. In a few years they would become successful lawyers,

Adolphe Neuman (right) at his atelier in Geneva

doctors and professors. In the evenings they gathered around the table to talk politics and world affairs. This was the first time since leaving Warsaw that Adolphe was leading a life that resembled the one he had led in his hometown. He thrived on the intellectual conversations that he had missed so much, and it was an interesting time to be engaging in political matters. Apart from the economic fallout from the Great War, they talked most about the 1917 revolution in Russia. Now that the tsar had been overthrown, Adolphe and his friends were convinced that finally everyone in Russia would benefit from freedom and equality.

Marie listened to her husband's conversations but was wary of taking part herself. She knew her place in the kitchen, and every night she religiously prepared Adolphe's favourite dishes, making sure there was enough left to serve the guests when they arrived. Over the years, the cooking of Madame Neuman – as Adolphe had 'Frenchified' his family's surname from Neyman – would become famous in Geneva's Jewish community. Marie was thriving in her new environment. With the move to Geneva she not only gained more independence and living space, but like her husband, was rediscovering the feel of a community around her. Adolphe's friends' wives got together to gossip and exchange recipes during the day, but most importantly, Marie had been reunited with her sisters.

Since first Paula and then Marie had left Warsaw to start a new life in Switzerland, the rest of the family also quietly migrated West. Paula eventually left Europe to settle in America, but her other sisters, Berthe and Mania, found themselves only a few minutes' walk from Marie's house in Geneva. Their visits to Marie's to say hello in the morning started a family tradition that would last long enough for their children and grandchildren to tell me about it. Aunt Berthe, a solidly built woman who would never shed her thick Yiddish accent and who would forever be mocked for it by her nieces; and the beautiful Aunt Mania, whose life would be tragically cut short during the Second World War, became permanent fixtures in the lives of Eva and Genia. With the discovery of their relatives, their cooking practices and the Yiddish they now heard frequently in the house, Marie's daughters also started asking questions about their Jewish identity.

For Eva, it all fell into place on the first day at school. She was sharing a desk with the girl who would become her best friend – Vera Diakoff. The girls were asked to complete a questionnaire – filling out their names, and the names of their parents, as well as their religious beliefs. When it came to the question about religion, Eva shook her head – she didn't know what that meant, and so she asked the girl sitting next to her to help her answer the question. Vera told Eva to put down the same thing she wrote on her paper – she was Russian Orthodox. That's how Eva discovered, later that day at home, that she was, in fact, Jewish.

Growing up in the small Swiss villages, Eva had been accustomed to speaking Swiss-German at home to her parents and spending time with the local children. She instinctively knew that she was different from the others – she had heard comments from other parents and had noticed the quiet exchanges in a different language between her parents at home, some of which she would eventually learn to understand. But for the first years of her life, she had been completely cut off from the culture and lifestyle her parents had left behind.

Neither Adolphe nor Marie ever wanted to deny their daughters their Jewish heritage. But living in a foreign country surrounded by Christian communities, they had felt safer keeping to themselves and integrating into rural life. Now that they had met other Jews in Geneva, they felt more confident and slowly returned to their old practices.

Passover, one of the most important dates in the Jewish calendar, became Eva and Genia's introduction to the Jewish life of the city. The Starobinskys, a notable family in Geneva that would leave their mark on the charitable and community work during the Second World War, invited Adolphe and his family for the first night of Passover – the first Seder – at their house. There were twenty people around the table, and Eva sat quietly, observing. The reading of the *Hagadah* – the book that sets the order of the night and tells the story of the Jewish Exodus from Egypt – took a long time to get through. Eva was hungry, but the food didn't seem to be coming.

Marie and her daughters, Genia and Eva. Geneva c 1923

She was wondering whether this would be the only night in the calendar where food was not actually on the menu – how terrible and unusual would that have been!

I laugh when I read her account of that night. I can't help but think back to my own first Pesach, experienced at a similar age to Eva. I was fifteen when we were first invited with my parents to celebrate Passover at the house of a family acquaintance in northwest London and, like Eva, I didn't know what to expect. From that year on, Passover became an important part of my life, an opportunity to gather around the table with friends and family, although due to their secular upbringing, never hosted by my parents. But that first night, even though I enjoyed the tradition and the ritual, I also remember being desperate to finally eat! As I reflect on that experience, I think of my cousins, Eva and Genia, and the parallels in our lives. Separated by history and a huge generation gap, our first discovery of our Jewish roots is an achingly similar experience.

Geneva was a revelation for the Neumans. The city became home for Marie and her daughters, enabling Adolphe to build up his business and realise his ambition for the future. But it also took him further away from his humble origins. In just over a decade, the poor boy from Warsaw's Jewish streets became an entrepreneur in one of Europe's prospering metropolises. His daughters would never know the misery of poverty or manual labour that he had endured. Adolphe would never forget the hardship and deprivation he had left behind, aspiring to help those in need and engaging with charitable and philanthropic organisations. Yet his success also set him on a path very different to that of his brother, widening the gap between their fortunes that would last for the duration of their lifetimes.

5

The road East

Russia, 1910s

The bullets that put an end to the lives of Archduke Franz Ferdinand and his wife, Sophie, the Duchess of Hohenberg, changed the course of European history. The chaos of war that swept across Europe within weeks of the death of the heir to the Austro-Hungarian throne was staggering in its scale. It has been engraved in our collective memory and in history books the world over. But what is less frequently remembered is that the lives of the people in Europe before the breakout of the conflict were more stable and prosperous than ever before. The European middle classes and aristocracy were of close kin and travelled across the continent to socialise and shop together. Kaiser Wilhelm II, King George V and Tsar Nicholas

II were cousins and even though rumours of a possible war were never far away, few were seriously alarmed. For those not privy to the luxuries of court life, it was still a time of many improvements to life thanks to the increased industrialisation of the continent and benefits of global trade.

Jews of Warsaw were also experiencing a revival. Despite frequent anti-Semitic attacks, they were now allowed to live anywhere in the city and could hold office and practice trades they had previously been barred from. Many thousands had assimilated into Polish life and were now speaking Polish and Russian on a daily basis. Political ideologies, including Zionism, socialism, positivism – for those who believed in integration of previously marginalised groups into Polish society through education – and various combinations of all of these, also contributed to the revival of Jewish society. The increased political awareness of Jews in Warsaw was mirrored in the rest of the Russian Empire – which wasn't as stable as the rest of Europe, despite Tsar Nicholas' closeness to the European elites. The attempted revolution of 1905 failed to achieve the desired result, and resentment was spreading.

All that was about to change. The war that the people of Europe were about to experience would throw out national borders and ideologies, and would turn out to be the deadliest conflict Europe had yet seen.

Where was Marcus on the fateful day of 28 June 1914? How did the news of the impending war affect him? Did my great-grandfather immediately know that this would be the moment his life would change forever? In the ten years since the departure of his brother, Adolphe, Marcus had matured into a determined young man. He followed political developments in Russia and abroad with great interest and made use of all the newspapers from across the political spectrum that were available to him in Warsaw. But he was restless. Picking up odd jobs and trying to earn a living to support himself and help his mother, he felt lost when he thought about his future.

In the post-Sarajevo world, opinions in Warsaw's Jewish community were as divided as on the rest of the continent. As European powers began to declare war on each other, it became clear to Marcus that his life was about to change, for better or for worse. Because of their deep dislike of the tsar, many Polish Jews declared their support for the Central Powers of Germany and Austria, hoping that eventually they would be liberated from Russian rule. But in the more politically inclined Jewish circles, Marcus saw support for Russia rise. Young men and women who were keen to prove to the tsar once and for all that they were loyal citizens were beginning to enlist for their country. Marcus felt that this was the decision he had been waiting to make all his life. For him, there were no doubts. As Russia ordered general mobilisation on its border with the Austro-Hungarian Empire, Marcus put on a uniform and joined the Russian Imperial Army.

My great-grandfather enlisted alongside many young men eager to serve their country, and would become one of at least 500,000 Jews fighting for the tsar. He would serve as a medical orderly attached to the Russian Second Army, which was formed from Warsaw military units and before the outbreak of the war was meant to serve as a reserve formation, supporting other units fighting against Germany and Austria.

There was no time for Marcus to settle into army life. Despite the initial plan, the Second Army was mobilised almost immediately after the start of the war and invaded East Prussia alongside the Russian First Army. Russia had a bold and ambitious plan of capturing East Prussia. They believed that upon their success Berlin itself would be threatened. It would, in fact, become Russia's worst defeat of the war. The first major battle of the war, the Battle of Tannenberg, put an end to the military careers and dreams of thousands of young men. Poor communications, a lack of modern equipment and un-coded messages intercepted by the Germans meant that Russia's Second Army was left virtually destroyed. An antagonistic and hostile relationship between the two commanders, General Samsonov, who was leading the Second Army, and the commander of the First Army, Paul von Rennenkampf, also led to a breakdown in communications, fatally exposing Samsonov's forces to attack.

Marcus was lucky. He was not among the dead or the 92,000 taken prisoner, and he went straight back into battle. The Second Army would continue fighting on the Eastern Front until the dissolution of the Imperial Army in early 1918.

Marcus Neyman during the First World War

My grandmother had always hinted at Marcus' military career, but without any specific information about his service I found it difficult to imagine the kind of man my great-grandfather had been, or had become, during the war. As I carried out research for this book, I came across some information that revealed more about the man he was than I could have ever imagined from my grandmother's stories, or from the details of his later life.

My great-grandfather was a hero. He was awarded the St George Medal for Bravery in December 1914, followed by two more Medals for Diligence in the two years to come. A man with no medical training, but of a strong build and, as it turned out, brave by nature, Marcus excelled in his dedication to his comrades and risked his life more than once to take the lead and rescue the wounded from the theatre of war. His zeal and dedication were noticed by his superiors. Even though he was not promoted in rank, he was respected and admired by the troops.

The army was an eye-opening experience for Marcus. Aside from the horrors of war that he no doubt experienced, it also became a political stomping ground for a man who had been interested in politics since early childhood but hadn't found his way in life.

The Russian army was huge in size, and at the beginning of the war the mood of the troops reflected the mood of the public – a feeling of patriotism and an expectation of a quick victory lifted everyone's spirits. But very soon it became apparent that the army was vastly unprepared for war. With a lack of supplies and resources, and a poor leadership, support for the campaign began to wane. Letters from home told the troops of food shortages, and talk of strikes dominated the mood of discontent. With morale hitting new lows, and a sense of a huge upheaval around the country, Marcus was one of many who became disillusioned with the Romanovs and the ruling elite.

Small communist cells became active among the troops, spreading the message of fairness and equality and calling for a revolution. The Communist Party had been suppressed by the tsar and had not posed a real political threat to his rule, but with the army in disarray and the mood becoming increasingly volatile, more people were taking note. Their aim was to overthrow the tsar, the aristocracy and the church, and to replace them with councils to represent ordinary people. Having joined the army to prove his loyalty to the tsar, Marcus would eventually be demobbed with firmly settled communist beliefs.

The overthrow of Tsar Nicholas in March 1917 led to the establishment of the Provisional Government and a very turbulent time in Russia. By the time the Bolsheviks consolidated power and Lenin signed a peace treaty with Germany to take Russia out of the First World War in 1918, Marcus was a different man. The news of his mother's passing had reached him at the front, and while he returned to Warsaw briefly to pay his respects at her grave at the Jewish cemetery on Okopowa Street, Marcus knew what he wanted from life. It was time to leave his hometown and head for Moscow – the city that would become the new capital of communist Russia, and for my great-grandfather, the land of hope and opportunity.

My grandmother learns of her father's decorated past when I tell her about the results of my research. I see a proud smile on her face as she thinks about the man who was ultimately severely punished for his choices in life, but who always tried his best to be a kind and protective father. Despite the medals and personal successes of the war, neither of us were surprised that he kept his military life a secret. Marcus' political transformation brought about a move to Moscow, where in the new communist world it was safer to keep your Imperial achievements to yourself. But the man who once followed his brother to the centre of Jewish life at Nalewki Street also chose to leave behind his past, and that included ties to the Jewish community of his childhood. His daughter would never know the traditions and festivals of the Jewish faith or go to a synagogue, but her ethnic heritage would closely follow her throughout her life in the Soviet Union. For my great-grandfather didn't shed his identity entirely. His name would still be recognisably Jewish – Abram Marcus Neyman.

An idealist, a communist, Marcus believed that something monumental was happening in his homeland, and he wanted to be a part of it.

After the Russian Empire had been overthrown, it would take more than five years of civil war and political turbulence before the Soviet Union was established. As he watched hundreds of thousands of young Jews head deeper into Russia towards the big cities, attracted by the prospect of greater urbanisation and the opportunities of city life, Marcus could not predict that his life would eventually be crushed by the very system he believed would make Russia a fairer place.

6

A broken dream

Moscow, 1920s

Anna lies in bed awake at night. Her memories take her back to the
Sretensky Boulevard of her childhood. She was five or six years old, and
she sees herself following her mother to their new home. Anna's nanny
was holding her hand, and Anna, half asleep and quickly dressed only
a few moments earlier, was trying to keep up. In front of them, a tall
man Anna recognised as her mother's friend Arkady, was carrying a large
wardrobe mirror above his head, his arms raised up high. The mirror was
heavy; his arms bent and swayed lightly at the weight of his burden. Her
brother and sister were struggling with the weight of her small children's
bed behind them. In the haste and nervousness of the moment no one

had thought to ask the children if they needed help. The sun had barely risen and everything around them was still. It was not long now until some traffic would return to the streets and the boulevard would fill with passers-by. But at that moment even the stray cats Anna was used to seeing rummaging for food scraps by the bins in the far corner of the nearby playground were nowhere to be seen.

Anna and her family had just been evicted from their apartment, most of their possessions confiscated by the authorities. As they crossed the boulevard, they looked around nervously. But there was no one to witness their humiliation. Their neighbours were either still asleep, or pretending that they couldn't see what was happening right in front of their eyes. Anna was still a child but she knew that in the blink of an eye her world had been turned upside down.

My grandmother started telling me about her past the day she met her cousin Genia for the first time. After lunch with our new family we headed back to the hotel we were staying at nearby to give the elderly relatives a chance to lie down. My grandmother was too animated and overwhelmed by the meeting to contemplate any idea of rest. She caught me completely unprepared. I grabbed a notepad and tried to keep up, scribbling badly in Russian cursive I was no longer used to using. She talked and talked, starting from her childhood, through her university years and later life, painting a very vivid, but very factual, picture of what happened to her and her family, a story no doubt influenced by what she had heard from her cousin earlier. The contrast between their two worlds seemed striking. As I jotted down the facts, I knew that I would need many more hours of conversation to get the full details of what happened to Marcus and his family during the early years of the Soviet Union, and the decades of terror and isolation that followed.

The belief that sent Marcus on his way to Moscow prevailed along with the 1917 October Revolution, changing the face of the country and determining its future. The post-revolutionary years were difficult for Russia. Civil war, waged with anger and brutality rarely seen before, was raging across most of the territory, and food shortages affected the population. So irreconcilable were people's views on Russia's past and its future, that they tore apart families and destroyed livelihoods. Hundreds of thousands fled the country, millions were killed in terrorist attacks, or died from hunger and disease and other war-related causes. Gangs of boys and girls, orphaned and left homeless by the war, roamed the streets, looking for food and shelter.

But the country was in motion. Eventually, as the war came to an end, new ideas gave way to new projects. For those, who, like Marcus, were eager to start building the new country, the spirit of revolution hung optimistically in the air. An idealistic young man, Marcus saw the situation as a positive challenge. In the calamitous years of the civil war, he married the woman he would spend the rest of his life with. In Russia, Zelda Zilbert was known as Zinaida, or simply Zina. Marcus adopted her two children – Solomon, his name later Russified to Salya, and Luybov, translated into English as 'love' and shortened in Russian to Lyucia.

I am too scared to interrupt my grandmother when she starts telling me the story for the first time in Geneva, but on other occasions I try

Marcus with Zina and her children, Salya and Lyucia. Moscow c 1921

to find out more about my great-grandmother's past and her first two children. More often than not, everything is covered in a shroud of mystery and silence. Salya, who would live to the age of ninety-eight, but whom I would never meet because of family quarrels and misunderstandings, and Lyucia, who died relatively young in the 1960s, do not feature prominently in my grandmother's stories. She tells me that her mother never told her anything about their father, or where she had met him. We know that the children were both born in Vilnius, the capital of Lithuania, which was then also a part of the Russian Empire. That's where the trace ends.

Zelda Zilbert was born in another corner of the Russian Empire, the Polish city of Bialystok. A good-looking young woman with a round face and short black hair cut to a bob, Zelda was one of at least five siblings. She came to Moscow with her sister Rahil and brother Benjamin – known as Venyamin in Russia, or Nyoma for short. Two other sisters, Bella and Bertha, later travelled to Western Australia, where they joined their three uncles – their father's brothers – and their big prospering family.

By the time Zina – I will call her by her Russian name for the purposes of authenticity – arrived in Moscow, she had decided that her past would forever remain out of reach of the future generations.

Moscow in the 1920s was a fast-changing place. Having taken over the tsarist city, the Bolsheviks were wasting no time in modernising and adapting it to contemporary life. The maze of small cobbled streets in the old centre of the new capital would soon be partly destroyed to give way to new infrastructure. Many churches and wooden houses would be knocked down. The multitude of trams and other forms of public transport would soon be competing with the many cars appearing on the roads, making the city busier than it had ever been. The capital, which was still recovering from the war and where most of the population lived on food coupons, was being transformed into a new Soviet metropolis. The slums on the outskirts were giving way to new apartment blocks built by the government, which were meant for the thousands of workers coming to take up jobs in the factories. For many of those arriving from rural areas, the houses were a revelation of modernity. With running water and quiet squares outside with benches under the trees, they amazed the residents who had until now lived in much more squalid conditions.

Marcus saw the changes in the city as a perfect opportunity to get involved. He found a small apartment in an old pre-communist building in the city centre and was spending all his time trying to make money – and, most importantly, contributing to the development of the new country. He set up a stall at Sukharevsky market in central Moscow where he traded in fabrics. He joined the commercial class of the city, and for the first time in his life he was able to bring money home.

The market, famous in Russia as the last stomping ground for private traders, legitimate and otherwise, was an institution. Thousands took up the Kremlin's new permission to trade on a free market basis. Despite its dubious reputation, Sukharevsky market was the main trading point for entrepreneurial types like my great-grandfather Marcus. It had existed in Moscow since Napoleon was chased out of the city. A chaotic place, there you would find people selling their wares on the sidewalks, street pedlars, beggars and homeless children mixing in and out of the crowds. A tram would go by, bringing with it more people who jumped off to join those already buying and selling: a woman offering seeds on the corner of a makeshift street in this town of stalls, and beyond her, a man displaying badges and pins with Lenin's portrait. Many of those selling food had come from the rural areas, hoping to shift their fruit and vegetables to make a living. Past the produce and into the non-perishable sections, the streets got cleaner and more settled. The smell of food lingered in the air but was quickly absorbed by the strong odours of leather and animal skins sold at a stall nearby. Marcus' new place of work brought together people from all walks of life.

My great-grandfather's desire to take part in building the country he believed in was finally being realised. He was entrepreneurial. He sourced his materials from different parts of the country and was successful at selling them. After years of deprivation, famine, strikes and general chaos, Muscovites were happily trading with each other.

They had Lenin to thank for this. The economy of the newly created Soviet Union badly needed a kick-start after five years of civil war, and Lenin's brainchild was the New Economic Policy (NEP). It was meant to bring capital to the state, and by encouraging people to trade and create small businesses, the government was hoping to increase production and bring cash to the economy. Lenin had to fight many staunch Bolsheviks in the party who did not agree with this radical break from the Communist doctrine – and until Gorbachev's 'Perestroika' in the mid-to-late 1980s, NEP would become the only time the Soviet Union experimented with the co-existence of public and private sectors of business. The policy would work – it would boost production and revive the economy. But its success would also be its downfall, as Nepmen – the name given to those taking part in the new initiative – and their families would find out in the near future.

With trade going well, Marcus moved his family into a bigger and more spacious apartment near Sretensky Boulevard – around the corner from the Sukharevsky market and in one of the most historic areas of the city. Today it's one of a series of boulevards encircling Moscow's historical centre, with cafe terraces and the Russian oil giant Lukoil's headquarters overlooking the square. My grandmother remembers it as a quiet neighbourhood. The little streets of her childhood are gone, to make room for new apartment buildings, but the area is still recognisable from old photos.

In a four-storey brick building hidden away from the chaos of the busy streets, Zina gave birth to her daughter Anna on 20 March 1923. Marcus' nieces in Switzerland, Genia and Eva, now had a cousin in Moscow. At seventeen years old, Eva was already an adult, and Genia was about to turn ten when news of his niece's birth reached Adolphe.

The world is a different place now to what it was in 1923. When Anna was born, Lenin had less than a year left to live. The first years of her life were fairly quiet, and the family was relatively well off compared to others. Her parents were enjoying the first years of stability under the new Soviet regime after the civil war. Zina worked at a tailor's shop during the day, and in the evenings she put in extra hours. She was an experienced dressmaker, and women would come to her house to place their orders. In front of the big wardrobe mirror in her bedroom, Zina took their measurements, sketched the drawings and sent everything away to 'her women', as she called them, who then made the outfits for the wives of the Moscow elite. She left the house early in the morning to go to work and on her return worked late into the night.

While Zina and Marcus were away from home during the day, the life of the family apartment was never quiet. When Anna's brother and sister came home from school they were looked after by the family cook, Akulina – an enterprising old woman who went around the neighbourhood shops during the day looking for food, often queuing for hours to buy basic ingredients. In the evening she had to cook up whatever she had found into a family dinner. The process was often interrupted by Salya, ever the naughty boy, who liked to tease Akulina and ran to one of his favourite hiding places whenever a tutor came to the house for a daily lesson of music or French, my grandmother tells me in a slightly disapproving tone. He once pulled out a chair just as Akulina was about to sit down, making her fall to the ground. He found it very funny, my grandmother says, shaking her head. But she treasures the childhood memories of the brother who liked to draw attention to his tricks. Lyucia wasn't amused by her brother's behaviour either. A quiet and curious girl, she often felt overlooked in the mayhem of the apartment, and while Akulina was chasing her brother around, Lyucia buried her head in a book or waited for her stepfather to come home so he could tell her about his day at the market.

Anna was looked after by her much beloved Nanny Lousha. Lukeria Egorovna, a stout no-nonsense woman from deep inside Russia who would dedicate the last fourteen years of her life to bringing up my grandmother, is irreplaceable in Anna's childhood memories. Her first steps and first toys, first trips to the park and memories of first friends are all connected to her nanny, who was always there to guide and reassure the little girl.

Sitting in her room in my parents' west London home, my grandmother describes the apartment where she spent the first five years of her life. 'It was in a nice brick house, four or five storeys high,' she says, the memory coming back to her slowly. 'The apartment was on the second floor and it was very spacious.' At the big wooden table in the dining room, the family would gather for their meals, prepared by Akulina. My grandmother's cot was in her parents' bedroom, and Salya and Lyucia had a room each.

The family set-up, with a large apartment as well as a nanny and a cook, was reminiscent of a well-to-do household in the tsarist times, and was certainly not very communist in spirit. The Neyman family were enjoying an almost bourgeois lifestyle, and the years of transition from the old ways to the new were relatively stable. Their friends came to the apartment in the evenings to discuss the events of the day and make plans for the future. They talked about Communism and the new government, certain in their belief that the new country was going to make their dreams of a new and equal life come true.

Did their new life reflect the ideas that had brought them to Moscow in the first place? Marcus and his friends had been able to make the most of the revolution so far, and their living arrangements and work opportunities reflected that. Did Marcus understand that for Communism to work in earnest, equality for the masses would have to become a little bit more equal? The Communist Party certainly saw it that way. The Bolsheviks blamed the NEP for the rise of the new middle classes, and they had people like Marcus and his family in mind.

Back in 1918, a new policy had been put in place to promote the correct way of thinking and to eliminate the bourgeois families whose ethos contradicted communist values. The Moscow Soviet – the city administration – called it a 'condensation' policy on families with large apartments, effectively making the well-off families share their homes with those less fortunate. To begin with, the policy targeted merchants and other leftover elements from old tsarist Russia. But after Lenin died and NEP went out of fashion, the policy was expanded and more people found themselves in the spotlight.

Suddenly, my grandmother remembers, there was another Jewish family, the Talalais, living in what used to be Salya's room. Lyucia had to vacate her bedroom for two sisters who had arrived in the middle of the afternoon and were happily settled in the small but comfortable room overlooking the courtyard. There was another family in the room at the back, right next to the kitchen, making the apartment noisy and cramped. Anna's parents were allowed to keep two rooms for themselves and their three children. Akulina was let go, but the Neymans couldn't have survived without Nanny Lousha, so she had to share the room with Salya and Lyucia. My grandmother's voice tenses up as she remembers the new arrangement; it is as if, in telling me the story, she is reliving the humiliation of the time.

The condensation policy gave birth to communal apartments – or *kommunalka* – the living arrangements that still haunt those who had to endure living side by side with people they didn't know, despised and often feared. Even though it started as a war on privilege and an attempt to create accommodation for more people moving to the big cities, the policy was also a helpful tool to promote the creation of a more collective way of life. With individual family space turned into communal living, the Bolsheviks believed that people would become better communists when forced to share their living space with others.

Marcus was still working at Sukharevsky market and making money, but it would have been hard to come to terms with the infringement on his living space. He knew that even though he could have afforded to rent a different, bigger apartment for his family, he would have only been squeezed out by the authorities once again. This was the communist reality he had signed up for, and he understood the politics behind the changes to his life. People needed somewhere to live and the country needed as many workers coming to the cities as possible, but when he came home stressed and exhausted after a long day at work, he was irritated by the new people in his – now shared – living room. Equality for the people meant that there was no more freedom for evening discussions in the apartment, and Marcus talked to his wife quietly in the privacy of their bedroom. Their whispering didn't wake up the sleeping child, but had she been awake Anna would have known that her parents feared that the new reforms were a sign of worse things to come.

Anna turned five in March 1928. Four years after the death of the leader of the revolution, Lenin's economic policy was finally under the hammer. The introduction of NEP had had its critics within the party from the beginning. Even though the policy revived the economy during its years of existence, the more hard-core members of the Communist Party had always seen a hidden capitalist agenda to enrich certain layers of society in Lenin's plan, and the emergence of a middle class in the few previous years had reinforced their beliefs. The condensation policy was not enough to crush the new bourgeoisie. When Stalin finally decreed that NEP was an evil capitalist idea that had to be abolished, things moved very quickly.

The hundreds of thousands of Nepmen who had contributed to what they thought was the development of their country, who had started businesses and built up the economy, were automatically branded as the so-called 'enemies of the people' and arrested. As 'enemies of the people' they also became *lishentsy (pl.)* – from the Russian verb *lishat* – to deprive someone of something.

A *lishenets (sing.)* was usually stripped of voting rights and other privileges, and effectively became a second-class citizen, disenfranchised from society. Thousands were sent into exile to towns and villages across Russia, often doing back-breaking manual labour in atrocious weather conditions. For those who used to own bigger businesses and factories, where their whole families helped them run the production, their wives and children were exiled alongside them. Smaller entrepreneurs often ended up in towns less removed from civilisation, and their families were left in their hometowns to fend for themselves. The government also stripped the *lishentsy* of all their possessions as punishment for enriching themselves during the previous years.

Marcus was no exception. Once the crackdown on Nepmen began there was nothing he could do but wait. He tried to find out more – who was being arrested, where people were being sent, anything that would reassure him that the rumours of arrests were exaggerated and he could move on with his life. He barely slept and spent hours going over the choices he had made.

How could his life have gone from such a promising start to this tragic new development in just a few years? How could he leave his family? He was hoping that maybe he would be spared; at the end of the day he had only had a stall at the market, and not a big business like some of the other Nepmen he had come across.

But the authorities were not taking any chances. The people who had been seen to be discrediting the government needed to be taught a lesson, and so very quickly Marcus was arrested, and, after several days in prison, he was sent to the newly renamed city of Gorky. Known in non-Soviet times as Nizhny Novgorod, this beautiful city sits on the confluence of the rivers Volga and the Oka, more than 400 kilometres east of Moscow. Marcus' place of exile was far from his family; he would miss his daughter's childhood.

Marcus was a broken man. When he followed the Bolshevik ideology to Moscow, he had hoped that communism would be a solution for simple, hard-working people like him. He dreamt of building a new country for the people, where freedom, opportunity and equality would prevail. Instead, his world was turned upside down by the physical separation from his loved ones, an exile cruelly imposed on him by the system he had believed in and trusted.

But Marcus was incredibly lucky that his exile was not political. As waves of arrests intensified, Zina's brother Nyoma was also arrested. He was less fortunate and was sent to a labour camp in Siberia. Family legend has it that in Nyoma's case, the authorities paid undue attention to his place of birth in Bialystok, which had by then become part of independent Poland, and demanded the evidence of Nyoma's crossing the border into Soviet Russia. Nyoma's explanation that he had come over before the revolution, when Bialystok was part of the Russian Empire, and therefore he hadn't needed an entry visa and didn't have any evidence for his arrival were deemed insufficient. He was exiled to a labour camp. Had the authorities been as vigilant in Marcus' case, he would have suffered a similar fate, for he had also crossed the border from Poland before the country regained independence in 1918. Marcus was either being dealt with by incompetent bureaucrats who lacked a working knowledge of geography, or he was simply fortunate – in Gorky he was allowed to rent an apartment, work, and receive visitors.

In Moscow, Zina and the children set off across Sretensky Boulevard to their new home. She had to be strong now, Zina told herself. But inside she was shaking. She thought back to their last few minutes in the old apartment when she had to beg her friend Arkady, who was helping them move, to get her mirror out of the wardrobe so she could take it with her. It was a huge risk to take it, disobeying the authorities who only allowed the family to take Anna's bed with them, but it was a risk worth taking. Zina knew that without her mirror she wouldn't be able to earn a living. Zina understood Arkady's hesitance – he had seen many people arrested and taken away, and he didn't want to do anything that could threaten him, or the family, further. But Zina was in a desperate situation, suddenly left on her own with three children and an uncertain future.

Unfortunately, this was not the first time that Zina had been left to fend for herself. The death of her first husband had left her a widow at a very young age, with two small children to look after. (I decide that it was most likely death that separated my great-grandmother from her first husband.) Marcus' exile felt like déjà vu, history repeating itself. But this was not the time to give up. My great-grandmother was entrepreneurial; she knew how to get what she wanted and when in desperate need would always find a way to provide for her children. Most importantly, and despite her grim photographic appearance, she was a friendly and forthcoming woman, and her great sense of humour helped her find a common ground with most people she came across. A lot of her clients became her friends, and some would eventually be able to help her in life.

With her husband gone, Zina sprang into action. Her matter-of-fact attitude and can-do spirit, at least in front of the children, meant that in a few days Anna, Lyucia and Salya had settled into their new routine. Their new home was only a few streets away and consisted of two rooms in a communal apartment that had been converted from an old neighbourhood stable. The ceilings were low and the house was made of wood, but there was a kitchen and a toilet, and the people living in the two other rooms seemed quiet and welcoming.

Anna's bed was placed in her mother's room. The only familiar piece of furniture, it brought comfort to the little girl amid the chaos and uncertainty of the move. Nanny Lousha and the two older children all had sleeping arrangements next door. The bigger room also served as a dining area, a hall and a living room. From her old metal chest, her only possession, which she placed by the window, Nanny Lousha looked over the family's new home. At the opposite end, a sheet of white linen hung from the ceiling, cutting off a corner of the living room to give Lyucia a bit of privacy. In her tiny burrow-like space, Anna's sister had a fold-out sofa bed and a wooden chair.

Salya's curtain was opposite, but he didn't stick around for long. At the age of seventeen, he was accepted to study at the Naval Academy in Saint Petersburg – a huge honour for a boy from a family with no connections, and the adopted son of a *lishenets*. Surprisingly, the authorities did not punish the boy for Marcus' sins. Salya was fortunate – he jumped at the opportunity to get away from the constraints of family life, hoping it would open up a path to a brighter future.

'You know,' my grandmother suddenly tells me, 'my childhood was the happiest time of my life.' We have been spending many afternoons like this, her sitting back in the old wooden armchair with its flowery English cover that has followed us around since our very first London home in Greenwich, and me, leaning against the wall on her single bed opposite. During the many hours of our conversations, my grandmother has never volunteered any emotional information about her past. I have become used to asking her questions that would make her think about her feelings, trying to catch a glimpse into the memories buried deep inside her. But I couldn't expect to be able to change her so easily. For too long, the uncertainty of life in the Soviet Union and the often complicated nature of her own personal life meant that it always felt safer and more natural to stick to the facts, hiding the true nature of her feelings. That's why I am so surprised by this sudden outburst of positivity, which comes during an episode of her life where I would not have expected it.

The truth is simple. As a child, Anna was sheltered from the realities of life by her nanny. When she thinks back to those years, she remembers the walks in the park where she could run around chasing the birds and admiring the beautiful flowers in the summer. With the sun shining and her nanny nearby, Anna would spend hours hopping along the squares on the pavement or turning the sidewalk into a walk of art with her multi-coloured chalks.

Every season brings back a different memory. Once the snow had fallen and it was sufficiently cold for the water in the lake to freeze over, Anna would start pleading with her nanny to take her to Chistie Prudi. Literally translated as the Clean Ponds, the nearby city lake was the best entertainment for the neighbourhood kids. The pond is still there today. Around it, the busy road is constantly congested with traffic, and even the trees cannot protect the passers-by from the noise and pollution of exhaust fumes. But when Anna was growing up, the elongated park-island in the middle of the road was quiet and empty, making it a perfect playground for the children. Anna glided along the smooth ice in her shoes, falling over and getting up again to continue. In these rare moments of happiness she could forget about the tense atmosphere at home and the worries she knew her mother was trying to hide from her.

7

Eva's big day

Geneva, 1933

Heinrich Heine, the German poet Anna and Genia quoted to each other on the day they first met, had prophesied the terrible fate of Europe's Jews: 'Wherever books are burned, human beings are destined to be burned too.' A hundred years later, and just months after Adolf Hitler came to power, an event unseen in Europe since the Middle Ages paralysed many with fear. On 10 May 1933, German students gathered in Berlin to burn books containing 'un-German' ideas. They were encouraged by Hitler's Propaganda Minister, Joseph Goebbels, who joined them at the bonfire and declared the end of the 'extreme Jewish intellectualism'.

In Geneva, on 10 May 1933, Eva was not thinking about the future of

Europe's Jews. With her wedding four days away, she was quietly resigned to the fact that her life was about to change. Her heart was torn between the man she had fallen in love with, and the man she was about to marry. Eva was twenty-six years old, a beautiful young woman with a delicate feminine face and a shy smile. Her short dark hair was elegantly arranged around her head, not a single curl out of place. But her quiet demeanour and grace hid a determined temperament. Eva had grown into a woman who knew what she wanted and was not afraid to go after it.

There was one man Eva admired, respected and feared almost in equal measure, one man who could stop her in her tracks – her father, Adolphe. Since the day she became aware of her disability as a child, she had tried everything she could to impress him and gain his respect as a daughter and as an individual. Now that she had to make the hardest decision of her life, she was not only thinking about herself and her future happiness but also of her father's disappointment if she made the wrong choice.

Only a few months earlier she had taken the train from Geneva's Cornavin Station to the Belgian city of Antwerp where she would spend the holidays visiting her father's friends. It was the cold month of December, and during the train journey Eva admired the frost-covered white trees and fields. She was tired of what seemed like the monotony of daily life at home and was looking forward to a change of scenery. I suspect there was another reason for Eva's visit to the city with the largest Jewish community in Europe. She was twenty-six years old and still unmarried by the time most young Jewish girls in Europe would already be wives and mothers. Perhaps Adolphe had been hoping that his daughter would find a suitable match in Geneva, but when it became apparent that Eva was in no rush to settle down, he organised a trip to Antwerp, hopeful that an eligible suitor might present himself abroad.

There is no way to find out whether a young man called Stanislas Zousman was that eligible suitor all along, or whether fate played its part and the meeting was a coincidence, but he was the man Eva met and fell in love with during that winter holiday. Stanis was a gentleman brought up with the best manners of European families, and made an unforgettable

71

impression on his guest. A young man of medium height with a round face and dark hair, Stanis didn't stand out for his looks. Fortunately, Eva was more impressed with his charm than his appearance. He would take off his hat when getting into an elevator, and when walking on the pavement he would always walk on the outer side.

For me he was a revelation. I had never met a nicer man, more caring than him. […] With Stanis, in the first fifteen days we saw everything, spoke about everything, went to the cinema, to the theatre, to dance – I felt appreciated, sought-after, and when he asked me to marry him, I said yes.

Two weeks was all it took for Eva's future to be decided, a hasty decision made at the end of a two-week holiday. Many years later, Eva would write that in meeting Stanis, she had felt that she met a man different to all her male friends back home.

We were friends, mates, we told each other our dreams, we were like brothers. When I first met Stanis, I was meeting a man, he was nine years older than me.

Back home in Geneva, Adolphe could not contain his happiness. Stanis came from a Russian Jewish family who had fled during the revolution and had been living in France and Belgium for many years. They were diamond traders, and even though the Zousman family was of a lower social status than the Neumans, Adolphe was satisfied that Stanislas would make a good husband for his daughter. The only man in the family who didn't work in the diamond industry, his job as a representative of a German silverware company in Antwerp gave him a standing in the community and stability to give his new wife the lifestyle she had been accustomed to at home.

Was Eva really happy to be getting married, or was she trying to please her father? The pages of her diary leave my question unanswered.

Was I in love with Stanis? Or in love with what he represented? Everyone at home was very happy, and when I saw a real diamond, I was really happy to think of married life with him, and I told myself that it will be good to live with him, that he will surround me with love and I decided to do the same for him.

Three weeks before Eva was due to be married, she met the man she would later describe as the love of her life. Eva and Genia were attending a party with their friends. It was the end of April, and with the weather finally improving, the two sisters were in a good mood. The gathering was a birthday celebration in a fashionable restaurant on the banks of Lake Geneva, and the young women were looking forward to an evening of dancing. Eva was proudly showing off her diamond engagement ring and with the wedding fast approaching, the conversation centred on the final preparations for the big day.

When, later that night, Eva was introduced to Simon Chaikhine, she was surprised that she hadn't met him before. A violin player and brother of one of her close friends, he was not part of their social group. Often away touring with the Geneva orchestra, Simon rarely socialised with his sister's friends. Eva could see that she had made an impression on her new acquaintance. A tall, gaunt man with kind eyes and a smile that suggested a contagious sense of humour, he was twelve years older than her, and Eva's coquettish instinct took over. She had always enjoyed the attention of men, and now that she was about to get married, she felt stronger, more powerful, and protected from the usual uncertainties of interaction with the opposite sex.

For the whole evening he didn't take his eyes off me, Eva would write in her diary. *Together we danced only one dance, the tango, 'La Cumparsita', without a single word and at the end he just told me that I had beautiful eyes.*

Eva was flattered. She wondered what would have happened had she met Simon six months earlier, but she brushed her thoughts aside. She remembered her first meeting with Stanis, her husband-to-be, and thought ahead to their wedding – a big event that her father had been planning for several months.

However, thoughts of Simon were not easy to ignore. At the end of the evening, he walked her home. When they arrived at the door of the family apartment block, Simon asked Eva if he could see her again. Eva told him the truth. She was engaged, due to be married next month. Simon was stunned. He had not noticed the ring and hadn't heard the earlier conversations about the approaching wedding. He politely said goodbye to Eva and walked away.

Eva was in shock too, but again, she tried to ignore it. As she lay awake that night, she told herself that she was probably never going to see Simon again, and it was just a girlish infatuation. But she was mistaken.

The next afternoon, as she left the office, she found Simon waiting for her. He was there to walk her home. He continued to come back every day for a week, and as Eva got used to his company, she decided that it would not be such a bad thing if she saw Simon every now and then. They never planned their meetings, she reasoned, and Stanis was still in Antwerp finishing a business deal before he came to Geneva, so with feelings of guilt and anguish, Eva continued her daily walks with Simon.

How long did it take her to realise that her heart had taken over her head and that she was in fact falling in love with this mysterious young man? Was this always Simon's plan, or had he simply not been able to stay away from Eva? It was certainly days, and not weeks, because with the countdown clock ticking, both Eva and Simon knew that their feelings for each other would soon need to be addressed.

And so we fell madly in love with each other, Eva would write. We didn't know what to say, or what to do. I wanted to break up with Stanis, which would have caused him a lot of sorrow, but he would have recovered. But Simon told me that he could do no such thing, that he could never be happy knowing that in the process he was hurting someone who didn't deserve it. For hours and hours we argued, he didn't want me to break off the engagement, and so we said our final goodbyes and I got married.

Writing in her diary many years later, Eva was abrupt with her memories, but as I keep flicking through the pages of the journal, a letter falls out onto my lap. Three fading sheets of paper with barely legible, beautiful cursive writing. I am struck by the discovery. Eva had mentioned that her best friend Hélène was one of the few who knew everything about what was happening to her in the spring of 1933, but this letter, written the morning after her last meeting with Simon, is more evocative and emotional than I could have ever imagined.

I wish I could sit next to you by the lake. I would put my head on your knees and weep, and weep. I don't have the right to cry at home – I am a happy fiancée. I can only cry in my bed at night.

So Eva began telling her darling 'Lène' about the tragedy of her love story.

Yesterday my wonderful romance came to an end. It was brutally cut, at the moment when the roots were becoming strong, stronger every day. And now I can only say: it is finished, finished, never again. These words are terrible because they contain so much. You know, my dear, all that they contain for someone who is in love.

My heart tightens as I read these words of a twenty-six-year-old woman, who had to make one of the hardest decisions of her life. Her handwriting is measured and stable, but her words are laced with the grief and misery of someone devastated by love for the first time.

Happiness is rare in life, very rare. You have to enjoy it while you have even a little bit of it. For me, what will begin on the 14th of May, will not be happiness. I do not yet know what it will be. I know that everything passes, even the good memories. But the bitterness of not being able to hold onto happiness while I had it will stay with me.

75

The depth and eloquence of the words leave me staring at the pieces of paper in front of me, aching for my cousin.

Did Simon panic when it became clear to him that Eva would break off the engagement? Would Eva have dared upset her father, with all the presents already received and the new Belgian family arriving in Geneva at Adolphe's expense? Writing in her diary with many years of hindsight, Eva was certain that she would have had no problem changing her mind had Simon asked her to be with him. She blamed him for not convincing her to be more decisive, and imagined that they could have had a very happy life together. But with the distance of many years, it is possible that Eva was looking for a simple memory. A memory of a man who swept her off her feet in just a few weeks, and whom she chose to abandon for a man who had similarly made an unforgettable impression on her during a winter holiday in Belgium only several months previously.

In the untouched pages of her diary, pristinely kept for decades, there are many conflicting emotions. Many years later, she would frequently

Eva and Stanislas Zousman. Geneva, 1933

write with nostalgia for her life with Stanis, never forgetting that it wasn't just an arranged marriage without feelings. She had been looking forward to marrying him, showing off her engagement ring to her friends and helping her father plan the wedding.

Eva's engagement photograph was taken at the Salon Américain studio in Geneva. The future husband and wife look very serious, and knowing what I know about the events leading up to their marriage, it is easy to assume that they were not happy. Before the wedding day Eva confessed to her husband-to-be that she had fallen in love with someone else. She couldn't have known that it wasn't the end of her story with Simon and that their paths would cross again many years later.

Stanis was heartbroken, but he promised his fiancée that he would win her love. And he did. Eva would reflect on the pages of her journal:

We were happy together, Stanis and I.

8

Diamond city

Antwerp, 1930s

I travel to Antwerp in the summer of 2015. I want to be able to picture the city where Eva and Stanis spent the first years of their married life. Antwerp has had a Jewish presence from as early as the thirteenth century, but it was only after 1794 when it was captured by the French that Jews were allowed to settle in the city freely for the first time. The community grew significantly in the nineteenth century when many Jewish immigrants arrived, fleeing the pogroms in Russia and anti-Jewish laws in other countries in Eastern Europe. Many were on their way to the United States and England but had to cut their journeys short due to illness or a lack of money.

The influx of refugees coincided with the growth of the diamond industry. Antwerp had an old tradition of diamond trade, and in the early 1900s there were already several hundred Jewish diamond-cutters in the city. The influx of raw diamonds from the Belgian colonies in Africa and the willingness of the new arrivals to work for lower salaries helped turn Antwerp into the main world hub of the diamond industry and trade.

Today, Antwerp has one of the largest Orthodox Jewish communities in Europe, and walking around the city you feel immersed in traditional Jewish life, where some beliefs and conventions have remained unchanged for centuries. The livelihood of the diamond merchants who greet me as I get off the train at Antwerp's magnificent Central Station still centres around the diamond district. The shop windows present an embarrassment of riches to all those arriving in the city by rail, but it's on the discreet Hoveniersstraat, or the Gardener's Street, hidden behind the first row of shops, that the real business takes place – eighty percent of the world's uncut diamonds are traded there.

Kippah-wearing men dash in and out of the shops and offices as the day gets going, catching up on the deals and the neighbourhood news. Today, not all businesses are run by Jews, with many Indian, Russian and Lebanese traders also prospering in the community.

Amid the chaos and the noise, I try to imagine the streets eight decades before my visit. As I walk away from the train station and towards the neighbourhoods I know to be predominantly Jewish, I realise that I don't need to try very hard to be transported back to 1933.

The Jewish life of the city surrounds me. Mezuzot, containing pieces of parchment inscribed with words from the Torah, adorn the doorframes of most houses. Boys and girls playing on the streets watch me curiously. The delicious smells coming from the bakeries selling the mouth-watering rugelach pastry rolls of my childhood lure me in for a not yet deserved break, but I am unable to resist. From inside one of the shops along the Simonsstraat, tightly packed with flour and sugar sacks as well as the freshly baked breads and pastries, I watch the world outside. Young mothers rush around the neighbourhood with their offspring, running errands and taking their children to school. The clothes of these women, the long skirts, and hats or wigs on their heads reveal their religious background. This is clearly an Orthodox neighbourhood, and as interesting as I find it to sit down and observe the daily life of the community, I know that this is not the life that my cousin Eva led when she moved to this city.

I have to walk further out of the city centre and get a tram to reach the street where Eva and Stanis first settled in 1933. Jan Van Rijswijcklaan, or Avenue Van Rijswijck to my French-speaking family, is a far cry from the small streets of central Antwerp. The long, leafy boulevard with houses dating from the turn of the twentieth century stretches from the King Albert Park near the city centre out towards its outskirts. The apartment building Eva and Stanis moved into was completed just before their arrival, and as I sit on the tram going along this never-ending street, I keep an eye out for a change of architecture. Just as we leave the city centre and cross the ring road flowing with cars under the bridge, I notice that the buildings have become more modern. This is my cue to hop off and continue on foot. Gone are the elaborate facades of the early twentieth century. I am now looking at the more square shapes of the 1930s, trying to identify the building I have only seen in a photograph. The faded picture of Eva's mother, Marie, posing with her granddaughter in front of their home will have to guide me. I bring it up on my phone, and it is not long before I realise that I am in fact standing right in front of number 164 – the tall white apartment block in the photo that I have spent so long studying.

It might have been repainted and smartened up over the years, but otherwise it looks the same. With its white panelling and the elegant rectangle-shaped windows, it is a typical house reminiscent of the art-deco architecture of the 1930s. I stand in front of it as cars whizz past me. The busy road, with three lanes going each way, is full of traffic leaving the city. It is the middle of an unusually chilly summer day and there is not a soul in sight. I try to picture it eighty-two years ago when Eva moved to the neighbourhood, and apart from the congestion on the road and all the new buildings lining the street behind, I imagine it was not very different. Nearby is a park and a little pond, and it is there that Eva went when she wanted to escape the apartment.

Eva frequently sought the fresh air of the small green space that became her getaway. Inside, the mood was often heavy and stifling. The spacious four-bedroom apartment certainly measured up to the lifestyle to which Eva was accustomed, but with her husband away at work during the day and no one to socialise with, Eva soon grew bored. The beautifully decorated living room, with its rosewood floors and matching furniture fabrics was luxurious, but when I look at a photo of Eva and Stanis seated at the heavy wooden table in the middle of the room, I can sense the contrived atmosphere of the moment.

Eva had tried to make the apartment her new home – a huge bouquet of roses on the table is testament to that. But she also discovered the challenges of being a housewife, and she was completely unprepared. At home in Geneva, her mother, Marie, was the queen of the kitchen, and the rest of the house was always spotless. Marie had made it her priority to keep the family home presentable for her husband's friends and colleagues. Eva, sheltered from the hard work involved in maintaining the high standards she had been used to, had to learn the hard way. She started by asking her sisters-in-law for help with her cooking skills, hoping to use the opportunity to get to know Stanis' family better. She was quickly disappointed. Brought up in a traditional household with men's and women's roles clearly defined and divided, Stanis' sisters looked down on the educated young woman who had grown up in luxury but couldn't put food on the table at the end of the day. '*What was the point of you getting a university degree if you can't even make dinner for your husband?*' were the words of one of Stanis' sisters that Eva would remember for the rest of her life.

The world of the wealthy and intellectual community in Geneva collided with the reality of Stanis' family's working-class and traditional Jewish background. '*I was scorned by the family who were all in the diamond business and had never read a book. […] I was bored, I couldn't get used to this life where all that counted was money and diamonds,*' Eva would write in her journal.

Eva never would become a great cook. Her dinners at home would for many years vary between the predictable veal ragout, roasted veal or veal escalope – with pasta, rice or potatoes doing the rounds. But Stanis didn't mind. He concentrated on making sure his wife was happy and tried to create a lifestyle for Eva that reminded her of her life in Geneva. The newlyweds didn't miss a single ball; they went to the cinema, organised trips to the sea and found other amusements for themselves.

Looking at Eva's family albums, I can see that she never accepted the lifestyle of domesticity, and it seems that Stanis was happy to let his wife lead the way. The couple spent their holidays in the mountains with Eva's parents and relatives. They visited Geneva, where Eva sometimes stayed for weeks at her parents' house, catching up on the news back home and going out with her friends. Between Antwerp and Geneva, Stanis and Eva led a lifestyle that is reminiscent of that of many wealthy couples today – where travel and holidays facilitate a happy life.

On 24 November 1935 Eva gave birth to a baby girl – Anita. Unfortunately, this was not a good time to be born Jewish in Europe. While Eva was recovering from childbirth and the many bedridden weeks she had to endure after she put on too much weight and walking with her disability became a problem, her mother, Marie, came to Antwerp to look after Anita. It was a joyous time for the family, and the bond established between grandmother and granddaughter would last a lifetime.

Stanis marvelled at his newborn daughter, and when he was at home, he tried to forget the rumours he had been hearing on the streets. In the past few years, life for Jews in neighbouring Germany had become precarious with the rise of the Nazis. Through family connections and friends, many of Stanis' acquaintances were sharing details of laws and decrees that were being introduced across the border to put pressure on Jewish businesses. Many companies were closing down or had been forced to sell to the so-called Aryan Germans after the boycotts of Jewish-owned businesses encouraged by the authorities. Stanis reassured himself that these horror stories were not completely true and a similar scenario would never happen in the prospering Jewish community of Antwerp. He was also relieved to know that Adolphe, who was closely following developments in Berlin, was not worried about the future of Jews in Belgium and Switzerland. But both men would be proven wrong within a very few short months.

Stanis became a victim of the new Nazi laws overnight. Once Jewish businesses in Germany started finding it difficult to source supplies and employ workers, many were forced to close and declare bankruptcy. The silverware company Stanis was working for was no exception. He was one of the first men in Belgium to be affected by the developments in Germany, and the loss of his job came as a huge shock. A Jewish refugee from the tsarist rule in Russia, whose family had successfully established itself in Antwerp, where he had been able to build a career and provide for his family, Stanis could now feel history going backwards, as he found himself out of work simply because he was Jewish. From the safety of Antwerp, it was hard to comprehend what was happening only a short distance away, but the restrictions being faced by hundreds of thousands of Jews in Germany were now a reality for Stanis. He knew that once a government turned against Jews, there was no easy way out; his family had seen it all before in Eastern Europe, and the stories of persecutions followed him into adulthood.

A man with a different personality might have taken this as a sign of worse times to come, but Stanis was an optimist. Already in debt due to his inability to put aside enough money each month, Stanis asked his father-in-law for help and hid the gravity of their financial situation from Eva. While another would have been devastated at not being able to provide for his family, Stanis never despaired at the first sign of trouble. He knew that despite Adolphe's support, he needed to try to find a new job. He remained hopeful. He was convinced that the Nazi government in Berlin was not going to last and that the temporary misfortune that had befallen Jews would come to a quick end.

In Germany itself, 1936 saw a slight toning down of the anti-Semitic rhetoric while the Olympic Games were being held, as Hitler didn't want the international community to criticise his government and move the Games to another country. But in practice the Jews were not seeing a respite in persecution. There were few reasons to be hopeful. Jews had been barred from many professions in the past few years, and, unable to do business and make a living, many were forced to leave the country. Belgium was one of the chosen destinations, where they joined friends and relatives, and the labour market, in the hope of finding work. In Antwerp, the city where Jews survived largely because of the diamond industry, Stanis was not well placed to find a new job.

For Eva, life went on uninterrupted. She supported her husband's attempts to find work, but despite her previous interest in news and politics she seemed oblivious to the wider significance of news coming from Germany. Supported financially by her parents, and therefore somewhat shielded from the harsh reality of what was going on around her, she continued to visit Geneva, introducing her young daughter to her hometown and her friends. She escaped the strain of Stanis' unemployment, and while he enjoyed the time he could spend with his family, his optimism proved to be contagious. Eva was certain that the situation for them, as well as for Jews in Europe, would improve with time.

9

The land of Zion

Tel Aviv, 1930s

A young couple stepped off onto the Haifa pier and were immediately surrounded by people greeting them. The man, with his handsome face, kind eyes and a somewhat square hairline, looked relaxed and happy. He was being hugged by an elderly couple who looked like his parents, and they didn't want to let go. The young woman next to him was nervously looking around, trying to take in the chaotic scene around her. Hundreds of men, women and children were unloading their bags and suitcases. Languages from all corners of Europe could be heard calling out to friends and acquaintances. Mothers were disciplining their little children as they tried to misbehave, hoping not to be noticed in the surrounding chaos. Porter boys were rushing around, trying to find customers who needed help with their belongings, and a few metres away horse-drawn carriages were waiting to take people to their destinations. The excitement in the air was contagious, and as she watched people around her weeping with happiness, Genia hoped that this would make for an auspicious beginning to her new life in Palestine.

But she was also apprehensive. An experienced traveller who had disembarked in many ports of Europe, she was carefully observing her surroundings. She could see that the port had been recently constructed and work was still continuing. Today, it is one of the largest ports in the Mediterranean, but when Genia arrived, Haifa was just beginning to assert its importance. On the sloping hills above the port, white buildings amid green bushes dominated the landscape. The coastline of the bay stretched out as far as the eye could see, and Genia found herself squinting as she studied her surroundings. The bright Mediterranean sun was shining over her, and soon the new arrivals began to feel the heat few of them would get used to for some time. Genia was yet to discover the sandy beaches of Tel Aviv, where she would settle with her husband, and the maze-like streets of ancient Jaffa and Jerusalem. But as she thought back to the wide streets of Geneva and the green mountains of Switzerland, she felt that she had arrived in an exotic and foreign land.

Nearby, hundreds of men were working on the smaller trading boats, taking away the big boxes that had arrived and replacing them with other goods. They carried them on their backs, some bent double under the weight, others showing off their strength and muscles as they went about their business. The men were dirty and unshaven, and Genia caught a whiff of their tobacco and sweat-saturated bodies. Many of these men had fled the repressions and persecutions of Europe; others had come for their political beliefs. Like Genia and her husband, David Ismojik, they had arrived in the Promised Land recently, and were now doing all the jobs they could to survive.

In many ways, they were the lucky ones. The politics of 1930s Europe determined their destiny. They chose to pack their bags and leave at the earliest sign of trouble, running for their lives and hoping for a better future in Palestine. The Zionist movement propagating a Jewish homeland in the Middle East first attracted followers at the end of the nineteenth century when it was envisioned and described by the political activist and writer Theodor Herzl. Tens of thousands fled the pogroms of Eastern Europe in the early twentieth century, but it was only now that the idea of a Jewish homeland became relevant for many of those who would have otherwise chosen to stay in Europe's Western parts. Thirty thousand people arrived in Tel Aviv in 1933, mainly from Germany where the first anti-Jewish laws were being introduced. But people were also coming from Austria, Poland, Romania and Hungary. Forty-two thousand arrived a year later, paving the way for many thousands still to come.

Genia looked over at her husband as he greeted his family and close friends. It had only been a few weeks since they had attended their wedding in Geneva, but David's return home to Palestine was a separate occasion to be marked. The thought of her wedding took her back to the beautiful Hotel D'Angleterre, where it was celebrated. Genia could still feel the buzz of the moment when she thought back to the Chuppa in the Grand Hall and the hundreds of guests watching her and David get married. She had waited a long time for that day. Ever since they had met as students at the University of Geneva, she had known that they would spend many years of their lives together. In her daydream she pictured the coffee breaks from their studies in Geneva's cafes and restaurants, and eventually dinners at her parents' house – once David had passed the fiancé test and was admitted into the family home.

Adolphe had always been sceptical of the young man, because of his Zionist ideas and idealistic world view, but Genia's father admired the dedication required to obtain a medical degree and hoped that his daughter would eventually change her mind about going to Palestine. Genia shook her head at the thought of all the arguments she had had with her father over this land. She looked at her surroundings; she could see the beach, the Mediterranean. The sunshine and the smell of the port and the sea reminded her of her holidays in Italy and the south of France, and she was sure that her father had been overreacting when he warned her of the turbulent region she was choosing as her home.

Genia knew that her choice of Tel Aviv was not entirely political, but nor was she blindly following her husband who had always wanted to return home at the end of his studies in Geneva. For her, Palestine was a break from the past. She had been craving freedom and new experiences. Life in Geneva had become unbearable and stifling. Growing up as the younger daughter in Adolphe's household, she had been looking forward to being able to make her own decisions in life, and with Eva married and gone to Antwerp two years earlier, Genia felt that it was time for her to also decide her future.

In David she found a companion and a soulmate. A Jew from a Russian family who had moved to Tel Aviv at the turn of the century, he enthralled her with stories of the opportunities in the Promised Land. At a time when Jews were being persecuted by the Nazis in Europe, it was the moment, David had told her, to take their destiny into their own hands, and build their future together, for themselves and their children. Genia wouldn't have called herself a romantic at heart, but she bought into the idealistic notion of a happy life built by Jews in their own land.

Without the rose-tinted glasses of idealism, Adolphe could see through David and Genia's dream of happiness and peace in Palestine. His heart was heavy when he thought of the Arab workers, who were heading to the cities to benefit from the economic development of the land, seeking jobs on British- and Jewish-run projects and construction sites. Adolphe was worried that eventually this would lead to violence and turmoil in the region. He did not believe that Zionism was the solution to the problems that Jews were facing in Europe, but he was eventually won over by his younger daughter's persuasive arguments and didn't want to stand in her way. He could see that in the last few years Genia had become a young woman with an exceptional force of nature and determination, and even though he found it difficult to agree with her sudden passions and beliefs, he was secretly proud to see himself in his daughter's resolve and fortitude.

Genia was twenty-one years old. A newly married woman, in a new land far away from her family, she was determined to enjoy herself. She arrived in Tel Aviv just as it was granted city status, and she watched it grow. Thousands of buildings were going up, built by the German and Austrian architects who were adapting Europe's Bauhaus style to make it Tel Aviv's own. The light-coloured apartment blocks with shaded balconies and small windows designed for the hot Mediterranean climate would earn Tel Aviv the moniker of the White City. While the city itself was being spruced up, so was the life its new inhabitants were leading. Like Genia and David, many of their new acquaintances came from wealthy families who had been able to move to Palestine with all their savings and belongings intact. They were grateful that they had been able to escape Europe and were now looking forward to living without fear.

A newly qualified radiologist with a medical degree from a European university, David returned to Tel Aviv to join the ranks of hundreds of doctors, lawyers, architects and professors who were coming to make

Eugenia and David Ismojik. Geneva, 1933

Palestine their home. Not all of them would find jobs in their original careers and some would struggle to adjust to life in a land that was seen as uncivilised and un-European, striving to make something of itself amid the chaos of the region. But the determination of the new arrivals to build a future for their families would see many doctors driving taxis and architects working as painters to fill the jobs that needed to be done to move ahead.

While her husband was receiving patients in his radiology clinic, Genia discovered a holiday-like lifestyle. Daily trips to the beach, which was only a few blocks away from her apartment and where young people mingled in the sun, became a favourite pastime. Thousands descended on the seaside at the weekend, but during the week Genia and her new friends could enjoy the sandy dunes to themselves, lounging on the beach chairs and discussing their new lives. Lunches and dinners on the terraces of the many cafes opening in Tel Aviv provided a much-needed getaway from the sun, which Genia became used to after the first few months, but which still occasionally proved too hot and tiresome for her European disposition.

Very soon, Genia and David found out that Adolphe's reservations about the future of the Middle East were beginning to be proved right. Palestine had been under the British Mandate since 1920, when the Great Powers carved up what used to be the Ottoman Empire after the end of the First World War. Great Britain accepted the mandate, incorporating a requirement to build towards a national home for the Jewish people, an idea that had first been embraced by the British government in the Balfour declaration of 1917.

By the mid-1930s the Arab population was getting increasingly frustrated. They watched as tens of thousands of European Jews arrived every year, and the British rule showed no sign of weakening. A general strike of Arab workers was quickly followed by a boycott of Jewish products and escalated into terrorist attacks against Jews and the British.

British policy in Palestine had once been influenced by the pro-Zionist thinking of Herbert Samuel, who as High Commissioner had attempted to mediate between Zionist and Arab interests in the region. But with the changing dynamics of world politics, Britain's increasing dependence on Middle Eastern oil and the likelihood of another war in Europe meant that the Foreign Office had to reorient its policy in Palestine. The British government was now increasingly intent on maintaining a good relationship with the Arab neighbours.

The fragile relationship between Arabs and Jews became increasingly strained by violent incidents, and in 1936, the land was engulfed in what would become known as the Arab Revolt.

As they watched violence unfold on their streets, Genia and David were not aware of the details that we now know from history books. Historians point out that the unrest was not sudden and the British Mandate rule could not have sustained a peaceful existence between the Jews and the Arabs.

Alone at home, Genia had no choice but to become a silent observer of the events. She had never seen clashes before and was shocked by the violence. She closely followed the investigation of the uprising by the British government, and when it was eventually recommended that the Mandate should be abolished and the land divided between the two peoples she welcomed the decision. She hoped that it would bring some normality back to her life, and the streets would become quieter. But the discussions over the future of Palestine would continue for decades.

Having arrived as a cheerful young newlywed determined to make a fresh start in life, Genia soon felt the weight of world events on her shoulders. News from Europe was not encouraging, and even though she took immense pleasure in knowing that she had become an aunt to her sister's daughter Anita, she worried about the intensifying persecution of Jews in Europe and Stanis' unsuccessful attempts to find work.

The violence around her kept her on edge at night, as she lay awake thinking back to the calm evenings in Geneva, when she could dance all night and not worry about the journey home. She was scared to share her feelings with her parents because she was too proud to admit to her father that he had been right to be worried about her safety in the Middle East. But there was another reason why she had suddenly become so concerned about the instability and violence around her. She had just learnt that she was about to become a mother, and she was now hoping for a peaceful future not only for herself, but for her child as well.

Ariane was born on 12 November 1937. Marie came to Tel Aviv to help her daughter in the first weeks of motherhood and brought with her gossip from back home. News of life in Geneva made Genia nostalgic for the city she had left behind, but she was happy to have her mother with her and showed off the streets and beaches of Tel Aviv. Together they walked for hours, pushing the pram and admiring the Mediterranean sunsets. Marie was relieved by the semblance of tranquillity and tried not to upset her daughter with worrying news from Europe. Swiss Jews were following updates from Germany with growing concern, but Adolphe was still convinced that the Nazi government was not going to last. In his mind the situation in the Middle East was more volatile and conflict unavoidable. At her husband's request, Marie tried to convince Genia to return to Geneva with her, but her pleas went unheeded.

Marie headed home after several weeks with a promise from her daughter that she would come and visit her parents in the new year. Genia would have liked to take her daughter to Geneva to meet the rest of her family, but she wanted Ariane to be a little older before making the trip to Europe. In the end, she waited too long. Ariane was about to turn three, when Italy bombed Tel Aviv in September 1940, putting an end to any thought of further travel.

Genia would have to wait until the end of the war to see her family again.

10

I do not have any relatives abroad

Moscow, 1930s

'There is something I haven't told you about my father, Marcus,' my grandmother tells me as we are having lunch at my parents' house in west London. I've come to say hello and see how she is doing. It's been six months since we finished the latest round of interviews, and I find my grandmother pensive and distracted. She is using her fork to shuffle the food back and forth on her plate, as if contemplating whether she should indeed continue with the story. 'He was a Nepman. He was arrested for being a Nepman,' she suddenly states in a decisive manner.

I look at her in surprise across the table. In fact, we had spent many hours discussing her father's arrest and the subsequent exile, and I reassure her that she didn't forget to tell me this tragic story. My grandmother looks confused and embarrassed by her mistake. She has forgotten that conversation, I realise. I want to remind her of what she has told me, but she shakes her head and looks away in silence. As I give her time to gather her thoughts I realise that in the last few years she has aged faster than I had noticed. But as I stare at her face I also remind myself that what they say about the women in our family is true; the lack of wrinkles on their faces makes them look decades younger than they actually are. Her hair, dyed close to her natural brown, takes another few years off her age and it is easy to forget that she is in the ninth decade of her life. She interrupts my reverie, and as she starts talking again I notice a sudden change in her voice.

'I spent my whole life hiding the truth about him. I had to conceal his arrest and exile long after he was dead,' she tells me. 'I was too scared of what would happen if anyone knew. Now I lie awake at night thinking about those days.' Her voice is strong but sadness is engraved in her eyes, and I feel guilty for making her relive the memories that had been buried deep inside. 'The fear never leaves you,' she adds, as she turns her attention to her lunch once again.

Anna was very young when she became aware of the world around her, and with that awareness came the fear. Stalin's repressions were already in full swing in the mid-1930s when my grandmother and her nanny were sent on an errand by Zina. 'That was the day when the bubble of my childhood shattered,' my grandmother tells me.

A schoolgirl of ten years old, Anna was quiet and conscientious. As she walked back from school that beautiful spring day, she was looking forward to spending the afternoon with her friend Malia. She didn't know that this would turn out to be one of the most defining days of her life. The day when childhood ended and adulthood began.

When Anna and her nanny got home that afternoon, Zina asked them to deliver a dress to her friend and client Zhanna Kissina. The dress had just been returned from the atelier, and Zhanna needed it that evening. As Anna followed her nanny across the courtyard that led to

Uralsky lane number 2, she was oblivious to her surroundings. It was the same courtyard that she crossed on her way to school and back, and she had stopped noticing its appearance. She didn't see the trees proudly showing off their first new leaves, or realise that very soon the little square would be transformed into a miniature paradise, a hidden getaway from the busy streets of the city around them. Anna was following her nanny down the path that split the square evenly in the middle, wondering whether this afternoon she would be allowed to play with her friend Malia or whether they would have to study.

Nanny Lousha was carefully carrying Zhanna's dress wrapped in brown paper, hoping that its owner was not going to find it creased on delivery. The wooden house they were going to was similar to the other houses on the square. It was a converted stable, and there were several families sharing the rooms inside. The wooden panels had seen better days, and the thin brown paint was beginning to come off after many snowy and wet winter months. Once Nanny Lousha had found the apartment she needed, she rang the doorbell.

An official-looking man answered the door. Nanny Lousha had never met any other members of the Kissin family, but the man's clothes and demeanour told her that he was an outsider. He stood up straight and looked at Nanny Lousha intently while she explained that she had been sent to deliver a dress to Zhanna and would like to leave it at the apartment. But the man had other plans. He told both Anna and her nanny to walk through the living room and take a seat in the next room. Inside, they found several people already gathered, sitting on chairs lined up against the wall.

'We didn't like this at all,' my grandmother tells me. 'This wasn't our plan, but the man looked stern and scary and so we sat down in the room with everyone else.'

Anna didn't recognise anyone. As she looked into the unfamiliar faces, she imagined the people to be Zhanna's neighbours who shared the apartment, or maybe a few friends who had popped by to visit. No one met Anna's eyes. The only child, it seemed she alone was brave enough to raise her head and look around. She was confronted with empty stares of people who were terrified of their surroundings. They seemed to have shrunk in their seats, trying to take up as little room as they could, and, if possible, disappear into a different reality. Nanny Lousha was staring at her feet, carefully studying her shoes. The same shoes that she had worn for years, they looked torn and lifeless. Anna could sense the fear in the air, and it told her that she should sit quietly and not make a sound.

They spent what seemed like hours in the room, waiting. In her memories of that day, Anna would block out the faces of the other people, or the china in the wooden cabinet in the corner. The only thing that comes back to her when she lies awake at night is the man who let them in – pacing slowly back and forth by the front door. The heels on his shoes echoed off the wooden floors of the apartment, giving his pacing a monotone rhythm. Every time he stopped, the people in the room tensed, expecting a rude interruption to their almost reverie-like existence. But the man carefully exchanged a few words with his colleague, and the pacing continued. An old wall clock was steadily ticking away the time, but the people in the room were silent. No one wanted to be the first to speak. No one knew what was happening, but that didn't make them talk.

Eventually they heard the lock turning in the front door. Anna and her nanny listened intently. A discussion followed, and the man who had unlocked the door, most likely Zhanna's husband, was led away by the men who had been waiting in the apartment. 'You need to come with us,' were the only words that were audible, almost as if they had been said louder than the rest of the conversation on purpose, and they were enough to send shivers down the spines of those who were trying to feign indifference to what was going on next door. After that, everyone else was free to go.

Nanny Lousha tried to avoid eye contact as she got up from the wooden chair and collected her belongings. She looked visibly shaken as they rushed back home across the courtyard, Anna's hand tightly squeezed in her palm. Nanny Lousha's firm grip on her fingers was beginning to hurt, and Anna felt that the tension and the fear of the afternoon would stay with her for the rest of her life.

At home, in the two rooms that formed their part of the communal apartment, Zina and Nanny Lousha didn't have a private place to talk, and despite their persistent whispering, Anna learnt that the men had been waiting for Zhanna's husband to arrest him and take him away. Zina was flustered, as she kept repeating the word 'arrest' many times over, worried about the fate of Zhanna's husband, but also about her own family. The memories flooded over her, as she remembered the detention of her own husband, the hours she had spent at the prison trying to find out more information and the details of where he had been taken, risking her own life in the process. Zina imagined the hours Zhanna would have to wait at the Lubyanka prison, or maybe the Butyrka, or Lefortovo – trying to find out where her husband was being held, listening to the rumours of the women in the queue, learning that days, weeks, and months might pass before she would be granted an answer. And sometimes, Zina knew, it was better not to know. She thought of her brother Nyoma, who had not been heard from since the day he was taken away, and for whom she had been fearing the worst, not daring to admit to herself that he was probably no longer alive.

As fears and emotions continued to flood her, Zina tried to stay calm. She worried that her friendship with Zhanna would be enough of an association for the authorities to come to her own home as well. There was nothing she could do but wait. That evening, she kept her daughter at home, afraid of letting her out of her sight even for a minute. She could tell that her play date was now far from Anna's thoughts as well. Zina tried to work as the mountain of sketches waiting for her by her bedside needed to be sent to the atelier as soon as she could finish them. It was not like her to be behind on the orders, but today she felt unable to continue.

Anna came to her mother's bedroom to find her lost in thought in front of her big mirror, a tape measure and a piece of fabric lying forgotten on her lap. Zina was not her usual cheerful self, but she tried to smile to reassure her daughter. Anna noticed that her mother was flustered and wondered if she had been crying. She sat on her lap, and Zina wrapped her hands around her daughter's small frame, but neither

Zina. Moscow, 1930s

mother nor daughter wanted to voice their thoughts. The conversation hovered around the events of the afternoon. Zina asked about homework and talked about the improving weather. There was nothing she could do to reassure her daughter. She would have liked to be able to tell her that Zhanna's husband had done something wrong and that his arrest was justified, but she knew that lying was not the answer. In the end, the only thing she could do was repeat the same words of warning that Anna had already heard before. Staying discreet and not talking about your family was the best way to stay safe, she told Anna. 'Don't talk about people who come to the house', 'Don't repeat what you hear at home', 'Don't pass judgement on your teachers', 'Don't tell your classmates your father is not around', 'Don't mention your family is from Poland', and the list went on and on. Anna was not listening. Her mother's words were floating around in her head. She could repeat them in her sleep and she knew that she would never say anything to anyone. She silently begged her mother to continue, so she could sit there, in the stillness of the moment, with her mother's arms wrapped around her, protecting her from the evils of this world. She thought back to the man's piercing eyes and tried to forget Zhanna's apartment, the tense atmosphere and the terrified faces of the neighbours, staring at the wall ahead to avoid any eye contact that would reveal their state of terror and anguish to everyone in the room. Anna knew that she would never repeat what she witnessed to anyone, as it would mean trouble for the whole family.

Zina was not exaggerating when she told her daughter to be careful. During the purges, Stalin killed anyone suspected of disloyalty – first in the party and in the military, and later in the general population. People were arrested after quarrels with their neighbours or for telling a misjudged joke, which would often be overheard by an informer. Colleagues, neighbours and even families discovered that betrayal was easy, as thousands reported back to the authorities. Innocent people were arrested and sent to labour camps in Siberia, where millions died from malnourishment, pneumonia and abuse. Zhanna Kissina was never seen in the house again, my grandmother tells me. She never found out what happened to her husband, whose arrest put the whole neighbourhood on alert and reaffirmed everyone's belief that it was better to watch your every word – what you said, and to whom you said it.

The day after the arrest, Anna was back at school. She tried to be a good student, but she was distracted. She thought about the previous day and looked around her class. Was it true what her mother told her? Should she fear all her classmates and teachers? Anna felt lost and confused and looked forward to the afternoon when she would be able to take refuge in a loving world familiar to her for many years – Malia's house.

Malia Braude, Anna's childhood friend from the neighbourhood, would become a friend for life. With Malia, Anna felt at home. She felt protected in her house where she went after school and even though she didn't yet think of the big words like 'trust' and 'friendship', eventually she would realise that those were the essential principles needed to survive and stay sane in the uncertain world she lived in. The daily routine of school in the morning, followed by an afternoon of homework and foreign languages taught to Anna and Malia by tutors hired by their parents provided the stability to her life that Anna still treasures today in her nostalgia for the days long gone. Twice a week the girls were taught German, immersed in the world of Heinrich Heine and his contemporaries made accessible by a strict German woman who came to Malia's house and didn't mince her words when it came to berating her pupils' lack of enthusiasm for cases and conjugations.

'Do you remember, we didn't like the German?' Malia asked Anna over the phone from her home in Massachusetts recently. 'I have a photo of the three of us and I had crossed her out with a black pen,' her childhood friend continued. My grandmother has no recollection of not liking the teacher, *Nemka*, the German, as Malia calls her. She smiles at the memory. English and French lessons followed during the rest of the week, opening up a world of literature that both girls enjoyed for its power to take them away from the daily routine of their own lives. After the lessons were over and their homework was done, the girls often played together late into the night, until Nanny Lousha came to collect Anna.

Listening to my grandmother recount her school days in so much detail, I am impressed by how successfully Zina was able to make the daily life of her daughter's childhood so normal and relatively free from the worries and the fear that she must have experienced herself.

The close bond of their childhood years helped Anna and Malia navigate the world around them as they grew up. They knew more about each other's lives and families than was common, but that knowledge only tied them more strongly together. Anna had noticed that Malia's clothes were often better made and more colourful than her own. As she got older, the realisation that the dresses and shoes came from abroad dawned on my grandmother. Malia's family had relatives outside of the Soviet Union – an uncle, as Anna later learnt, who lived in Palestine. Until the eventual crackdown on all communication, he was able to help Malia's parents by sending them parcels, and sometimes currency, which they spent in specially designated shops, only available to those with such connections. But Anna never asked for details, and Malia didn't volunteer the information. There was an unspoken understanding between the two girls that could only exist between the closest of friends – an acceptance of the facts as they were, without questioning the motives behind them or asking for more details. They had learnt this from their own parents. The less said aloud the better.

Marcus' return from exile brought the girls closer together. When he came back to Moscow one day, surprising his wife and daughter with his arrival, Anna was terrified to share the information with anyone. She didn't know how to feel about her father's return. A man whom she remembered only vaguely was suddenly back. He was shorter and heavier than she recalled, but she was not sure if she should be happy that her father was back. In the evening, Anna watched her parents disappear into their room, and tried to listen to their conversation late into the night. The whispering eventually stopped and she fell asleep, but the hushed, nervous pace of the discussion revealed more than she was supposed to know.

Zina was worried that her husband's return would put the whole family at risk, with the authorities still watching him and keeping an eye on his relatives. Marcus reassured his wife that there was nothing to worry about. He was allowed to live and work in the capital again and he hoped to make up for lost time with his wife and daughter.

It was while he was trying to get to know Anna better during a walk around the neighbourhood that they bumped into Malia. Anna's eyes first shone in recognition, but as she realised that she hadn't told her friend about her father's return, she averted her gaze. She wanted to disappear and hide her head in shame, as the guilt for hiding the truth immediately overwhelmed her, but she needn't have worried. The next day Malia gave her friend a hug, and Anna knew that there was nothing else to be said. Her friend was happy that Anna's family had been reunited, and she was there if she ever needed to talk about it.

As the 1940s approached, life became no less tense and uncertain. More people were arrested, more suspicions raised and more whispering

Adash Malach, Anna and Marcus. Moscow, 1934

This photo was taken after Marcus' return from exile. Adash is quite a mysterious character. He was Marie Neuman's brother, known to Anna in Moscow as Ilya. He visited Anna and her family several times while he was in Russia for business. Not much is known about him, he is said to have died in the UK.

overheard coming from the kitchen. Anna was in the last years of school as news reached her of the outbreak of the Second World War in Europe, but because of the Soviet non-aggression pact with Germany, it would be a while before Russia became a battleground itself.

My grandmother was applying to continue her education at one of Moscow's universities, and the first hurdle she encountered was the questionnaire. This questionnaire, or the application form, comprised a long list of questions that every Soviet citizen of every generation would come to hate. It was omnipresent in everyone's life. It was required when applying for a university place, a job or a promotion. Some forms were relatively straightforward; others were so complicated it was impossible to fill them out. Most of the time, the difficulty and the number of the questions depended on the job you were applying for. The application for further education was fairly easy, but as Anna soon discovered, its purpose was to filter out those applicants the authorities deemed unsuitable for the privilege.

As she sat at the dining table at home one evening and stared at the questions in front of her she already knew that she would have to be careful with her answers so as not to be caught out by the Soviet system. 1. Surname. 2. Name. 3. Patronymic. 4. Date of birth. So far, so good. 5. Ethnicity. 6. Party membership. It was getting more treacherous. Anna glanced down at the long list of questions she had to answer before she could proceed with her application. Some questions you wanted to lie about but you couldn't. Ethnicity, famously known as the 'fifth clause', or the 'fifth paragraph', after its numerical order on some Soviet documents, was one such question. Anna couldn't hide the fact that she was Jewish – one of the 'problematic' ethnicities for the authorities. Her passport clearly stated her ethnic origin and so the questionnaire had to have the same information.

The 'fifth clause' was finally abolished by Russia in the years before it was my turn to apply for my first internal passport, aged fourteen, in 1999. With the Russian surname from my non-Jewish grandfather, I became the first member of my family, the first in many generations of Russian Jews, not to be identified as a Jew on my documents. But with Jewish names like Neyman or Braude you could barely hide your Jewishness from the Soviet authorities.

Even though unfavourable, the fifth clause on its own was not enough to cause serious problems for my grandmother. As she continued scanning the paper she came to the question she knew could make or break not only her career, but also her life. It asked about the existence of any criminal record for Anna or any of her relatives. To reveal the truth about her father's arrest and exile for being a Nepman would have meant revealing her status as the daughter of a *lishenets*. The road to university would have been closed. But the consequences for concealing the truth could be a lot more severe if the deception was ever uncovered. Anna stared long and hard at the list in front of her but she had already made her decision. She knew that she had a future ahead of her, and if she had learnt anything in recent years it was that if she found a way around the restrictions and the barriers, she had a chance at independence, and possibly happiness. She chose to ignore the question. She denied having grown up with a father in exile, and hoped that nothing else in her application form caught the eye of the authorities.

As evening set in, Anna was still at the dining room table grappling with the moral compromise she had made with herself. She waited for her parents to come home from work so she could talk to them about her decision, but she knew that they would not contradict her choice.

When my grandmother and I sit down to look through the hundreds of photos she has kept all her life, I discover some documents in one of the piles that I take out of a Marks & Spencer plastic bag. I am not aware of their existence and can't believe my eyes when one of the papers turns out to be an autobiographical letter my grandmother wrote in 1950. A modern-day cover letter outlining the main events of her life, its aim, along with the questionnaire, was to catch out those whose biographies were unsuitable for employment. On three yellowing sheets of paper, my twenty-seven-year-old grandmother outlined her life from the day she was born. She listed her education and all the jobs she had already had. The last sentence sends shivers down my spine: '*I do not have any relatives abroad.*'

It was another lie that she eventually got used to living with, for she had no choice. Revealing the truth about her cousins in Switzerland would have meant serious consequences for the family. For authorities terrified of foreigners and connections with the West, no matter how tenuous, a confirmation of relatives abroad could have meant a suspicion of disloyalty, further investigation, or worse. Arrest, interrogations, the Gulags. Who knows what Stalin's men would have decided in each case, but the possibilities were all too obvious. Lying to survive became second nature, but it also had an impact on even the strongest-willed. When I ask her about it now, my grandmother tells me, very firmly, that there was no other way, you just had to get on with it and live your life. As I dig further and further into her old life, I find that I am discovering a new side to her. A strong woman determined to survive.

My grandmother goes on to tell me that the power of friendship should not be underestimated. Even though they were cautious with each other when it came to details about their family lives, Anna and Malia knew that they could count on each other's support if they ever got into trouble. Over the years they helped each other in moments both happy and sad. The bond the two girls established on the playground of Sretensky Boulevard is still alive today. Whenever my grandmother calls Malia in the United States, they still talk of all the things they used to do together. Across the world, between London and Boston, their memories fly, and they are freer with each other than they could ever have been when they lived next door.

What a turn of fate, I tell my grandmother. Could you have ever imagined, back then, that you would be living in London, and she across the Atlantic, in Boston, and that you would talk on the phone every week? My grandmother looks at me. I am getting used to this look. Every time I try to fantasise a little bit about the past, I get the look. It is a look that says that she can't possibly understand why I would ask such a question.

'We didn't think about the future,' she tells me. 'We had to get through the present.'

Part Two

11

A holiday in De Panne

Western France, 1940

The great powers of Europe were at war. It was not yet felt on the streets of Antwerp and Geneva. The Swiss army had been mobilised since Germany invaded Poland in September 1939, and even though eight months later everyone was still tense, people didn't seriously believe that they were in danger.

Eva studied the newspapers. The coverage was dominated by the Battle of Narvik in northern Norway. The British were holding out against the Germans; they had the support of French and Free Polish troops that had fled to France following Poland's surrender in October 1939, and the war in the north of Europe felt far away. As she pored over the press, Eva was reassured that the pages were dominated by analysis and strategy. There was no urgency to the conflict, she thought. The anti-fascist sentiment on the streets of Switzerland gave her hope that her country would be able to maintain its neutrality. The Maginot line of defence along the French-German border was believed to be resistant to most forms of attack, and with Belgium's declaration of its neutrality there was thought to be no immediate threat to the civilian populations in the two countries.

Eva was restless. She felt that her life had been suspended between her parents and her husband. Between Geneva and Antwerp. Between the holiday-like feeling of the family bubble and the daily reality of the married life she had committed to. She told Stanis that she didn't want to leave Geneva, begging him to join her. It might have been a premonition. Despite all the reassurances, she knew that war was possible. She would rather be in Geneva when the day came.

Photographs from the family album tell me that Eva and Anita spent many months in Geneva. In the summer of 1939 they were taking trips to the mountains and picnicking in the sun with their friends. In September of that year, then October, and the New Year's celebrations at the end of the year, snapshots reveal an idyllic life of a family unburdened by the approaching war and the news reaching them from Germany and Belgium.

I am struck by photographs of Eva. In a fashionable black fox fur stole draped over her shoulders, the elegant woman was at ease in front of the camera, happily posing with her daughter and friends. In February 1940, Stanis made an appearance in several pictures, but his sojourn in Geneva didn't last long. Soon he was back in Antwerp trying to find a job and an income to support his family.

Stanis was forever optimistic about his job prospects. It was becoming obvious that most Jewish businesses in the city were struggling and he would have no alternative but to continue relying on Adolphe's financial support for his family's daily expenses. Eva felt that without a job for Stanis in Belgium, there was nothing to keep them there. She would have preferred to stay in Geneva where she could be closer to her family.

Eva with her daughter Anita. Geneva, 1939. Eva is wearing a black fox stole
that would later become one of her most treasured possessions.

In the end, she gave up. In early May, Eva packed her bags and told her parents that she would be back to visit again in a few months. Once her decision was made, she didn't linger. She didn't want anything to change her mind, to convince her that she was making a mistake. She packed a few of her belongings, and with her fur stole over her shoulders, despite the warming weather, she set off for the Cornavin station. Anita was by her side, and as she waved goodbye to her grandparents she looked forward to coming back to see them as soon as possible.

On Monday 6 May Eva and Anita left Geneva. They were heading to Paris where they would spend several hours before continuing their journey to Belgium. That day, and for the next four, French and Belgian intelligence officers received a steadily increasing number of reports of intense German military activity immediately opposite the Luxembourg border, but they didn't react.

On 7 May Eva and Anita were in Paris. They walked the streets of the city and Eva took her daughter to some of the parks that she remembered from her visits as a child. As they walked past a newspaper kiosk Eva glanced at the headlines, but they reassured her. *Paris-soir* wrote that the Battle for Narvik was continuing despite the snow storm. The war felt far away.

On Wednesday 8 May Stanis welcomed his wife and daughter to Brussels, and he couldn't hide his happiness. He didn't know that the French and Dutch embassies in Berlin and Switzerland had already been informed by reliable sources of the coming attack. He didn't let Eva ask him for the latest news of the war. He announced to his wife and daughter that to celebrate their return they were going on holiday. In fact, he had rented a small apartment on the coast and they were going to stay there for three weeks.

The rest of the day was spent planning the journey to the seaside. Stanis' brother Michel and his family would join them, and Anita looked forward to playing with her cousins Sylva and Izzy. Stanis' father, Abraham, a disabled elderly gentleman in a wheelchair, was accompanying his family to escape the stuffiness of Antwerp. He was hoping to enjoy the sea air, thought to be beneficial for his health. On the morning of

9 May they bought the necessary provisions for the trip. That Thursday evening the family reached their destination – the Belgian seaside town of De Panne. In 1940, the coastal town attracted visitors from all parts of the country. With white sandy beaches stretching as far as the eye could see, it was perfect for a family summer holiday.

The dates float past me and I feel like I'm in a bad dream. I am trying to make them stop. I want to turn the clock backwards, make Eva and her family turn back. Having first left the safety of Geneva to travel to Brussels, and then deciding to leave the Belgian capital and head for the coast, they would be caught up in one of the war's biggest and most defining moments.

The name of De Panne doesn't immediately bring up the horrors of the Second World War, since in the British collective memory it has been overshadowed by the events that unfolded in the town's southern neighbour – the French resort of Dunkirk, some twenty kilometres away.

For the Zousman family, there was no time to enjoy the beauty of their surroundings. From the moment they arrived at their apartment on the evening of 9 May, they could see planes overhead. They were circling in the distance above them, menacingly approaching the coast but then turning back and flying away. They returned again and again, raising the heads of the local population and the holidaymakers, but there was no way to find out what was happening. Stanis reassured his family that they were just German planes dropping propaganda leaflets.

In a few hours those planes were dropping bombs.

'On the 10th of May, in De Panne, we were woken up at 5am by the sound of the planes and the bombs.' Eva recorded the events in her diary.

It was only in the morning when they turned on the radio that they found out that Belgium, Luxembourg and the Netherlands had been invaded by the Germans. For Anita, a man in a uniform with drumsticks hanging around his neck would forever remain in her memory as the bearer of bad news. As the local police warden made the rounds of the neighbourhood in the early morning, his cries of *'Avis à la population'*[4]

---

4   Notice to the population (French)

were drowned out by the commotion of people waking up to the news of the war. The drumming accompanied the man wherever he went, but when he arrived, he was already late. Warned by the planes the night before, the radios had been on since dawn, and the news that he had come to bring was already on everyone's lips.

The army had been put on alert the previous evening as an attack was thought to be imminent. Overnight, Belgian forces took up their defensive positions. But they didn't have much chance against the numerical superiority of the German Luftwaffe. By the end of the first day, more than eighty Belgian aircraft were destroyed.

Eva didn't remember any panic. As soon as she learnt that her adoptive country had been invaded, her heart sank. She knew that deep down she had always been right. Her intuition had told her to stay in Geneva, but now it was too late. There was chaos on the streets and local officials were urging people to stay calm, but it was unclear what the family should do now. Attempt to return to Brussels? Or to Antwerp? It would have been wiser to go to Switzerland, and Stanis was trying to organise for the whole family to travel there, before it was too late. But time was not on his side.

Thousands of Nazi troops were marching across the Low Countries towards northern France. Eva and Stanis found it impossible to comprehend the scale of what was happening. They knew that as Jews they would be the first to be targeted now that Belgium had been invaded. It was difficult to imagine how little time it could take the German army to reach them on the coast. They couldn't get news of the offensive. The newspapers were outraged by the invasion and they were following the developments as fast as the printing presses and the technology allowed, but in the Belgian provinces it was impossible to anticipate the best move forward.

Eva and Stanis decided that it would be best to wait a few days, to see how the situation developed. They didn't know that thousands of British troops were running for their lives in the direction of Dunkirk just across the border from them. From De Panne, the horizon looked peaceful and tranquil, the birdsong only occasionally interrupted by the announcements to the public. They hoped that the fighting wouldn't come near them, and they went to the beach where they created games for the children to distract them from the worried glances they had picked up from their parents. When a telegram from Geneva reached Eva, urging her to come back, she ignored it.

In two or three days' time, when they decided it would be best to leave, it really was too late. Trains had been suspended to allow for military movements in the area, and there was only one way to go – on foot.

Stanis was optimistic. As the family began their walk south and towards northern France, he kept everyone's spirits up. He pointed out flowers to the children and told them funny stories that he made up along the way. But the pace was slow. Eva limped heavily as the family made their way along the narrow road heading away from Belgium. Abraham's wheelchair struggled along the badly paved path as it was rolled slowly by Stanis' brother Michel, leading this small family procession. Anita and her cousins, at first terrified of what was happening, were soon distracted by the views of the sea and ran ahead.

Stanis knew that they would not be able to get very far on foot, but luck was on their side. In one of the villages along the way they bought an old car, big enough to carry eight members of the Zousman family. A young local man was hired to drive it, and once all the bags and belongings were loaded into the car, they continued their journey towards the border. The driver assured Stanis that he knew a guesthouse on the other side where they would be able to rest and spend the night. After several hours' walking, Eva and her companions were desperate for a break and some food.

Determined to continue the journey as soon as possible, the travellers only brought with them the necessities for the night. Eva would not be separated from the fur stole that she had brought from Geneva. A token reminder of a life that seemed distant and full of illusions, it would now accompany her every step of the way. At the last minute, she came back to the car to bring a duvet inside for Anita, a wool blanket, her pillow and a thermos – having deemed the comforts of the guesthouse not satisfactory enough. She would later thank herself for her foresight.

In the morning they discovered that the driver had disappeared with their car. Their only means of transport was gone, along with all their belongings.

Safely in France, the family stayed at the guesthouse for several days to reassess their situation. They were hoping to find another car to take them further inland. Eva rested her feet. She was tired after the walk and in pain, but she was impatient to continue. The proximity to the Belgian border was uncomfortable and reports about the progress of the war left her sleepless at night. Battles raged around them in France, Belgium and the Netherlands; the Germans were trying to advance towards the coast from all sides.

Walking was the only option. The children were excited as one morning they bade goodbye to their hosts and set off on a long walk. Anita was reassured by her parents' jovial mood as they got on the road leading south. Everyone seemed to be talking at once. The tension of trying to decide how to proceed gave way to a vocal animation of a decision that had been made and agreed on, and the entire family was temporarily taken in by the sense of relief and progress.

On 15 May the Netherlands surrendered to Germany. The news reached the Zousman family on their way to Dunkirk.

When they eventually arrived in the city several days later, it felt unnaturally quiet. Bomb explosions were heard in the distance and smoke could be seen rising in the north, but it was the stillness of the air that put everyone on edge. There was no noise on the streets, no one made a single sound, terrified of missing a sign of approaching hostilities or a notice to evacuate. Eva searched for provisions and a place to stay, and was lucky when a farmhouse on the outskirts of the city provided both. She was still hoping that escaping the area was an option, that a solution would miraculously present itself and rescue her and her family from the nightmare they could have never imagined. For the moment they were relieved to have found shelter for the night and interrupted their journey to recuperate.

We didn't know that the entire English army was back in Dunkirk as they were trying to escape back by the sea. [...] We spent a terrible night under bombardment in Dunkirk, we didn't know what awaited the soldiers on the beach. Stanis thought we should board one of the boats heading to England as well – what a utopia!

A utopia indeed, and it must have seemed like it to the thousands of British soldiers when the order was given to evacuate. By 21 May British, French and Belgian troops were effectively trapped along the French coast. A French division had been successful in holding the Germans by the city of Lille and giving the Allies time to gather in Dunkirk, but now their time was running out. British prime minister Winston Churchill's call for all small private boats and ships to gather along the coast to help the evacuation process sounded like a crazy dream.

Stanis and his family didn't wait around for the evacuation. They joined other civilians fleeing the bombs and the explosions. They were now heading southeast, hoping to find a train that would take them further away from the fighting, the smoke that had penetrated their clothes and the terrifying screams of the people witnessing the disaster unfold in front of their eyes.

Stanis and Eva didn't realise that they were entangled in the middle of one of the biggest Allied evacuation operations of modern warfare. Operation Dynamo, later also known as the Miracle of Dunkirk, would continue for almost ten days, during which the local population and everyone who found themselves in the area would experience war at first hand. More than 20,000 civilians would lose their lives in France in May and June 1940.

The family continued walking. They were now joined by thousands of people. Bikes, carts, horse-drawn carriages, trucks, pushchairs and prams, young and old, women and children, people were walking away from the fighting and towards central France. They carried their bags on their shoulders. The horses were laden with food and necessities, and many brought their cattle with them. Along the roadside, people stopped to give the elderly and the young a chance to rest and to catch their breath. Nobody knew how long the journey would last. No one could predict where they would spend the night. The locals knew the area and they found the shortcuts. Everyone else followed. They crossed the fields and went past abandoned farmhouses. Many had been burnt to the ground; others were still blazing. The refugees – and that's what these people had become overnight, having been forced to abandon their homes – were a wave of human suffering. Many would die along the road. Some would reach their destination. Few would ever speak of the traumatic experience. Many would choose to forget.

Anita remembers the warmth of her mother's fur stole. She slept on it and covered herself with it when it got cold at night. It became more of a treasure than Eva could have ever imagined when she first bought it the previous winter in Geneva.

Anita also remembers the shoes she wore. Her Scottish slippers, as she called them because they were made of velvet, with a black top and a small button loop and a button. For many days she looked down at her feet and saw those slippers. They were not proper footwear and were not meant to be worn outside, but the niceties of her middle-class upbringing had gone out of the window many days ago. Anita's slippers looked out of place amid the burnt-out fields and all the people fleeing. Her legs were hurting, and she was hungry.

When an opportunity presented itself, Stanis bought a motorcycle with a sidecar. A young man was found to drive it. Stanis insisted that his wife and daughter should continue the journey with the driver. He would look after his father and his brother's family, and they would find another means of transport and follow Eva as soon as they could. Their destination was Lyon. They were far away; the road could take several days, but Eva and her husband agreed to meet at the hotel nearest to the train station. They were sure that they would be reunited in a few days.

As Anita recalls, 'My mother and I found ourselves with a man who was happy to drive the bike with us in the sidecar. And like that we drove. We drove along the roads congested with all the people fleeing. We found ourselves among this river of people, with little carts that they were pulling, kids' prams, where they had put food or mattresses, or in cars, if they had them. It was awful. And we were among these people, trying to get further into France, escaping the encirclement by the Germans.'

Once the petrol ran out, they parted ways with the driver and abandoned the motorcycle and the sidecar. They had been able to advance further into France, but the flow of refugees prevented them from going fast. Once again, Eva and her daughter started walking. The summer of 1940 was warm and dry, which no doubt saved the lives of many of those who were trying to escape the fighting

Even now, Anita remembers the hunger. They went with little or nothing to eat for days, sometimes buying bread and vegetables from the locals they came across on their journey. It had been weeks since they'd had a full meal, as Eva would be reminded one day.

I will never forget a farmer who gave me an egg for Anita and a lady who wanted to snatch it from me to give it to her elderly husband. I kept it for Anita, I was able to boil it, she ate it very happily and she vomited it straight away.

Finding shelter for the night became one of the main priorities. People were sleeping under trees and in the bushes, but Eva hoped for a safer place to escape the occasional chill of the night breeze and the dew of the morning grass. The duvet and her fur stole still provided them with shelter, but it was warmer and drier inside. When they came across a farm that was still inhabited, Eva was hoping for some food, as well as a place to sleep. When she knocked on the door, she was expecting some sympathy – a young mother with a child was easier to accommodate than a family of eight, and she had been lucky in her previous attempts to find shelter. She was turned away. The owners were afraid of the numbers of refugees arriving on their doorstep. Their state of fear and uncertainty forced them to turn away people who had been walking across their lands for days.

Fate saved Eva again. As she took cover in the nearby fields at night, she was awoken by Stuka planes, their howling sounds warning of an imminent attack. In horror, Eva watched the German aircraft dive as it approached its target, machine-gun bullets spraying everything in their wake. A bomb was dropped and the farm went up in flames. Eva and Anita ran as far as they could to escape the heat of the flames and the danger that the fire would spread to the dry fields nearby.

A common sight over the French beaches and surrounding areas, Stuka planes terrified the people. The sirens would forever be engraved in the memories and nightmares of those who survived the war. They left chaos and destruction that was equally difficult to forget. The bodies of those who were not quick enough to hide. Those who ran in the wrong direction, or those who were simply too close to the target of the Nazi fighting machines – the terrifying sight of war that was witnessed by women and children trying to run for their lives.

Eva threw herself on the ground, or in a ditch, trying to cover Anita with her own body. What would happen to her child if she died, she thought? She would have died too. She was too young to understand what was happening, too young to realise where they were. It would be better if they died together.

Eva was surprised when one day they approached a German checkpoint. Along the way she had come across French soldiers who often shouted to them that the Germans were coming, but no one understood that they meant to say that the Germans had surrounded the area. Eva was convinced that they had been walking away from them all this time, but in fact the German troops were also ahead of them.

Eva could barely see the checkpoint, for all the people who were attempting to get through. Long lines of trucks, carriages and those on foot were patiently waiting for their turn. They were hoping to cross into occupied France. Eva had been clinging onto a shred of hope that there would be a chance to go to Switzerland, but it soon became clear that Belgium was her only option. She came face to face with the first Nazi soldier she had ever seen. She didn't know how to voice her request. She didn't know how to behave with this man, the occupier, the man who was fighting for Hitler. But she was in a desperate situation. She could speak German, and she had to use all that was in her power to get herself and her daughter out of these French fields that had been their home for the past six weeks and back to the Belgian capital.

It was Anita who eventually came to her mother's rescue and saved the day. 'It was the time of daisies,' she tells me. 'There were lots of them, in the fields, everywhere. Long daisies and poppies, very fragile wild flowers. They were almost as tall as me. I hurried over to my mother and the officer, and handed him a bunch of flowers, telling him that they were for him! So he took me in his arms with the flowers, and told my mother that he had a daughter my age at home. He would have probably got a photo out. He asked us where we came from and what he could do to help. When mother said Switzerland, he laughed.'

There were no open roads into neutral Switzerland, but he could help get them to Brussels. The officer took a liking to Eva and her daughter, and he offered them his driver, who would take them to the Belgian capital. To the envious stares of everyone else in the queue, Eva and Anita got into the chauffeur-driven car, their nightmare almost over.

Eva was relieved. In the last six weeks she had walked more than she had ever done in her life. Her legs were now stronger, but the exhaustion was making itself known. In the hours it took to get to Brussels, Eva came face to face with devastating reality. There were German troops everywhere, Nazi flags flying on many buildings. People seemed to be getting on with their lives, but the air was thick with tension. Eva noticed the forced politeness, the cautiousness when a German patrol was spotted in the area. As she got out of the car and thanked the driver, she was aware of the curious looks in her direction. A tired, dirty, unwashed woman with a little girl, who had both seen better days, got out of the car in front of the Hotel Le Palace – one of the most luxurious in the city. The porter wasn't sure whether to open the door for the strange pair or to chase them away, but Eva's demeanour told him to hold back.

Inside, in the mirrors of the expensive décor, Eva gave herself a curious look similar to those of the passers-by outside. She glanced at the ragged woman and for a second didn't realise that she was looking at her own reflection.

Eva asked for the biggest room with the biggest bathroom, and after taking five or six baths she was finally happy to go to bed. However, sleep eluded her. Having spent so many nights lying on the ground or in haystacks in the middle of French fields, she couldn't settle in the luxury of the expensive hotel bed and ended up finding more comfort on the floor.

In the morning, Eva and Anita went to the Swiss embassy with the intention of sending a note to Eva's parents to let them know that she and Anita were alive, but there was news waiting for her. She learnt that Stanis had been able to reach Belgium several days previously and was waiting for her at a hotel nearby.

With the chaos of the war, and the country newly occupied by the Nazis, Eva and Stanis were fortunate to be reunited.

12

Life under occupation

Brussels, 1940–1942

I sit in front of an ancient white computer monitor waiting for it to come to life. Under the table, the hard drive whirs away. The dusty room is home to the Archives department of the Jewish Museum in Brussels. Thousands of old books and files fill the shelves, their labels laconically describing the documentation relating to the rich and recently tragic history of the Jewish community in Belgium. Its sealed windows and a stuffy smell suggest that it hasn't been aired for weeks, but the few rays of sunshine that do manage to seep through the windows give it a mysterious, almost library-like, feeling. The archives room on the top floor of the museum is not usually open to visitors, but

I have come across Olivier who has offered to help me look through the database of the Jewish Register created by the Nazis in 1940 and which required the compulsory registration of all Jews living in Belgium – the *Jodenregister*.

From Eva's diaries I know that the family were registered in Antwerp – after initial resistance from Eva herself who wanted to avoid any contact with the authorities and those who were helping the Nazis put in place their anti-Jewish measures. Today the database provides a further glimpse into her past, and as we put the names into the search bar, I have to remind myself of the grim reasons for the existence of these documents, despite my anticipation.

Several minutes later I am looking at the proof of the Nazis' terrifying ideology. The names and all the details of Eva, Stanis and Anita are meticulously written down, noting their full names, the names of their parents, their dates of birth and home addresses for the years they lived under occupation in Belgium. Across the page from their names – a large capital letter: J. Jude, Juif, Jew.

When they were reunited after the unfortunate holiday in De Panne, Stanis and his family settled back in Antwerp. Their apartment on Avenue Van Rijswijck had been taken over by German officers, all their possessions confiscated. There was no time to mourn their belongings. With the help of Stanis' family they found more discreet and furnished lodgings to rent on Kleinehondstraat. In the middle of the Jewish neighbourhood, and around the corner from the historic Eisenman Synagogue, Eva found herself in the heart of the largest Jewish community in Western Europe. Stanis was seeking reassurance in the small streets of the quarter and the close proximity to other Jews, but Eva felt claustrophobic. This was not her world. The rented apartment was small and stuffy. There was no air, and no matter how long Eva kept the windows open to be able to breathe better she felt that she was suffocating. She missed the luxury of her previous homes. The apartment on Avenue Van Rijswijck, where she could leave the house and seek the quiet green spaces of the nearby parks, suddenly felt like a palace and Eva dreamt of being able to return there. What made it worse was that she was surrounded by the alien world of religious Orthodox Jews who lived in the area. She found it hard to identify with the working-class families with their many children, and the bustle of busy streets during the day.

Eventually Eva convinced her husband to move to Brussels. News of the pogroms and attacks on the Jewish quarters of German cities persuaded her that it would be better to live in a bigger city, and away from the Jewish community, where they could feel more anonymous.

Having escaped the Jewish neighbourhood of Antwerp, Eva found herself on Avenue Louise – one of the most beautiful, and today one of the most prestigious, streets in Brussels. But the move didn't help her escape the worries about the occupation and the war. Soon after, German SS Security Police requisitioned a building on the other side of the street for their headquarters.

Number 453, originally an apartment block with a pale sandstone facade and a balcony for every window, would soon fill people with dread, and many would refuse to walk past it. It was there that thousands of Jews and resistance fighters would be interrogated and tortured before they were sent away to concentration camps. Two other buildings on Avenue Louise would also be used by the Nazi administration; Eva's neighbour in the apartment below was a German officer.

Eva was terrified by the proximity to the Germans, and by the worsening situation for Belgium's Jews. Within a few months, more anti-Jewish measures were passed, and Jews were now forbidden from owning a radio and having jobs in business. Eva tried to think of ways to protect her family. Although her status as a Swiss citizen didn't help her in day-to-day life, with the aid of the Swiss consulate Eva was able to obtain a plaque that she put on the door of her apartment. It read 'Under the protection of the Swiss embassy'. It was not much, but she hoped that it would stop the Germans from forcing themselves into her apartment if they were ever searching the building.

One night Eva came much closer to the German neighbour than she had ever intended to. That night Anita was very ill. High fever and an incessant cough brought on by an outbreak of measles meant that she hadn't been able to sleep properly for several nights, and Eva was sick with worry. A party was underway in the apartment downstairs. Eva had grown accustomed to the sounds of women dancing and champagne corks flying open at her neighbour's soirees, but Anita's illness and the sleepless nights brought her to a state of near hysterics. She was desperate. She found a piece of paper and a red pencil, and in big letters wrote a note asking the neighbour to keep the music down due to her daughter being unwell.

As she left the apartment, she was determined to avoid a direct confrontation, but she knew that she couldn't sit still any longer. She slipped the note underneath her neighbour's door, rang the doorbell and quickly walked away. The officer appeared almost immediately.

'I don't care about your child!' he shouted and slammed the door shut.

Eva went back inside and collapsed on the sofa. She felt powerless and unable to do anything to change the situation. She looked at the concerned face of Ti – her friend and a doctor who had been helping her look after Anita. Emotion overwhelmed her. In Ti's presence, she felt her heart flutter. She hadn't been able to admit this to herself, but without his help and support she wouldn't have been able to get through the past months.

Stanis, suffering from stress and panic attacks, had been tirelessly job-hunting to improve the spirits of his family. It was Ti who helped her when Stanis was unwell, and now with Anita, he had been by her bedside day and night, waiting for the fever to die down. Eva thought of all the evenings she had spent with Ti and his wife, Betty, the two couples confiding in each other and trying to look forward to a future brighter than their present.

It was a chance encounter at a neighbourhood park that brought Ti and his family into Eva's life. The Sternbergs had moved to Brussels following the Anschluss, when Austria was annexed into Nazi Germany in 1938 and conditions for the Jews in their home city of Vienna worsened. The family were a revelation to Eva. Szygmund, known by everyone as Ti, his wife, Betty, and their son, Paul, were perfect companions for the

Zousman family. In Paul Anita found a perfect playmate, and in Betty Eva found a friend. In Dr Sternberg Eva saw the qualities she missed since her departure from Geneva. Ti was intelligent and cultured. In his spare time he played the piano to entertain the children and talked about cinema and literature to Eva and her husband. With the world seemingly breaking apart around her, Eva had finally met someone – and a family – who could help her replace the friends she had left behind in Switzerland.

While the children were at school, Eva and Betty helped each other find food for the day, often going from one shop to another and queuing for hours to be able to obtain basic goods. The experience was made easier by their growing friendship. They shared their secrets of the past and fears for the future, and made plans for the evenings when they would be joined by their husbands to discuss the events of the day. As the two women grew closer, they also confided in each other and learnt the truth about each other's marriages.

Betty found out about Eva's affair with Simon in the weeks before her marriage to Stanis – a marriage of friendship, as Eva called it – but her new friend didn't seem shocked. It had been difficult for Eva to admit the truth, and she told Betty that she admired her marriage to Ti and wished that her own marriage was more like theirs – that her husband would find work and have an opportunity to prove himself to his family. But Betty didn't let her friend idealise her marriage. Eva was surprised to learn that it was, in fact, falling apart. Betty didn't mince her words when she told Eva about a lover who was waiting for her in England and her plans to travel there to join him as soon as the war was over. Eva's high esteem for Dr Sternberg made it difficult for her to understand Betty and her reasons for wanting to leave him.

From the pages of Eva's diaries, I had sensed her admiration for Ti, and I had long suspected the truth that eventually Eva spelt out for me in black and white.

After the unpleasant encounter with the German neighbour, Eva was overcome with gratitude towards Ti. She looked at him, a tall, dark-haired man, his eyes reflecting the kindness of his spirit. Ti got up to leave and brought Eva back to reality. She didn't know that the daydreams she often experienced were almost identical to the reveries that came over Ti himself. As she walked him to the door, she was about to find out his true feelings.

I told him I didn't know how to thank him for his dedication (he obviously never wanted money), and he told me: "Love me, because I've loved you for months without having the courage to tell you. But not knowing what tomorrow will bring, and if you leave for Switzerland on your own, I want you to know it," and he held me tight and kissed me. I was struck by lightning; I couldn't have been more surprised. I was shaken by this and realised that it wasn't just friendship that until now attracted me to him.

After the first confession of their feelings towards each other, Eva and Ti tried to find time to spend together. Very quickly, their mutual admiration grew into a wartime romance, lived out with the passion of a time where every day could have been their last, every minute the moment before the final goodbye.

13

Under enemy fire

Moscow, 1941

'*Grazhdane, vozdushnaya trevoga! Grazhdane, vozdushnaya trevoga!*'[5]

Anna looked up at the loudspeaker at the nearest lamp post and knew that she had seconds to act. She was not going to make the same mistake she had made last time an air raid was announced. This time she was not going to run to the nearest bomb shelter. She shuddered at the memory of the crowded basement and the terrified screaming children clinging to their mothers. There had been panic on the streets, and too many people had tried to squeeze into the shelter, pressing their bodies against each other, making her more scared about suffocating

---

5   *Citizens, an air raid warning! Citizens, an air raid warning!' (Russian)*

underground than being killed by a bomb on the streets of Moscow.

Anna kept running. She was around the corner from her house in the small lanes off Sretensky Boulevard, and by the time she reached the old square of her childhood she could see the first incendiary bomb lighting up ahead of her. The cylindrical-shaped bombs dropped by the Germans on Moscow caught fire instead of exploding, making it possible for quick-thinking volunteers determined to protect their city and save people's lives to put them out. Anna knew exactly what to do. Quickly, she put on the special gloves that she had been given and ran towards the fire. Once she retrieved the bomb she could safely drop it into a big barrel of water in the courtyard. By then all the neighbourhood volunteers had gathered to put out the fire. They didn't wait around. They knew more bombs were coming, and they scattered around the local rooftops to carry on their work.

While Anna was relishing the opportunity to contribute to the war effort, her mother was reluctant to watch her daughter put herself in danger. Since war had been declared a month earlier, on 22 June 1941, measures were put in place to evacuate citizens of the biggest cities closest to the front line. Hitler was emboldened by his successes in Russia over the past month; the Axis destroyed most of the Soviet air force on the ground and advanced deep into Russian territory. Hundreds of thousands of Soviet soldiers were taken prisoner. The Russians knew that the next target would be the Kremlin itself – a great symbol of state and power. But Hitler's advantage was not going to last. Only 195 bombers were deployed to attack the Russian capital on 22 July – enough to send terrified Muscovites running for their lives, but not enough to ensure any significant damage to the city. The bombing continued in the following days, but the Luftwaffe was confronted with intense air defences. The Russians were not going to give up easily.

In less than a month Moscow residents had built mock houses and roads around the Kremlin walls and painted the roofs of the buildings to blend them in with the rest of the city. The massive area covered by the Kremlin had changed beyond recognition, and when the Luftwaffe

Anna with her brother Salya Neyman while home on
one of his visits during World War II

forces flew over it, they did not immediately recognise the heart of the Soviet Union. Due to the Soviet creativity and a limited German air force available for the mission, it soon became clear that the Kremlin was not in any real danger. It did get hit on the second day of the strikes, but the historic fortified complex in central Moscow didn't suffer serious damage; in Stalin's apartment, only the windows had to be replaced after they shattered. The German air force was unable to maintain even the relatively low levels of engagement, and by the end of the summer the number of bombers eventually decreased to thirty, and later fifteen. The raids resulted in substantial civilian casualties, but caused only minimal damage to important targets.

When it became clear that the Germans were not going to give up despite their failure to destroy Moscow from the air and that the war was going to intensify, Zina announced to her daughter her decision to join one of the organised evacuations. From all over central Russia and Ukraine, factories and plants were being moved to safety far from the front line. Schools, hospitals and universities were taking employees and their families out of the capital and relocating them further east. Places on the freight trains heading east were in high demand, but Marcus was able to organise for his wife and daughter to join the exodus. His job in the supply department of one of Moscow's universities, always considered to be run by resourceful and entrepreneurial people, opened many doors and allowed him to make sure that within days Zina and Anna were heading to the city of Ufa.

The regional capital and the biggest city of the Republic of Bashkiria, Ufa is almost 1,200 kilometres southeast of Moscow, towards the border with Kazakhstan. In the first year of the war it welcomed more than 100,000 people. To be able to accommodate all the newcomers, the authorities uprooted many of the local citizens, prioritising accommodation for those families working for strategically important industries.

Today, a train journey from Moscow to Ufa can be made in just under a day. More than seven decades since it took place, my grandmother recalls her journey with horror. She was most terrified of falling ill. She witnessed hundreds of people offloaded at small rural train stations when they were too unwell to continue their journey. Their relatives disembarked with them, left to fend for themselves and care for their loved ones, often in vain.

Days and nights merged into each other as the freight train continued its journey. Days of living on the food they had brought with them and occasionally exchanging ration coupons for hot water and bread at local stations. Nights spent sleeping on the floor with hundreds of others, suffocating in the smells and bodily odours of people who had not been able to wash for weeks or use appropriate bathroom facilities. Stopping for hours in the middle of nowhere to allow passage for military trains taking supplies and soldiers to the front. It took a month for the train evacuating Anna and thousands of others to reach a village outside of the Bashkir capital.

Anna was relieved when the train stopped and they were told that they journey was over. She didn't care that the train would not take them to the city, and that it was up to them to arrange accommodation locally or find their own way to Ufa. She would have been happy to stay there, in this remote place that was further away from anything than she had ever experienced in life. The exhausting journey of the previous month had made her appreciate the peace and quiet of her surroundings. But her mother was determined to get to Ufa, and eventually she found a driver to take them to the city they would call home for the next two years.

In Ufa, the days floated past one another, filled with news of the war and updates on the wounded. Anna shared a small room with her mother. Next door they could hear their recently retired landlady, who was supplementing her income by hosting people fleeing the war. Zina took up sewing and occasionally made a dress for a client to support herself and her daughter. With the little money she earned, she was able to buy food at the local market, but the shortages were becoming widespread and Zina had to improvise. In the evenings, for lack of anything else to do, they listened to the radio. Hitler was concentrating his efforts on

Ukraine; Moscow was still under siege. Zina tried to reassure herself that Marcus was safe and would be able to find provisions to feed himself. But she knew that sooner or later the Germans would redouble their efforts in trying to reach Moscow, and she was right.

Capturing the seat of Soviet power would become crucial to the success of the war, and on 15 October 1941, with the enemy approaching, Stalin ordered the evacuation of the government from the capital.

14

White City

Tel Aviv, 1941–1945

Pinsker Street, Trumpeldor Street, Bograshov Street – walking around the old streets of Tel Aviv today, it is difficult to imagine the days when the war first came to the White City. The Italian aircraft appeared out of nowhere, dropping their bombs on the quiet residential streets in the middle of the afternoon. One hundred and thirty-seven people were killed and three hundred and sixty-six more injured when they were caught going about their daily lives. It took several days to get the bodies out of the destroyed buildings, and for many weeks those who survived walked past the half-ruined houses where their friends and neighbours had once lived. Eventually, the streets were cleared up and life returned to normal.

Children once again ran towards the sea, and sounds of the radio through open windows filled the summer air.

Among those quiet streets there was another, smaller lane named after the founding father of modern Yiddish literature – the Shalom Aleichem Street. It is here that Genia found an apartment in a white Bauhaus building she loved. She decided that lightning didn't strike twice, and moved to the street with her family. Genia and her daughter were three blocks away from the beach.

Today, it is almost completely dominated by tightly parked cars on both sides. The buildings look run-down and in desperate need of at least a fresh coat of paint. When I visit Tel Aviv I stare into the top-floor window that Ariane told me used to be their apartment, and I try to imagine life in the city of my cousin's childhood.

As soon as she woke up in the morning Ariane wanted to run to the beach. The beautiful white sands of the city were in her dreams every night, the sandcastles she could build with her friends growing more and more elaborate every day. A confident and animated four-year-old, she was happy to spend all her time outside, enjoying the sunshine and running after her friends around the neighbourhood. The other children were the sons and daughters of European refugees and émigrés who had made Palestine their home. Very soon they were speaking Hebrew to each other, and even Genia had to learn the language to speak it to her daughter, as Ariane didn't understand anything else.

Genia made her daughter's life as carefree as possible. She protected her from the news of the war and made sure Ariane didn't feel her father's absence. On 18 February 1941, David signed up for the British Army's Royal Medical Corps. Genia could see that he had been desperate to fight for the future of his country, and he was one of many Jews from the local community to join the British Army. He also took on a more English-sounding name, and would now be known as David Jerome-Newman. The Jews in Palestine didn't have their own forces, as the British didn't want to end up with an armed force beyond their control after the end of the war, and those who could were joining British divisions and battalions.

Ariane. Tel Aviv, 1943

David had always felt that it was his duty to participate in the war and make a difference. He was a committed Zionist and an opponent of the fascist ideology that had already murdered so many Jews in Europe. Now, he had his chance.

Genia was proud of her husband. He was hired as a specialist radiologist and would follow orders to different British military hospitals serving the Allies in the North African campaign. Genia didn't know that it would be years before David would return to Tel Aviv. Weeks and months passed without him, and with only her daughter to keep her company Genia felt abandoned and forgotten in this foreign land. She had friends, of course; her love for social gatherings always made it easy for her to develop friendships. Nevertheless, she felt alone.

The opportunities to visit David were rare. When they did arise, Genia didn't hesitate. She took Ariane, and together they travelled the region. Port Said, Alexandria, Cairo and Beirut were just some of the places that Ariane discovered as a little girl. All these cities were crucial for the Allies' efforts and were certainly not the best destinations for a child, but this was the only opportunity Genia had to keep her family together – despite the war.

Ariane was fascinated by the military hospitals. She spent time with her father while he was working and quickly got to know the ins and outs of his routine. David protected his daughter from the worst cases that he saw, making sure she was away from the men crying out in pain and devastation as they lay in bed waiting for the agony of a treated wound to subside. Ariane doesn't remember the cries. She remembers playing leapfrog with some of the patients, the ones who had been touched lightly by the fighting or the ones about to be discharged. She remembers the nurses – helping people and alleviating their pain, often simply sitting down to talk to them and listen to their stories. She watched in fascination as they kept the hospitals running, blissfully unaware that many years later she would follow in their footsteps.

Cairo in particular lingers in Ariane's memory. Living at the historic Shepheard Hotel on the Promenade while they were visiting David,

Genia discovered that there were bedbugs everywhere and decided that she could not let her daughter sleep in the bed. To Ariane's great amusement she learnt that evening that she would be spending the night in the bath. Her mother arranged a makeshift bed for her in the tub to protect her from the bites. A far stronger memory is the hotel lift – the first lift she had ever seen, which for many days provided so much entertainment and fascination that only a visit to her father's hospital could drag her away from its perennially opening and closing doors.

Life slowed down when Genia and Ariane went back to Tel Aviv. They could enjoy the comforts of being away from the front line, but the feeling of anxiety didn't leave Genia. The relatively peaceful years between 1940 and 1945 in Tel Aviv were lived against the backdrop of the war in Europe. The letters she received from her parents took many weeks to reach their destination and often caused her to worry even more. The paragraphs on the progress of the war didn't get through the censors; the black lines crossing out words and sentences hung over her as she tried to guess what her parents wanted to tell her. Genia worried about her sister, Eva, and her family. She tried not to believe all the rumours she heard about the deportation of the Jews from Germany. She knew that while her sister was in Belgium she was not safe from a similar fate.

The distance and the sense of being cut off from her family overwhelmed Genia. An onset of depression brought with it a stomach ulcer, confining her to bed for weeks. David's parents did what they could to help their daughter-in-law, trying to provide comfort and support, as well as looking after Ariane, but Genia knew that only time and good news would bring her relief.

David returned on leave to see his family, but the visits were rare. For Ariane those stays bring back conflicting memories. She tells me her parents would go out in the evening leaving her alone in the house. Eventually she learnt to entertain herself, but at first the fear of strange noises and the darkness overwhelmed the little girl. She never got over the air sirens.

'I was taught to go down to the basement when there was a siren. It was below our building, and there was a shelter with sandbags. If there was an alert when I was alone, I went downstairs on my own. A few times they came back in the middle of the siren because they knew I was by myself. But I remember going downstairs, with bare feet – I was five, six years old. I wasn't scared because it was normal. We were used to it,' she tells me.

When David went back to the front line, Genia made an effort to lead a more normal life. She responded to lunch and dinner invitations from her husband's friends that had gone unanswered, trying to make herself socialise again. She attended parties in the evenings. The lifestyle that she had enjoyed in Geneva and in her early days in Tel Aviv was still to be found in the war years, and overcoming her loneliness and fears she tried to rediscover her former self.

Ariane also assures me that her mother did not lack attention from male admirers. Genia couldn't have known that it would be her attempt to distract herself from the routine of daily life that would eventually lead to the end of her marriage and life in Palestine. Through private tuition in French, which she started after an acquaintance suggested it as a way of passing the time and earning some money, she met Kurt B. An émigré from Berlin, he shared Genia's passion for culture and intellectual debate, and very soon they were spending many of their evenings together. Kurt confided in Genia that he missed Europe and would like to return once the war was over. Admittedly, this was something that she had been thinking about herself. Even though there was no end to the fighting in sight, Genia started planning her return to Geneva. All she needed now was for the war to be over.

15

A lucky escape

Brussels, 1942

It was New Year's Eve, 1941. Eva, Stanis and Anita arrived at the Sternbergs' apartment on rue de la Vallée in Brussels. They were dressed up for the occasion, determined to celebrate the arrival of the new year. It was not yet eight o'clock in the evening. The residential curfew for Jews had not yet started, and the two families had hours to put the final touches to the apartment and the festive table.

They were celebrating the end of the year, hoping that the new one would bring peace and security. They were not naive. They knew that in the past few weeks, Jewish students had been banned from attending public schools, and the strict curfew from 8pm until 7am meant that many more households were now struggling to hold down the jobs that they were still allowed to have, or to gather with their friends in the evening.

Yet Eva was feeling hopeful. She was enjoying the holiday surrounded by her family and friends, and they were welcoming in the new year with a parcel that Eva's parents had sent her for the holidays. As a Swiss citizen she was allowed to receive gifts from abroad – the humble seasonal provisions of cheese and chocolate obtained by her parents despite the rationing. She tried to put aside everything she had been agonising over for the past few months and imagined a safe future for her family in Geneva, away from the uncertainties of war.

She glanced over in Ti's direction and her heart beat faster for a few seconds, overwhelmed by momentary sadness. She already knew that despite their growing feelings for each other, the circumstances of their lives had a stronger power over their fate. Ti was sitting at the piano playing children's round dances. His handsome face lit up as he watched Betty, Stanis and the kids dance in a circle. Their shadows jumped up and down on the wall, magnified out of proportion by the candles lit for the celebration.

Eva was overwhelmed by emotion and struggled to hold back tears. She hadn't seen everyone so happy and so relaxed for many months. You could almost imagine that they were leading a normal life where Jews were not persecuted and their lives were not in danger. Eva thought back to the past six months and promised herself that she would never send her daughter away again. What had she been thinking when she decided that Anita would be better off in Geneva with her grandparents? Of course, she reminded herself, the promise of better food and security, and the rumours of deportations that were intensifying last spring played their role. Panic was setting in when she had made the decision, but she had regretted it almost immediately. She lasted several months before finally asking Adolphe and Marie to put Anita on a train back to Brussels. The months of tears and anxiety were now over, and as she watched her daughter twirl around the living room, she was reassured by her happiness, and her expression of joy at seeing the adults pretend to dance with the children.

Eva knew that there were many difficult decisions ahead of them. If it had been possible for them all to leave the country with the same ease that the Red Cross had first evacuated Anita with the other children, they would have been on the next train to Switzerland. For now, their future was far from decided. Eva didn't want to spoil the celebration. She didn't want Stanis or Ti to notice her tears. She quickly looked away to compose herself. '*It was the last holiday that we spent together,*' she would write in her diary many years later. '*All that followed after was the war and anxiety.*'

The start of 1942 was a grim reminder that things could – and would – still get worse. Dr Sternberg came home one night a shadow of his former self. His job had kept him going, providing stability and comfort. Ti always thought the status of a doctor would protect him and his family from the fate suffered by thousands of others. His many non-Jewish clients seemed to respect him and value his opinion, and he was reassured to have their support. The latest anti-Jewish measure, announced to take effect overnight, was a brutal reminder that no one was safe. No Jew was protected from Nazi ideology. No family doctor, surgeon or dentist would now be allowed to treat their non-Jewish patients.

Ti's world collapsed, leaving him naked and exposed. His inability to protect his family came so unexpectedly that he spent days not leaving his study. He needed to readjust to the new reality. Now that it touched him directly, he was able to see it for what it was: a persecution of a people for simply trying to live their lives.

Ti might have been late to the realisation that it was no longer safe to be a Jew in Brussels, but all around him people were trying to find ways of leaving the country. The lack of food and the restrictions faced by Jews made it almost impossible to lead a normal life. The rumours of deportations and concentration camps, the suspicions, the conversations overheard on the street and news whispered quietly to a friend filled everyone with doubt. Together, Ti and his friends spent hours in the kitchen – talking and arguing, imagining the best-case and worst-case scenarios and trying to work out what to do. Once the children were safely in bed, they could talk freely to each other, but they preferred to whisper, their hushed words filling the small kitchen in Eva's apartment with anger and anxiety.

They knew that they should have tried to leave. But Stanis would never be allowed out of the country. His only piece of identification was his Nansen passport. Once the official status of a stateless refugee issued by the League of Nations, it was now a worthless piece of paper. Without an exit permit he would be taken off the first train, turned back and probably arrested and deported along with thousands of others attempting to flee the Nazis.

Eva and Stanis hoped that in Brussels they could remain invisible – hiding right under the noses of the Germans who were busy arresting Jews elsewhere.

But the Germans had other plans. In May 1942 they announced that all Jews would have to wear a yellow star when they left the house. The new measure made the Jewish population an unmistakable target: to be humiliated on the street, to be taken in for questioning and then arrested. There seemed to be no respite.

Eva was furious. She had already had to have her passport stamped with the letter J. She had felt ashamed and incredulous when she learnt that the idea had come from Switzerland.

It was the chief of the federal Swiss police who came up with the good idea. In fact, this Rothmund (who went down in history as the worst of the bastards) who asked the Germans to put the letter J (Jew) on the passports, to identify the people who had to be driven away from the Swiss border.

Eva despised the idea, but what could she have done?

Not to register and try to pretend to be Christian with names like Zousman or Sternberg or Kahn? If they caught a Jew whose passport didn't have the letter J, he was shot. What should we have done? We talked for hours and hours, not knowing what we were discussing – if we could hide in a safe place we could avoid having the J on our passports. My friend Anne was the only person we could trust, but she had already put up her mother who barely spoke French. And also hiding meant having a lot of money to be able to pay those who would hide us. And so we went to the Kommandantur, all of us, thus identifying ourselves for the slaughterhouse. We couldn't leave the house without a proof of identity and when one of us went to buy food, we shook from fear if their absence extended.

Eva was determined to stand by her beliefs. She was a Swiss citizen, protected by the neutrality of her country, and she refused to put on the ugly yellow star imposed by the occupying powers, instead putting on a pin with the Swiss cross on her lapel. Nothing would change her mind. She was lucky that she didn't get stopped.

Eva and Stanis knew that it was time to act. They were determined to save themselves and leave the country. It was almost too late by then; Eva could tell they should have left earlier. Thousands of Jews had already been taken away by the Germans, and thousands more would follow. Eva and Stanis started looking for a way out.

In spring 1942 Jews were beginning to get scared, there was talk of arrests, of camps near Brussels, but that was it. We knew that we really needed to find a way of leaving together. Anita and I with our real papers as Swiss citizens, the others with fake papers.

Anita remembers the day their lives changed forever. That afternoon she was surprised to see her mother arrive in the middle of the school day in a panic. She could see the tears in her eyes as she rushed over to hug her daughter. She told her that they were going home. Eva didn't explain that she had just got a phone call from Anita's teacher, who got in touch as soon as she could get to the telephone to warn Eva that there had been a raid at another school in the neighbourhood where all Jewish children had been taken away. The teacher's voice was shaking with fear, but Eva was already running out of the door to bring her daughter back home to safety.

Eva was in tears that evening as they decided that it would be safer to send Anita back to Geneva once again. She remembered the sleepless nights she had spent next to her daughter's empty bed the last time she was away from Brussels and she had promised herself she would not be apart from her again. But she knew that she needed to make a responsible decision. If the raids on schools continued she risked losing her daughter forever. Once again, she went to the Swiss Red Cross to sign Anita up for one of the trains taking children across the border. Officially they were going on holiday but no one was under any illusions about the true reasons for the evacuations. Many Jewish children would survive the Holocaust in Belgium thanks to the Red Cross trains and to the many families that fostered them during the war. Despite her hesitation and heartbreak Eva was grateful to have the option of sending Anita to safety.

Of all the horrors of the war Anita lived through as a child, it is the evacuation itself that she remembers most clearly. As we sit in her apartment in Geneva, she tells me that the journey was a terrifying experience. She doesn't pause or hesitate as she recounts the moment more than seventy years ago when she said goodbye to her mother and father at the platform. They were surrounded by crying children and their parents, many saying goodbye to each other for the last time. Anita was being reassured by Eva and Stanis that the move was only temporary and that they would be joining her as soon as they could. Her father gave her a hug and reminded her to eat well and listen to her grandmother. As he let her go, she looked up to see him wink at her, trying to reassure her, but the familiar attempt to bring a smile to his daughter's face failed. Anita's bottom lip trembled as she got on the train, fighting back tears and trying not to let her parents out of her sight. She was not to know that this would be the last time she would ever see her father.

Anita with her father Stanis in Brussels during World War II

The train was full. Children of all ages, many silent now that their tears had dried, took in their surroundings. The youngest ones were looked after by the Belgian nurses who were allowed to accompany them across the border. Anita tells me she didn't know whether she was more terrified of the German soldiers who were standing guard in every carriage, their faces stone cold and their rifles at the ready, or whether she was still crying at the image of her parents waving her goodbye as the train pulled away from the platform. She lost sight of them very quickly among the wet faces of hundreds of men and women waving goodbye to their children, their white handkerchiefs flying in the air like confetti.

The force of her fall woke her up in the middle of the night. Anita had rolled off the wooden bench she was sleeping on and, even though she was still half asleep, she was terrified to see a German soldier heading in her direction. She was crying uncontrollably by the time he picked her up and put her back on the bench. Unsure what to do with the screaming child, he smiled at the little girl and disappeared. Anita laughs as she tells me the story, convinced that she probably scared herself even further through the force of her cries.

Eva and Stanis spent an agonising summer in Brussels. Eva felt trapped. In an emotional letter to her father, she wrote of her wish to go on holiday in the Swiss mountains of the Jura. She knew the letters were being censored and she hoped that her father would be able to read between the lines and would recognise his daughter's cry for help. The Jura was a favourite holiday destination for the family, but Adolphe didn't see the letter for what it was.

Alas, nobody understood us and for the rest of my life I will remember the letter where my father wrote that we didn't need holidays, that I must have forgotten that there was a war and who thought of holidays?

There were few options available for escape. Stanis and the Sternbergs needed fake papers to hide their true identities and Swiss visas to be able to cross the border into the country of Eva's birth. She tried the Swiss embassy, where she was told that Switzerland was only able to issue transit visas at the moment and she would have to find a country willing to grant her husband a visa if she wanted to get out of Belgium.

And so started the exhausting days. One after the other I went to all the embassies of South America, promising them money that was in Switzerland for a visa to one of their countries, the countries that we had no intention of going to after the war, something the embassies knew well. And I was the only one who could do all these approaches as I was the only one who was 'neutral'.

Hours on the tram were followed by hours waiting in small obscure rooms. Eva was exhausted by the gruelling days. She thought that she had a chance of getting a visa from one of the countries of South America, but she was too late. Once friendly to the plight of Jewish refugees from Europe, many were now more hesitant to welcome them on the other side of the world. Rising anti-Semitism at home and populist fears over competition for the few jobs available to the local people meant that what had once been a way to safety was no longer an option. Eva felt the weight of rejection on her shoulders. She tried not to lose hope. She thought of her daughter in Geneva and tried to believe that they would be reunited in the near future. But as she continued trying to organise an exit visa for herself, she learnt that without her father's help the Germans were not going to make an exception for her to leave the country.

The pages of Eva's diary read like a tragic novel of hope and suspense. Written many years after the events, she relives the uncertainties of the summer of 1942 when she was beginning to feel that if they didn't leave Brussels they would all be rounded up before the end of the year. Deportations had been going on for months in Germany. In July that year, notices were sent to hundreds of thousands of Jews in the Netherlands, and to several thousand in Brussels. By writing everything down so many years later, it is as if she was trying to miraculously change the outcome.

By the middle of the summer, Eva and Stanis had a plan.

We sought the advice of my friend Anne and her husband (Belgian, Catholic). We were able to buy fake papers, and stick in real photos for a lot of money. With Anne's advice we decided that Stanis and the Sternbergs shouldn't leave all together. Betty, blonde with blue eyes who doesn't look Jewish, would leave with Stanis and Paul. They had different identities – they were friends on holiday together, and their partners would join them later. The main thing was to find a smuggler to cross the Belgian border. Stanis would speak for himself and Betty (because of her strong accent. Paul spoke good French). And when we had news from them in Geneva, Ti would leave with a smuggler (his trip would be the most dangerous because he had a strong Viennese accent). I would be the last to leave as soon as everyone else was safe.

We didn't think this would be easy, but we didn't know that the Swiss border was hermetically sealed with barbed wire, no one knew that. At the end of June Stanis left, like he was going on holiday. Betty left with Paul, who was carrying a bucket and a spade. The smuggler was a lovely woman from Brussels who lived on the top floor of our building.

Ti and I waited with pounding hearts. After three days, she came back, telling us that everything went well and she left them in northern France where they were looking for another smuggler to get them through the Jura. We waited.

While they were waiting for news of their families, Ti moved into Eva's apartment. They didn't get many opportunities to spend time together, and as they nervously waited for news from Stanis and Betty, they could distract themselves with each other's company. They talked all day and all night. About their fears and their hopes for the future. About their families – Eva's husband and Ti's wife, whom they loved deeply despite their passion for each other. They thought of a time when there would be no more war and Europe would no longer be gripped by Nazi ideology. Eva nervously woke up every morning wondering whether there would be news from Stanis, hoping that he would be able to send her a note once he had safely crossed into Switzerland. Ti woke up from nightmares about his wife and son being captured and arrested, but he tried to reassure Eva that there was no need to panic.

They barely left the apartment. They had everything they needed and it was safer to be inside. Eva's feelings were tearing her apart. Her love for Ti and her worry for her husband were fighting inside her, trying to win over each other. She knew that she loved them both. She couldn't imagine Stanis not being in her life. And yet when she looked at Ti she felt alive, she felt young and hopeful, and wished that their self-imposed honeymoon at her apartment would never come to an end.

Ti asked Eva if she would marry him once the war was over. He was picturing an idyllic life for the two of them in Geneva – a dreamlike illusion brought on by the craving for love, passion and, above all, freedom. Eva was hesitant. She was worried about planning too much ahead, but she also knew that for the past nine years Stanis had been a perfect husband and a perfect father to her daughter. It was during one of these conversations that they were interrupted by a phone call.

Ten days after their departure, a bombshell. A female voice on the phone was telling me that my husband, the lady and her child were arrested and were with the German police and my husband had – by greatest coincidence (and risk) given my phone number to the lady. This woman was giving me a rendezvous in a cafe to tell me all the details in person. I was terribly bewildered, suspicious and scared to go to this meeting. I asked the secretary at the Swiss embassy (we knew each other well) if she could go instead and pretend to be me. She was happy to help and learnt that Stanis, Betty and Paul were arrested at a small train station and we didn't know what was going to happen.

More discussions with our friends the Mellers (Anne and her husband) who advised us to go to the Belgian police and tell them that my husband ran away with Ti's wife and that we would like the Belgian police to

get their hands on them and make them come back. And we went to
explain... What a comedy, what a comedy! But our reasoning told us that
maybe Belgian police would launch an appeal and the Germans would
give them back to the Belgians. Those who read these pages 50 years later
will laugh at our plans, but we still lived with hope. I can see myself going
to the police station with Ti to make a complaint against my husband
who abandoned me after telling me he was going on a business trip, and
Ti against his wife, who was meant to be on holidays on the beach. They
asked us a lot of questions, we had to lie a lot and the wait started again
without much hope.

Eight days later, they arrived at Avenue Louise, all three of them, happy to
be there, not thanks to the Belgian police, but because the German border
police (not the Gestapo or the SS) believed what Stanis told them. Yes, he
had brown hair and dark skin, but everyone knows that Belgium had
been occupied by the Spanish for a hundred years and between them and
the Flemish there had been a lot of mixing. Stanis and Betty pretended
not to speak and understand Flemish. They kept them at the police station
for 48 hours, fed them and laughed with them, and let them go. As simple
as that. We were happy and distressed, we had to find new fake papers,
new smugglers, and time was running out.

When I first read the story I couldn't believe how far-fetched and
implausible it was. It also left more questions than answers, but Eva
moves straight on to continue recounting their eventual escape from the
country.

A breakthrough came when Adolphe informed his daughter that
she and Stanis would be able to go on holiday in the Jura Mountains
after all.

It was then that we understood that he obtained a visa for Stanis to enter
Switzerland and when I asked the same question on behalf of our friends
the Sternbergs, father told me it was out of the question.

Adolphe was also able to obtain an exit visa for his daughter, securing her escape from Belgium and her future.

Father had a lot of trouble getting a visa for me, and it was Professor Babel (my history professor at University) who accompanied him to that bastard Rothmund at the Federal Council (the worst anti-Semite) who finally and thanks to Prof Babel allowed himself to yield and had the Reich in Berlin issue me with an exit visa despite the letter J on my Swiss passport.

The exit permit that Adolphe was able to obtain for Eva was issued for a specific date, and on 12 September 1942 she received a note informing her she had twenty-four hours to pick up her documents and leave. She panicked. Stanis and the Sternbergs were still trying to sort out fake papers for themselves to leave the country; Eva would have preferred to make sure that they were safe before leaving herself, but she didn't have a choice. In the morning she travelled to the German embassy to pick up her exit permit.

In the courtyard of the building she hesitated. She was not sure how to find the office that she was looking for, and when a German officer appeared, she asked him for help.

'An exit permit?' He was surprised. 'Are you Jewish?'

'Yes,' replied Eva.

'But you are not allowed to leave the country!'

Eva explained that she could leave because as a Swiss citizen she had been given a permit, and showed the officer the letter telling her to pick it up. She was simply asking him to point her in the direction of the correct room. The officer became aggressive.

'No!' he shouted. 'You are not allowed to leave and you are going to come with me now!'

He grabbed Eva by the arm and started to drag her from the courtyard. Eva tried to resist. She knew that if she didn't escape from this man her life would be over. But he had the upper hand; he was stronger and had already managed to drag her away from the courtyard. Eva was about to call for help when another employee of the embassy appeared in the corridor. Eva begged the woman to listen. She waved the piece of paper in her hand and shouted that she was only looking for the office where she could collect the document that was waiting for her.

It was Eva's lucky day. She would later describe the appearance of the woman as the most miraculous moment of her life. The officer had no choice but to let go of Eva's arm when he learnt that it was his colleague who had Eva's document on her desk and Eva could follow her to pick it up. He watched Eva straighten her dress and follow the woman across the courtyard, his fists clenched in frustration.

Having escaped arrest and obtained her permit, Eva hurried home. She didn't have time to stop and think about her lucky escape. She had to pack her bags and get to the hotel near the train station before the start of the curfew. The train didn't leave until three o'clock in the morning, but it was not safe to travel to the station in the middle of the night; the risk of arrest was too high. Now that she was so close to leaving the country she would make sure no one else stood in her way.

At home Eva finished packing. She took her most valuable possessions, but tried to keep her luggage light. She could see Stanis pacing outside the door, nervously looking into the bedroom. They hadn't had a chance to sit down and discuss their future. Eva could feel her heart swelling up with emotion as she prepared to leave. She packed some of Stanis' clothes as well, as she imagined that he would have to make most of his journey on foot. She was so sure that they were going to see each other in five to ten days' time that she even brought his tux.

At the tram stop on Avenue Louise later that afternoon, she said goodbye to her husband. They kissed as they saw the tram approaching. They held hands, wishing they had more time to talk, to plan, to prepare for her departure. The tram was almost at the stop. Eva hugged Stanis, reassuring him that they would see each other the following week. Stanis looked pale and tried to smile. His hands were shaking, and Eva had to summon all her energy not to break down in tears as she climbed the two steps of the tram and found a seat by the window. Time stood still. They watched each other, their faces wet, the palms of their hands damp from sweat, their hearts beating faster and faster. As the tram started pulling away, Stanis ran after it.

'I feel we will never see each other again,' he shouted.

Eva's heart jumped. She feared his words. She wished he hadn't said anything, but she knew that he was wrong. She shouted back, promising that she was looking forward to seeing him next week. She was too far for her words to reach him. As she looked back she could see her husband standing at the tram stop, his face buried in his hands, shaking uncontrollably as tears finally overwhelmed him.

At the hotel Eva tried to compose herself. In a few hours she would be boarding the train that would take her to safety. She tried to read, but instead replayed the emotional goodbye to Stanis, telling herself once again that he was wrong. She knew that they had a plan. They had almost succeeded in getting to Switzerland; this time nothing would stop them.

Eva was woken by a knock on her door. Her heart jumped. Two knocks, pause. Three knocks, pause. Then one. It could only be him, she thought. Their secret knock, announcing his arrival.

Ti explained that he couldn't let her leave without saying goodbye. He held her in his arms. He kissed her and stared into her eyes, trying to memorise every little thing about her. There were no words that could reassure them of their future. Nothing they could add to everything that had already been said a million times over. They could only hope that they would see each other again under different circumstances.

They went over the details once again, Ti promising to write to Eva as often as he could, until it was time for them to leave Brussels and head for the fields and mountains of France and eventually – hopefully – Switzerland.

Ti got up to leave. She knew that he couldn't stay long. He had a long walk home ahead of him, and he would have to be careful. He couldn't take the tram in case he got stopped for being out during curfew, and she was grateful and overwhelmed that he had been willing to risk his life for her. As they said their final goodbye, Eva was torn by the emotion of the day. The guilt of deceiving her husband and the sadness of not knowing whether she would ever see her lover again made for a tearful departure.

It was the middle of the night when Eva boarded the train. She nervously looked around at the German soldiers surrounding her. She took a deep breath. She had a long journey ahead. From Brussels the train would take her to Basel, via the German city of Cologne and the French Alsace. Crossing into enemy territory was the only way to get to safety. In her first-class compartment, Eva was the only woman. The officer sitting in front of her helped to put away her two suitcases, and the train finally left the sleeping city behind.

They rode in darkness. The German officer made small talk. He smiled and asked Eva where she was going. Eva was cautious but decided that she had no reason to lie. He told her how lucky she was to be going to Switzerland. Then he talked for a long time. Eva drifted in and out of his monologue. She tried to concentrate on his words but her mind was racing ahead, trying to anticipate the problems she might still encounter.

As her companion kept talking, she noticed his elegant hands. She learnt that he was a pianist. He told her of his passion for music, his life interrupted by the order to put on a uniform and serve in the army. He was devastated. He knew that even if he survived the horror of war he would never be able to play the same way again. Eva was moved by what she heard. To her shame, she realised that not all Germans were united in their cause and that this young man was certainly not the only one to have a different opinion. In the morning, she woke up to find that he had brought her some food.

When they had to change trains, he helped Eva with her suitcases. He called her an 'Honourable Frau'. Eva smiled, but her hands kept playing with the hem of her blouse, scrunching it up and straightening it back again as she continued her conversation with the officer. She spoke quietly and quickly, trying to make sure the other passengers couldn't hear her. The rest of the journey passed in a haze. She would vaguely remember the two-hour break in Cologne where they changed trains and went to the buffet. More conversations with more soldiers who joined their cabin – they all told her how lucky she was, and she tried to smile. The document checks made Eva's heart sink so low she thought she might faint each time. She didn't dare look up and see their faces. Before the train crossed the Swiss border and reached Basel, her 'pianist colonel', as she now called him, disembarked, and Eva continued on her own.

She arrived in the middle of the night and checked into a hotel. She took a long shower and tried to stop herself from shaking. She found it hard to believe she was out of danger. She looked at herself in the bathroom mirror, her face puffy from the tears and the sleepless night. She tried to arrange her hair into place, but the curls seemed as bewildered as she was, refusing to stick together. Eva gave up. She thought of Stanis back at their apartment on Avenue Louise. She thought of Ti, so passionate and tender the last time she saw him, only hours ago but already it felt like an eternity had passed since their goodbye. She called her family to let them know that she had safely crossed the border, and collapsed on her bed in exhaustion. She wept.

16

A safe haven

Geneva, 1942–1945

The road leading to the cemetery is easy to miss. The sign is barely visible. Those in the know usually look for the small petrol station or the private car park across the road to remind them of the turning. An old stone wall and fields border the narrow lane leading to the cemetery. At the bottom of the road a small oratory adorned with a Star of David marks the destination.

The Veyrier cemetery in Switzerland is unique. A large metal gate welcomes you at the edge of the car park. Walk through the gate to the graveyard and you find yourself in France. This historic peculiarity doesn't matter to the people who visit the graveyard to tend to the tombs of their loved ones today. But it is this uniqueness that enabled smugglers to use the cemetery as an escape route from France into Switzerland during the war.

The graves face east, according to Jewish burial tradition, with the heavy stones set in straight lines to give the burial ground an orderly and dignified appearance. Big Hebrew letters spell out the names of the men and women of the Jewish community of Geneva who found their resting place on this small and intimate plot of land. If the stones commemorating their lives could talk, they would recount the most daring stories of escape and survival during the hardest years of Jewish persecution.

Joseph Ghielmetti, a quiet, hard-working man in charge of burials at the cemetery during the war, was one of very few people who could go back and forth between the two countries, and he used this privilege to save countless lives. Leading people through the cemetery under the cover of darkness or during a funeral, he made sure they crossed the invisible line at the metal gate at the entrance and reached the other side of the border unobserved by the Italian border guards.

Thousands were saved by crossing into Switzerland from France with the help of smugglers. They crossed rivers and mountains, hid in forests and in special hideout places, helped by farmers and their families, hidden for days and weeks until the path was clear for them to continue. For many, Switzerland was their only hope of survival. But the Swiss government was terrified of refugees. By 1942 it required all foreigners to obtain a visa before crossing into the country. Even those who were suspected of facing considerable personal dangers and risks in the countries they were running from – and that would include all those fleeing the risk of arrest and being sent to a concentration camp – were no longer admitted. As many as 20,000 people were turned away at the border, some betrayed by the smugglers, many others stopped by the border guards who arrested them and sent them to their deaths.

Those who did make it were relieved to find that despite Switzerland's refusal to pay for them, local Jewish communities and men like Adolphe Neuman were ready to provide food and shelter.

Adolphe's house was always open to those in need of a hot meal in the evening and sometimes a bed for the night. Daily dinners were held in the family apartment on Avenue Bertrand, often seating up to twenty people. Sitting at the head of the long table covered with a white tablecloth of old European lace, Adolphe led the conversation, frequently jumping from politics to the cultural life of the city. For those present it was hard to concentrate on what was being said in the room, for the smells coming from Marie's kitchen reminded them of the homes they had left behind. Despite the shortages and strict rationing, Adolphe was able to obtain enough food to feed his guests. When the dishes came out, conversation fell silent. It was not until the war was over that Marie would be able to feed her guests her signature chicken soup and gefilte fish. Nevertheless, even in the days when food was scarce, she created delicious meals by experimenting with the Swiss-grown produce that was available to her. People appreciated Adolphe's generosity, and many of those who first found a helping hand in his house became firm friends.

Adolphe was a stern and intimidating man, but also elegant and charismatic, always dressed in the best suits with carefully chosen accessories – either his favourite tie pin topped by a pearl, or a carefully folded handkerchief in his breast pocket. His appearance was a reminder to those who had known him for many years of what it was possible to achieve through hard work and dedication.

Adolphe was equally at home in the simpler attire of a grey shirt and nondescript trousers with a huge ladle in hand, serving steaming hot soup to hundreds of children of all ages. His huge smile was a rare emotion amid the stress and uncertainties of war, and he chatted to the children as he continued to dip the ladle in and out of the huge metal barrel-like bowl.

At La Mensa, a kosher restaurant Adolphe had opened with his friend Salomon Kagan, refugees and students who could not afford a hot meal elsewhere came to spend an evening to rebuild their strength and socialise. In the first four months of the restaurant's existence more than 12,000 hot meals were served to children, students, artists and refugees. Marie and her sister Berthe made hundreds of matzah balls for

Passover one year, and other members of the family often popped round to volunteer their services.

Despite his standing in the Jewish community and his extrovert nature, Adolphe was a private man. For many years his family was not aware of the extent of his involvement in the different charities and organisations that helped refugees and those struggling to stand on their own two feet in the post-war years.

Decades later, one busy Sunday morning at the flea market in Geneva, Anita's son Youri was taking a stroll through the Plainpalais Square. He was keeping an eye on the multitude of antique stalls, vintage merchandise and old books. It was then that he came across a portrait of a stern-looking man in his fifties, painted on a canvas and carefully framed in old lacquered wood. There could be no doubt, Youri realised seconds later, that he was staring at his great-grandfather Adolphe – the man whose life he had heard so much about from his mother and aunt, the both beloved and feared patriarch of the family. The man at the stall had found it at an old school building on the banks of Lake Geneva where he was allowed to look through the old furniture when the building was closed.

The school, as Youri later learnt, was run by the ORT[6], a charitable organisation that set up facilities to provide education for young Jewish boys and men who had left their homes and wanted to pursue further training and education in Geneva. Many of the early students had fled the Nazis in Eastern and Central Europe, and for them, ORT was a chance to obtain further training to help them get a start in life. Adolphe was among those who first saw the potential for such a school, helping to pay for the renovation of a building, which was opened in the post-war years and housed the school for five decades. A man who deeply appreciated books and languages, he also paid for the school library. It was there that for many years young men from all over the world could look up and see Adolphe's face watching them from an oil canvas, encouraging the students to persevere in life and achieve recognition for their abilities.

6   From Russian; ORT stands for 'Association for the Promotion of Skilled Trades'

Despite Adolphe's involvement with this and other organisations, it is not easy to find his name in the annals of their histories today. He didn't boast about his support and the numerous donations to the ORT school or the Mensa restaurant, and he continued to facilitate opportunities for young men and women long after the war was over.

Adolphe could not accept the wartime foreign policy of the Swiss government – the government of the same country that once welcomed him. Stricter entry requirements for Jews fleeing Nazi persecution and a refusal to accept responsibility for Swiss citizens who, like his daughter Eva, had found themselves under Nazi occupation, left him indignant and disappointed. He knew that Jews were being stopped at the border and turned back to where they came from, effectively sending them to their deaths. Adolphe felt helpless in the face of government policy and public opinion; both were against the opening of the borders to the tens of thousands of people fleeing from all corners of Europe.

Determined to act, Adolphe helped thousands. Unfortunately, today it is impossible to know just how many lives he touched, and just how many people went to bed at night grateful to the man who had done so much for so many, but who always preferred to remain in the shadows.

17

'Lapti'

Ufa, 1942

It was 1942 and Ufa had escaped the worst horrors of the conflict, but Anna's war experience was not over. Along with her friends and classmates from the Bashkir State University where she had been studying German language and literature for a year, she was being sent to the *TrudFront*. A typical Soviet shortening of two or more words to create another, *TrudFront* is short for *Trudovoi Front*, which roughly translates as the labour front line. While most of the male population was fighting in the war, everyone else capable of contributing to the war effort was mobilised to help the country. Anna's war effort included another Soviet concept – *ZernoSovKhoz* (*Zernovoe Sovetskoe Khoziaistvo*) – essentially a Soviet grain farm, although the words make it sound like something very official and important. These farms were first created in 1918 and, along with factories and plants, were the most popular destinations for the mobilised populations as that was where their help was needed the most. This practice of sending students to help out, created during the war, survived the war itself and became both one of the most feared and the most loved student experiences. For my intellectual father, going to the *KolKhoz*, a *Kollektivnoye Khoziaistvo*, a collective farm, during his student holidays in the 1970s was pure torture; manual labour was not for him. But my fun-loving mother, although no worker either, loved the spirit of the student labour movements, where young people met, fell in love and stayed up all night by the fire playing the guitar. That's certainly what she took away from her farm trips later on.

However, it was 1942 and the Soviet agricultural machine was in overdrive. The most recent five-year plan was suspended with the onset of war after only three years, and all efforts were being put into the production of armaments, tanks and weapons. Food was still needed to feed the massive Soviet army, as well as the general population, and Anna was packing for the village of Davlekanovo. I look at my grandmother, now a strong-minded ninety-two-year-old living in west London. What was going through her mind as she prepared to travel deep into the Soviet republic of Bashkiria? Was she anxious about going off on her own and leaving her mother behind? Was she worried about the course the war was taking? She didn't dwell on such details. Her life had already been turned upside down by the evacuation, and this time she was ready for the new challenge. Her best friend Malia, with whom she was thrilled to reunite at the University of Bashkiria after several unsuccessful attempts of writing to each other, was coming with her. The biggest decision she had to make was which shoes to take. She had her good, simple leather shoes, but she didn't want to ruin them by wearing them on the farm. The choice was not huge, as she did not own another pair. But this desire to protect her only good pair, which she knew would have to survive for many more months, if not years, prompted her to think creatively. She would bring her ice-skating boots, without the blades, for the wet weather. For the dry weather she brought *lapti* – bast shoes, which are made out of fibre from the bark of a birch tree. They had been in use since prehistoric times and were popular in Russia's rural villages. They were cheap to make but not particularly durable. Anna would fit right in at the farm in these shoes.

Russia was ravaged by war. After being caught off guard by the Nazis' shocking progress deep into Russian territory in previous months, the Soviet war machine was gearing up for a fight. Anna and her friends were following the news on the radio every night and were doing what they could to help the war effort, but they were still young girls on a summer break from their studies, and the gravity of the situation had failed to sink in. Anna was the butt of many jokes. Every morning she looked out of the window of the barn she was sharing with the girls and tried to work out whether it was going to rain or not. Should she wear her *lapti*, or would she be better off in her skating boots minus the blades? '*Nadet lapti?*' It is almost as pensive in Russian as 'to be, or not to be'. The girls found Anna and her *lapti* provided enough entertainment to last all summer.

Speaking on the phone to Malia recently, and recounting all the stories she had shared with me for this book, my grandmother reminded her best friend of their *TrudFront* experience during the war. '*Nadet lapti?*' she heard immediately in return, on a distant phone line across the ocean. A memory bubbled up to the surface from more than seven decades ago.

Of course, it wasn't all jokes and laughter. Everyone had to work at the farm. It was still dark when Anna left the room and made her way to the fields. It was back-breaking work for an inexperienced city girl like her. Harvesting grain, weeding potatoes, preparing hay for the cattle, Anna felt that she had been transported to an entirely different world. She wrapped her mother's old shawl around her shoulders to keep warm, yet still her teeth chattered. It was the middle of summer, but the cold damp air coming from the empty fields wrapped around her, penetrating her body, taking the last bit of her inner warmth away with it. With no proper clothes to keep warm, she shivered in her skate boots and wished for the night to end.

Anna with her friends Malia Braude and Tonia Alyoshina
during World War II

Two months at the farm felt like an eternity, with endless days of hard work and very little food. As autumn approached Anna was looking forward to going home and resuming her studies. It soon transpired that no arrangements had been made to take the girls back to the city, and so began a long wait. Anna was convinced that the farm bosses wanted to keep the students there as long as possible so they could get as much extra help as they could. She was devastated. She couldn't wait to get home, and suddenly the room she shared with her mother in Ufa and her own small single bed was an image of luxury. After another two weeks, in a spirit of defiance she organised a couple of other girls who decided that the time had come for them to leave by their own means. I am surprised to hear that my grandmother was the one leading the rebellion, but she tells me that by then she had had enough and could not tolerate the farm any longer.

It was not easy to leave the village of Davlekanovo. During the war a permit was required to be able to get on a train to travel to some cities, including Ufa. Having made their decision, the girls had no choice. They had to walk. In the middle of the night, they set off along the train tracks towards the city. Having led the uprising, Anna felt responsible for her classmates, so when they reached a Tatar village and needed a rest, she negotiated with a local woman to let them sleep in her house in return for a nice piece of linen that her mother had thoughtfully packed in her bag. The plan worked. Leaving their shoes in the doorway, as Tatar custom required, the girls fell asleep almost immediately.

It is eighty kilometres to Ufa. Under the cover of darkness, the girls walked a second night and by morning reached the town of Chishmy, their adventure almost over. From Chishmy they could get a train to Ufa without a permit, and several hours later reach home.

When Anna finally reached Ufa, she was quite a sight. As it turned out she had not returned alone; while brushing her hair that evening Anna realised that it was full of lice. She sighed. Her dreams of her bed would have to wait a little while longer, for the only solution to this was to pour kerosene over the hair, wrap a towel around the head and sit for hours waiting for the lice to die. Anna's short black hair was scraped into a bun and wrapped in an old faded towel, and she cautiously sat down on the sofa next to her mother to begin the wait. She had to repeat the procedure again and again, eventually washing her hair to try to get rid of the toxic smell of the kerosene.

The best thing, my grandmother tells me happily, is that the *lapti* survived the experience intact.

18

When there was hope

Brussels, Besançon, Drancy, Auschwitz, 1942–1943

Eva stared at the letter in her hand. She was terrified to think of its true meaning and the circumstances that had made her husband write to tell her that their 'holiday' had to be postponed. For the past six weeks she had lived letter to letter, both from Stanis and Ti, checking her mailbox several times a day for more news, writing to them of her feelings and desires to see them both safe in Geneva. She didn't dare mention their plans of escape, but she knew that they were making the final preparations for departure.

In her bedroom, Eva tried to come up with an explanation for their delay. She carefully re-read all the letters of the past weeks, wondering whether she had missed a detail, hoping for a hidden meaning she should have found and understood between the lines. There was nothing. She continued writing to Brussels, asking for a clarification, but without any real hope of receiving a clear answer.

On the 5th of November, the day I turned 36, I received from Stanis thirty-six lovely chrysanthemums, and I said to myself that these would be my favourite flowers. Weeks went by, the flowers were wilting and I didn't want mother to throw them away. December came and she threw them out.

Eventually Eva learnt from her friend Anne that Stanis and the Sternbergs had set off at the beginning of November. Anne was there to wave them off, but after their departure she had no more news to share.

It was September 1942 and Stanis, Ti, Betty and Paul were rushing to prepare for their departure. Every extra day they spent in Brussels carried the risk of arrest and deportation. German soldiers were patrolling the city, checking papers and removing Jews from the streets and their homes.

It took weeks to get hold of new fake documents and to find a smuggler who would help them cross from Belgium into France. Stanis, usually a cheerful man with a wide smile and an ability to tell jokes in every situation, became pensive and withdrawn. Ever since he had waved goodbye to Eva at the tram stop, he felt that something had shifted inside him. He hoped that his premonition would prove to be false, but with his wife's absence he felt luck had abandoned him.

Stanis and his companions set off from Brussels on 5 November, the day of Eva's birthday. They were hoping the date would bring much needed fortune at this moment in their lives. For Stanis, Betty and Paul this was their second attempt at reaching Switzerland. Like most refugees escaping war, they would make some of the journey on foot.

There were many different routes Stanis and the Sternbergs could have taken. It is only when I decided to look into their arrest further that

I learnt the facts. They were arrested on 16 December 1942 in the French city of Besançon. It is some seventy kilometres from the Franco-Swiss border, which means that they had been able to successfully get out of Belgium and make most of the way towards Switzerland before their luck ran out. They would have been planning to cross from France to Switzerland in the Neuchatel area, a popular yet treacherous route due to a river and a deep forest growing on a steep hill separating the two countries.

I learn the details of their failure seventy years after it took place, but it doesn't change the journey's terrible end. It does, however, affect Stanis' daughter deeply.

Anita always believed, having been told the story as a child, that her father reached the Franco-Swiss border at Moillesulaz, near the town of Annemasse, only six kilometres from the family home on Avenue Alfred Bertrand. She spent seventy years of her life thinking that her father was one of many men who were turned away by the Swiss guards, despite having an entry visa to Switzerland. The story she had heard from her mother, was that the Germans guarding the French border into Switzerland had seen Stanis as he was attempting the crossing, and so when he reached the Swiss border post, the guards turned him back to France. Once he was arrested, Anita told me, her father's real papers were found hidden in his sock, the Nansen passport stamped with the letter J revealing his true identity.

The story of Stanis' arrest at Moillesulaz makes more sense. Until 11 November 1942 that part of France was still in the free zone, and it would have been easier for Stanis to attempt a border crossing there. Even though the border with Switzerland was closed and he would have still had to be smuggled in despite having an entry visa, at least there would have been a smaller chance of arrest while in the French free zone. Trying to cross in the region of the Jura and going through Besançon would have been a much riskier undertaking, as that part of France was occupied and the risk of arrest on the streets during the journey would have been much higher. But I am sure that Stanis and the Sternbergs didn't have any other choice.

In an email to me on the day of discovery, Anita finds it difficult to conceal her emotion. *'My mother always told me that he was arrested at Moillesulaz, on the Swiss border, after being turned away by the Swiss border guards, because the Germans across the border in France had seen him! I believed this story until today, and I always blamed the Swiss for their actions!'*

After their arrest, Stanis, Ti, Betty and Paul were sent to the Fresnes prison near Paris. Despite the terrible conditions at the prison, Stanis was optimistic. Now that the worst of his fears had become reality, he felt that all he could do was sit and wait for whatever fate had in store for him. He refused to believe the horror stories and rumours about what awaited them once they left the prison. There was talk of the Drancy internment camp and concentration camps that followed from there, but Stanis blocked out the sound of people crying at night and trying to escape. He was confident that there was still a way out of his predicament. He was sure that Eva was doing everything she could to get him out. When he bumped into a family friend at the prison, he told him he was optimistic about the future. Leon Aleinik was eventually freed and contacted Eva – the first news she'd had of her husband for many weeks.

> *At the beginning of January 1943 Leon Aleinik called me to tell me that he spoke to Stanis and Ti at the Fresnes prison where he himself had been detained but later freed because he was Swiss. He told me that Stanis hoped that I would be able to free him. I told Leon everything I had tried to do with father's help in the last months. But by then Stanis and Ti and Betty and Paul were in Drancy.*

Family legend has it that Adolphe was indeed able to secure a laissez-passé for Stanis to get him out of Drancy and permission to travel to Switzerland, but by then it was too late. By the time the paperwork arrived at the internment camp, Stanis had been moved on.

Back in Geneva, Eva's hands shook as she opened the letter. It had been weeks since she had heard from Stanis, and although she dreaded to think what news the letter would bring, a letter gave her hope that her husband was still alive. As she put her hand on her heart, trying to stop it racing, she hoped for some good news at last. There was no stamp on the letter and the once-white envelope was creased, the corners softened by the long distance it had travelled. She recognised her husband's handwriting. As her shaking hands struggled to tear open the envelope, she imagined that Stanis had written to tell her of his escape, and that he was now in hiding, or maybe he was telling her that miraculously he would be freed. Eva didn't know that the contents of the letter would make her relive the guilt and the emotional turmoil she thought she had left behind.

She collapsed on her bed. The two pages of the letter, abandoned as her fingers slowly lost their grip, found their way to the floor.

He was accusing me of having not done anything to free him. He couldn't know that we tried to move mountains and continued trying to move them even after he had been deported for many months. There was also this sentence, the sentence that I never wanted to hear, because I didn't want to cause him any grief. "Ti told me everything and showed me the little photo that you gave him." I cried for him after I read all this, I was ill because of it. But I understood Ti, who loved Stanis very much and feeling that for them it was almost the end, he preferred to be honest with his friend and tell him the truth. I felt so much pain for both of them, especially Stanis. But Stanis added in his letter: "Despite all that, until my last breath I will think of you."

Eva never imagined that Stanis would learn of her affair with Ti. The guilt that she felt in the moments after their separation had been replaced by incessant worry about all her friends – Stanis, Ti, but also Betty and little Paul. She had almost forgotten the anxiety of the last days in Brussels, the fear of being found out and the moral dilemma of her affair.

Now, Eva was overcome by guilt. The emotion of her final goodbye with Stanis, followed by the passion of her final moments with Ti in the hotel room by the train station, the happy years she had shared with her husband and eventually even her brief affair with Simon before her wedding, all the memories came flooding back, tears glistening in her eyes, but she only blamed herself for her betrayal. She imagined her husband's pain, alone in prison, terrified of what the future held for him, knowing that the only woman he had ever loved had not been able to keep her promise to him. Eva felt that she needed to be able to explain herself, to help Stanis understand her actions, and beg him for forgiveness. But there was no return address. She wrote letter after letter, telling her husband of her feelings; the letters, sodden by her tears, all ended up in the wastebasket under her desk. She could not bring herself to finish them; she could not find the words to explain her actions.

Eva barely had time to compose herself after the nights she had spent lying awake when she received another letter, this time from Ti. His only request was for toothpaste. She spent hours looking at the once familiar beautiful cursive writing of the man she was in love with. She was trying to find hidden meaning, hoping to decipher a concealed message of love and passion that was once so easily exchanged between the two lovers. But on these pages Ti was almost unrecognisable. From his words she could feel how withdrawn he had become, how badly his detention had affected him. She didn't know when the letter had been written and how long it had taken to arrive at her address, but she went to the post office and sent the biggest parcel they would accept. She packed it with toothpaste, toiletries, chocolate, biscuits and other things that she thought might be useful.

Many years later Eva imagined that Ti, like Stanis, must have died thinking that she didn't do anything to help him.

Eva waited. She believed that Stanis and Ti would return. She cried in the middle of the night, awoken by a doorbell, only to realise that the bell had not rung, that it was all a dream. She dreamt of a happy future for her daughter where she was growing up with her father, and with each passing day she refused to believe that she would never hear from them again.

*

The sound of the doorbell was so sudden it made Eva jump from her chair. She stared at the door. She had been sitting on the balcony lost in thought. Memories of her childhood entangled together with hope for news of her loved ones swirled in her head, but secretly she wished for the silence to continue, hoping to delay any confirmation of her worst fears. The sound of the door interrupted her reverie and sent blood rushing to her face.

Hesitantly, she made her way across the apartment. It took her a moment to remind herself that it was the middle of the day and whoever was responsible for interrupting her thoughts was unlikely to bring news of her loved ones. At first she didn't recognise the young girl at the door. It was her niece Sylva. With short dark hair and a light complexion, the daughter of Stanis' brother Michel, and Anita's playmate during the unfortunate family holiday in De Panne, Sylva had turned into a young woman of sixteen. She was standing alone on Eva's doorstep. At the sight of her aunt, she fell into her arms, sobbing uncontrollably, finally relieved to have reached her destination.

Sylva's long and arduous journey to Geneva started in Antwerp. She had returned home to discover it ransacked. The doors of the house were thrown wide open, the cupboards turned upside down, and there was no sign of her father, Michel, her mother, Bluma, or her little brother Izzy in the house. It was a Sunday, a day the family usually spent together, reading books and resting before the start of the new week. Sylva felt her legs give way as she collapsed on a hard wooden chair in the dining room. In front of her she could see a fashion magazine her mother had been looking through when she would have been ruthlessly dragged away. Sylva's eyes were full of tears when she noticed that the corner of one of the pages of the magazine had been torn out and on it, a quickly scribbled note in her mother's writing. 'Go to Aunt Eva's', the note said.

The journey took several months. When she arrived, without a penny in her pocket and with only the few belongings she had been able to carry, she told stories of the nights she had spent on farms and the days where she stayed behind to work to get food. She changed location every few days, relying on the kindness of strangers and doing her best to avoid walking through populated places. She walked across half of northern France under the cover of darkness and was lucky to find a smuggler to help her get to Switzerland. She crossed the cold and tumultuous waters of the river Rhône, fortunate not to be swept away by the currents and not to be spotted by the guards watching over the seven-kilometre stretch of the river.

In Geneva, Sylva found family and protection. Heartbroken to find out that there had been no news from her uncle Stanis, she became the only person who could provide comfort to her aunt. In her sixteen-year-old niece, Eva found a companion and a sympathetic ear.

It would take Eva several years to learn what she already knew deep in her heart. Stanis Zousman, Szygmund Sternberg, his wife, Betty Sternberg, and their son, Paul Sternberg, were killed in Auschwitz on 9 February 1943, a few short months after they were first picked up and arrested in France. Michel Zousman, his wife, Bluma Zousman, and their son, Ignace Zousman, were killed in Auschwitz on 29 August 1942.

19

A day to remember

Moscow, Geneva, Tel Aviv, May 1945

Since the middle of the night people had been gathering on Moscow's Red Square, their faces illuminated with pride, cheeks puffy from tears of happiness and relief. It had been a sleepless night of celebrations, and as the news spread over the city, more and more people were joining in the festivities. Cannon fire and fireworks exploded over the Kremlin overnight, as reports of the ceasefire came in on the radio, and the spontaneous outpouring of emotion continued as thousands made their way to Russia's most iconic landmark. They waved flowers, greeting each other like long-lost friends, hugging strangers and kissing loved ones. They danced to the music blaring from the loudspeakers, singing the songs that they had forgotten over the five years of Russia's involvement in the hostilities. The war that left up to thirty million soldiers and civilians dead and decimated an entire generation of Soviet men was finally over. On 9 May 1945, the Red Square, the scene of so many future military parades in Russia and the Soviet Union, belonged to the people.

'It felt like the page had turned,' my grandmother tells me. 'Suddenly, there was good news. People had been listening to the radio and analysing the victories and the defeats of the army, checking the latest casualty figures and praying for their fathers and sons still at the front. And now, after years of losses and deprivation, after the months of tears on news of the deaths of young men and women, it was overwhelming.'

The Soviet people were proud of their perseverance and endurance during the years of the war but it would take survivors many decades to be able to describe in detail the horrors that they had lived through.

When she returned to the capital in 1943, two years after evacuation, Anna almost didn't recognise the city of her birth. Victory Day was two years away and the streets were dark. The blackout policy was in place and no lights illuminated the roads. At the first onset of darkness people escaped to their homes, where the windows were covered by tape and blackout blinds. The city was struggling.

Queues formed outside shops with people desperate for food. By the middle of the war the Germans controlled much of the Soviet Union's most fertile land. Feeding the population, including a massive army, was a huge problem. Food had to be obtained through coupons, and queues stretched for miles even for the most basic goods. The coupons were meant to last a month, and when you found something to buy, the shopkeepers cut off one of its corners, the treasured block of paper becoming smaller and thinner each time you made a purchase. It didn't matter though, as Anna soon discovered, because more often than not you had coupons left over at the end of the month; there was simply not enough to feed everyone.

People tiptoed around each other, aware of their grieving colleagues and neighbours. Death was everywhere. People shook when they came to open their mailboxes, dreading the news from the front. Death notifications arrived every day. The pieces of paper, with their formal language and official stamps, were brutal in their finality. On the streets, women dressed in black rushed to hospitals and morgues around the city, checking the reports for the latest casualties, looking for their husbands, sons and sometimes daughters. The fatality numbers were staggering. No one was spared the pain. Boys from Anna's school and childhood, boys she had been friends with growing up, the sons of her parents' friends and acquaintances were not coming home.

Day after day, night after night, Muscovites lived in fear and in hope that the enemy would soon be defeated, and they would be able to start rebuilding their lives.

'It was the people's victory, their day,' says my grandmother, returning to the day when people could forget about the tragedies of the previous years. 'Everyone was hopeful for the future, but we knew that the Soviet power didn't care about the people; it sent them to their deaths.'

When victory finally came, it was welcomed with open arms, tears of joy and pride washing away the anger and frustration of the heavy price the Soviet Union had to pay – at least temporarily.

The black-and-white photos of people hugging and kissing, crying and dancing in those early May days across Europe fill the screen of my computer. I am sitting in the comfort of my London flat as I look at the smiling faces of men and women, boys and girls, some barely old enough to have fought on the front line. Their happiness and relief looks the same – in London, Moscow, New York, Tel Aviv or Geneva.

In Geneva, Anita woke up on 8 May to find her grandmother, Marie, at the door. She was not the usual picture of elegance and grace. Her white hair was pointing in all directions and there was no hat in sight – an unimaginable occurrence, Anita tells me with a laugh. Around her grandmother's neck was draped a long crown of flags and flowers that someone had covered her in on the street. She was out of breath by the time she reached her daughter's apartment.

'The war is over!' she shouted. She wanted Anita and her mother to come down to join in the celebrations.

From her balcony, Anita saw people dancing and hugging each other on the street below. The accordion was in full swing and amid the noise of the beeping cars, the music faded under the singing voices. Celebrations would continue across the country for many days. A heavy load had been lifted from their shoulders, and people wanted to start looking forward to the future.

A sadness ran through the merriment. A sadness for all those who had been missing for years, gone, not known where. For Eva, this was also a moment of hope – that those loved ones would come back. In tears, she hugged her mother and daughter and promised herself that she would do everything she could to find out what had happened to her husband.

In Tel Aviv, people poured onto the streets even before the official announcement was made on the radio. Rumours had been circulating ever since Germany had surrendered the night before, and people were impatient to celebrate. There were parades, concerts, parties and fly-pasts. A flag with black borders was flown in memory of those who had been killed. Ariane describes the moment she remembers from her childhood as collective hysteria. Worse was still to come before the Jews would have their own country to call home, but on this day they were celebrating their survival. The Ashkenazi and Sephardi Chief Rabbis of Palestine declared a day of thanksgiving, with psalms and special prayers to mark the occasion.

The scenes of joy and happiness were almost unparalleled in the history of modern Europe. Eva, Genia, Anna, Anita and Ariane, as well as millions of others whose lives were irreversibly changed by the war, would never forget the years they had endured and the hope they felt when Europe was finally liberated from the evil ideology of Nazi Germany.

Part Three

20

Reunited in Geneva

Geneva, 1945

Ariane jumped off the train as soon as it came to a halt at Geneva's Cornavin train station. She was restless. The journey from Toulon in southern France had been long and boring, and she was impatient to run around and stretch her legs. The bright red hair of the seven-year-old girl was tied into two pigtails, which bounced jubilantly with each step. Hundreds of freckles covered her tanned face, a wide smile illuminating it as she turned to watch her mother carefully descend from the train. Genia was calm and elegant. No one could tell that only moments ago she had had to compose herself and readjust her make-up. It was the view of the Salève Mountain as they approached Geneva that made her heart beat faster. Tears started rolling down her face, and soon she was sobbing uncontrollably as reality finally hit her. She was back home for the first time in many years.

Genia scanned the platform for her mother and sister. She knew they would be waiting for her even though she had told them that it would be better if they met at home. Before she knew it, Genia was in her mother's embrace, breathing in the familiar scent of home. Then Ariane found herself in her grandfather's arms and curiously observed the commotion around her. She recognised Aunt Eva – she remembered her smiling eyes from the photographs. Her grandmother, Marie, who Ariane had been told visited her when she was just a baby, hugged the child and mumbled something amid sobs, but Ariane could barely make them out, and she didn't speak any French. Grandfather Adolphe winked at her, encouraging the little girl to smile. He seemed to be enjoying the reunion, even though Ariane could tell that he was not one for openly expressing his emotions. When the porter loaded their bags onto a carrier, Adolphe signalled that it was time to go, relieved to get away from the hustle and bustle of the train station.

Ariane was excited to be in Geneva. Since the end of the war two months earlier Genia had been making plans to visit home and finally introduce her daughter to her family. She told Ariane that they were going on holiday and would be back in Tel Aviv by the end of the summer. She was trying to reassure herself that she would return to the Middle East and to her husband, but in her heart Genia had already left Palestine behind. There was nothing for her in Tel Aviv. After the end of the war, David had decided to continue his military service, delaying his return by another three years. Genia's wartime friendship with Kurt had blossomed into a romance. Together, they dreamt of moving to Paris and starting a new life.

In Geneva, Ariane met her cousin Anita for the first time. Ariane and Anita. Anita and Ariane. Cousins, sisters, friends since they were little girls. Now both in their eighties, they live metres from each other, and often exchange WhatsApp messages in the evenings to catch up on the day's news. But for the first years of their lives they were almost unaware of each other's existence.

Ariane is sitting in her kitchen on Avenue Bertrand, four floors below the apartment where the girls' first meeting took place. 'When I saw Anita I thought she was like a sister to me, because I didn't have a sister, I was on my own. We couldn't speak to each other because I didn't know any French, but we understood each other as only children can.'

She remembers being seven years old and immediately finding the perfect place from which to observe her new surroundings at her grandfather's apartment. Her grandmother, Marie, was tidying the spotless apartment before the evening's celebratory meal to welcome her daughter and granddaughter to Geneva. Ariane, fascinated, stared at the dark green box. Shaped like a train, it slowly trailed across the living room as Marie vacuumed. Ariane promptly sat on top of this curious machine, which she decided had to be a toy; it easily carried her weight, transforming into a sleigh.

Ariane and Anita. Geneva, 1947

185

The Electrolux model, which Marie had been using since it was introduced just before the war, was a novelty for her granddaughter. In Tel Aviv, the tiled floors were washed three times a week to get rid of the sand blown across the city from the beach. For Anita, the hoover was not an exotic new discovery. As Ariane found out when her cousin walked through the door later that afternoon, she wasn't the only one who thought the sleigh-train was the best spot in the house.

Over a cup of tea, Anita also happily recalls the story of the hoover. 'Oh, that day we met for the first time!' she exclaims. 'I walked in and there she was, sitting in my spot!'

A sisterly rivalry had begun. Anita was used to being the only grandchild in Marie's and Adolphe's lives, and she spent a lot of time with her grandmother. From her vantage point at the top of the hoover, she closely monitored her grandmother's movements, anticipating the next turn as they vacuumed together, calculating the distance to the next room.

Everything changed with Ariane's arrival; she would go on to spend many years living with her grandparents. Despite the rivalry marking their first meeting, the two girls quickly became close friends. Aged nine, Anita was two years older than her cousin and became a neighbourhood guide and a perfect playmate for Ariane.

With Genia and Ariane's return to Geneva after the war, the whole family was reunited in Switzerland. Eva and Genia, once closely tied by their sisterly bond, relished their time together, living in the same city again more than a decade after Eva first left. A traumatic chapter of distance and separation was finally closed. Yet the dreams that had brought Genia back to Europe didn't centre on Geneva. In her reveries, she was going to Paris. After a few months of soaking up the family environment and rebuilding her energy, Genia was restless to move on with her life. Only 400 kilometres away, Kurt was waiting for her in Paris.

Genia moved to the French capital – the mythical city of fashion, poetry and art. She had often imagined herself in the city of light with Kurt, attending glamorous soirees and spending evenings at the opera.

The reality was very different. In 1946, Paris was recovering from the war. The rationing of bread, coffee, cooking oil and rice would continue for several years. A shortage of housing made life difficult for the burgeoning population of the already struggling city. Genia arrived in the cold, grey winter, and the snow-covered streets were far from the dazzling avenues of her imagination. However, in a rented apartment in the well-off sixteenth arrondissement, Genia and Kurt found a life together that they had only dreamt of in Tel Aviv.

Genia didn't realise how the trauma of the move would affect Ariane, who stayed behind in Geneva with her grandparents. Marie would bring her her mother's letters. Genia didn't write very often, and for Ariane every new message was a painful reminder that she had been left behind with her grandparents, uprooted from her country, her house and her friends. In her weekly telephone calls to her daughter, Genia encouraged Ariane to study hard at school and listen to her grandmother. She knew that her daughter was finding it difficult to settle into her new life, but she was certain that she would soon get used to her new surroundings.

Seven decades later, Ariane speaks of the toys and books she left behind in Tel Aviv. The trip to Geneva was supposed to be a holiday. She was looking forward to coming back to the sandy beaches of her hometown. For many months she would wake up dreaming of the sea, often crying out in the night for her mother and the life that was lost with this never-ending trip away. She no longer thought of the terrifying wailing sound of the wartime air sirens and the steps that led to the bomb shelter in the basement. Those memories faded to preserve Tel Aviv as the image of a perfect childhood that she would never get back.

Seeking to recreate the lifestyle of her early years, Ariane spent hours in Park Bertrand across the road. It was there that she rediscovered the freedom to run around, exploring corners and creating games that busied her outside for hours. The greenery of the many trees and bushes of the park were far from the sparsely planted boulevards and beaches of Tel Aviv, but Ariane enjoyed being outside, returning indoors only for dinner.

Many of the happy moments of those years are connected to her cousin, and Aunt Eva who would pop over almost daily to check on her niece and catch up on the day's events with her parents, often staying for tea and dinner.

Surrounded by the warmth and affection of the Neuman household, Ariane was living a life similar to that of her mother when she was a girl. As an eight-year-old, Ariane was oblivious to the social status of her grandparents. Her first big family event was Marie's sixtieth birthday party. The exquisite blue dress with a silk ribbon that Marie had picked out for her granddaughter for the occasion was not to Ariane's liking; it was tight and uncomfortable. Ever the tomboy, she felt like an impostor wearing the dress of a princess. However, she didn't want to upset her grandmother ahead of the celebration. At the party, she couldn't help but marvel at the glamorous surroundings. From the children's table, Ariane watched men and women arrive; her mother and Aunt Eva, both wearing elegant evening gowns, greeted their parents' friends with smiles and kisses on the cheek. Later, Ariane would learn that the guests were some of the most notable figures of Geneva's Jewish community. Adolphe's friends and business partners had supported each other since their arrival in the city and during the long years of the war. Marie was well respected in the Jewish community in her own right; she had spent years cooking meals for charity and organising fundraising events to help those in need. Though Ariane preferred to be playing outside, she was fascinated by the exquisiteness of the dresses and the splendour of the occasion.

There would be many similar events in Ariane's childhood. Eventually, she would become accustomed to their sophistication. Her mother's visits, short but frequent, provided a welcome interruption to the endless school days and afternoons in the park with Anita. A year passed. Her father's letters informed her that he was to be discharged from the army in the new year, and he was hoping to visit his daughter while he was on leave. Ariane didn't know that he had been trying to convince Genia to return to Tel Aviv. He was unsuccessful. Palestine was not a stable place, and Genia didn't hide her worry in her letters to her husband. The Second World

War was over, but the Jews were fighting the British for an independent Jewish state. David was involved with the Jewish Resistance Movement and promised Genia that the fighting would come to an end soon and life in an independent country would be different. But while the promise of a Jewish homeland might have been enough to convince Genia to move to the Middle East in the early 1930s, she was now a different woman. Her husband's arguments didn't sway her decision to stay in Europe.

For over a year David and Genia continued their correspondence, David first promising a life of paradise in Tel Aviv, and eventually, when he could tell that he was going to lose the battle, asking Genia to send Ariane to live with him in what would soon become Israel. David would not have his way. His wish for his daughter to live a 'normal life' rather than what he saw as a protected life of privilege, would go unanswered. By the time the State of Israel was created on 14 May 1948, Genia and David were divorced.

Genia's Middle Eastern adventure officially came to an end. She was not there to toast to the future of the newly created Jewish state with the man she once loved, the father of her child. The idealism of her youth had led her to follow David to a life full of promise in Tel Aviv, but after years of isolation in the faraway land she was seeking the comforts of Europe.

In Paris, Genia's life was about to take a new turn. Kurt's dream of starting up his own electrics factory came true. Adolphe was doubtful of the venture and did not appreciate being treated like a bank by his daughter. He only relented and agreed to a loan after hours of loud fights during Genia's visits to Geneva, during which Ariane would hide in the attic to avoid the confrontations between her mother and grandfather. Adolphe was proven right less than a year later. Kurt went bankrupt and all the money was lost. Genia knew that she could not simply walk out of the project as well as the relationship. Her lawyer, a man who would play an important part in the next stage of her life, was called Jacques Meyer-Morton.

21

A close call

Moscow, 1946

A year after the war was over, Anna had her dream job in Moscow. She was a translator for a team of scientists and engineers from the East German city of Jena. Their employer, Zeiss, once made photo-optical lenses, but under Hitler adapted itself to equip German armed forces. The Allies held Zeiss responsible for its contribution to the Nazi war of aggression; the factory was dismantled, bringing some of its operations – and staff – to the Soviet Union.

Anna, unaware of these details, was grateful for a job where she was able to practise her German daily, and didn't ask any questions. It was rare to have daily interactions with foreigners in the post-war years of the Soviet

Union, even if they were being held in the country against their will, but Anna was young and had the language skills. Her clean record meant they had no reason not to employ her.

The factory was in the Sokolniki district, a leafy neighbourhood in the northeast of the city mostly taken up by the massive park of the same name. Anna looked forward to going to work, where every day was different. The engineers didn't speak any Russian, and Anna translated for them while they worked, sometimes also helping with their day-to-day life. The Germans lived in a nearby sanatorium where they were fed twice a day. On some days Anna was lucky and could accompany her foreign colleagues to their residence for dinner. Food shortages in Moscow meant that on these occasions she would eat better meals than what she would have been able to prepare for herself at home. Yet these opportunities were not frequent and most of the time she left the factory at the end of the day.

'Were you able to learn anything about their private lives, and life outside the country?' I ask my grandmother. 'No,' she tells me. 'People were very cautious, sticking to professional conversation, at least when I was around.'

The Germans were effectively prisoners – or guests, as far as the Soviet regime was concerned – and they were aware that they would be better off revealing as little as possible. In Russia people were too nervous to ask personal questions.

Anna was enjoying her new life as a young graduate living and working in Moscow. The city was still suffering from post-war hunger and deprivation, but changes were becoming noticeable on the streets. Cinemas, theatres and exhibitions were putting on more shows and events to welcome people on their days off. Moscow's 800th birthday was celebrated with a sense of great pride but without undue pomp out of respect for the difficult period in most people's lives.

Anna was now an adult. She tried to put the difficult evacuation years behind her and concentrate on her future. She was looking forward to the opportunities it would bring. She was not to know that she was about to come face to face with the reality of the Soviet system that had already inflicted so much suffering on her family. It would make her re-evaluate her life under the Soviet regime, reminding her that it always paid to be on your guard in Russia.

Anna had been working at the factory for six months when she was called in by the management. When she walked into the small office, where she felt it was only yesterday that she signed her employment contract, she encountered stern faces. She was told to sit down. Her boss, trying to appear friendly and relaxed, told Anna that from now on she would have extra duties at the factory. At first Anna was happy to be given more responsibility, but as she listened, she realised that she was, in fact, being asked to spy on the German engineers she spent her days helping. She was reminded that she was a young and valued specialist in her country, and that her country needed her. She would have to listen very carefully to what the Germans said and report back to the management about everything she heard, no matter how trivial or insignificant it might have appeared. They wanted to know all the details.

Anna was close to tears. She realised that if she refused to cooperate her life would be over. But spying on the Germans, whom she only knew in a professional setting, was unfathomable to her. Collaborating with the Soviet regime that had wrought so much terror on its citizens would have never crossed her mind. As she stared at the piece of paper in front of her, she slowly shook her head. She was not going to sign it, she told them. She was not going to give away her freedom. She would not live with a guilty conscience, she thought to herself. In an instant she knew that this was only a job. She would survive if she had to look for another one, or if she had to be unemployed, but she would not sign away her life to become a state informer.

Her boss was stunned by her insubordination.

Anna tells me what I am already thinking; her refusal alone was enough to put her behind bars, and everybody in the room knew it.

The men got up from their chairs and walked out of the office; Anna was told to think about her decision. The door was locked behind them. Anna was left with her thoughts. She was surprisingly calm. She waited

Anna. Moscow, late 1940s

for someone to come and arrest her. Hours went past. She stared at the empty office room, deprived of anything other than the wooden table and chairs. As she watched the arms of the clock move, she knew that it could be many hours before she would be allowed to leave. Her thoughts and fears were her only company. When the door finally opened several hours later and her boss returned, she jumped, startled by the intrusion.

She was asked again whether she would sign the paper. When she declined, she was told to come back the following morning.

It was late when she got home, lost in thought and worried about her future. She didn't share her fears with anyone, preferring to go to bed. The morning is wiser than the evening, she thought, recalling the popular Russian saying. She would sleep on it, and maybe it would be possible to find a way out of the situation.

The next morning, she was summoned back to the small office as soon as she arrived at work. 'How can you do this?' she was asked. 'The Germans killed so many Jews, and now you are defending them!' But her mind was made up. She was not going to become an informer. She was not going to become one of them. She knew she had a long and dangerous battle ahead of her. They locked her in the room, again, to think.

In the evening she went home. The next day, and the day after, it continued. She was left alone with her thoughts. Days merged into one. She was tired and hungry. Anna no longer slept at night. She lay awake, wondering whether eventually she was going to give in. She knew that if she became an informer, sooner or later she would have to spy on her own family and friends. She had to find another solution, but as the days went by without change, she hoped for inner strength. She remembered the trips to church from her childhood, her nanny, Lousha, guiding her to the altar. She had been too small to pay attention, but for want of any other religious experience, she now wondered whether it would have been easier if she had a God to pray to.

Anna knew that this was a trap. She had found herself in an unsustainable situation and she realised that she would need help to get out. Again and again she asked to resign, but her request was denied.

Anna started to feel paranoid on the streets and thought that she was going crazy. She imagined that she was being followed. She jumped when the doorbell rang and at every phone call. Eventually she went to her mother for help.

Through word of mouth and years of hard work Zina had established a close network around herself, which had brought her many clients and contacts. One of her regulars was a woman from a Ukrainian village, Maria Tikhonovna Mogila. In Russian, a '*mogila*' is a grave, and it's ironic that a woman with such a surname should be my grandmother's saviour. Maria Tikhonovna was the party secretary of one of Moscow's districts – effectively the highest-ranking party official in her area – and she had been coming to Zina for her skills and taste in garment-making for many years. Anna had met her many times, as the women discussed clothes and talked about their lives. Anna often thought that if it hadn't been for their different social status, Maria Tikhonovna and Zina could have been friends.

As soon as Zina explained that her daughter was in trouble, Maria Tikhonovna picked up the phone to her colleague, the party secretary of the Sokolniki district, and asked him to spare the young girl who had found herself on the wrong side of the regime.

After another nerve-racking day within the four walls of the office, Anna was fired for 'refusal to work'. The wording was a black stain on anyone's file, but nothing could have been further from Anna's mind at that moment. She tried not to show any emotion as she collected her employment papers and walked out of the door a free person, the weight of the last ten days lifted off her shoulders.

Maria Tikhonovna saved Anna's life. Why did she help? Anna thinks that she had no reason not to. She was an intelligent woman, who understood the situation of a twenty-two-year-old girl who got into trouble. 'People's lives depended on people like Maria Tikhonovna; they were at the top, and the rest of the population were at the bottom, by their feet,' my grandmother reflects.

The truth might be a little more complicated. Maria Tikhonovna would have been risking her own position by saving Anna. Her act could have been interpreted as suspicious by the authorities, and she could have been accused of covering for an enemy of the state.

But Anna was lucky.

My grandmother tenses as she recounts that period of her life. Sitting in a spacious living room in my parents' west London home in 2016, it is hard to imagine that these events happened less than seventy years ago. And yet, in post-war Russia the terror of the 1930s didn't stop. People found themselves denounced to the authorities for the smallest of slip-ups. Trust was still a commodity worth its weight in gold.

22

Escaping reality

MOSCOW, 1948

It was a cold winter's day in Moscow on 15 January 1948. The streets were covered in thick layers of snow, and Muscovites rushed about their business to avoid spending more time than was necessary outside. It was only when you approached Tverskoy Boulevard from its southern neighbour, Nikitskyi Boulevard, that you noticed a stream of people heading in the direction of one of the side lanes. The side street, Malaya Bronnaya, was already packed. The people, all dressed in their warmest hats and coats, were there to mourn their hero, a beloved actor of the Soviet Union who had been killed several days earlier on a trip to Minsk. Solomon Mikhoels was a name that was familiar to all Jewish families living in the Soviet Union and possibly around the world for his indefatigable acting and directing skills, and, most recently, for his stance against fascism.

Anna and Malia were in the crowd. The theatre world had provided the girls, now young women, with a rare glimpse into a different reality and they had often sought the best plays and performances to brighten their days. That day they were paying their respects to one of their favourite actors – the star of the Moscow Jewish Theatre. Inside the theatre, a wake was taking place, and Mikhoels was lying in an open coffin. The injuries he had suffered when a truck ran him over were covered up by stage make-up but were difficult to hide completely. As the sounds of the fiddle reached the mourners outside, people began to weep, some openly, others hiding their tears, but all remembering the actor who made the impossible possible, the man who brought Yiddish language theatre to the masses of the Soviet capital.

There are not many people alive today who saw Mikhoels on stage. But once you saw him, once you breathed the air he breathed as he transformed himself into any one of his characters, you didn't forget that face for as long as you lived, my grandmother tells me. He had a recognisably ugly face, but it was so ugly, it made him beautiful, the founder of the theatre, Alexander Granovsky, once said. Mikhoels' performance of *King Lear*, translated into Yiddish, became the highlight of his career, hailed as a triumph of Soviet theatre and praised by reviews at home and abroad. Writing in *The Times* of London, Gordon Craig said that, 'Only now, after having returned from The Theatre Festival in Moscow, do I understand why we have no Lear worthy of the name in Britain. The reason is quite simple: we have no actor like Mikhoels.'[7]

But most of the roles performed by Mikhoels were much closer to home for his audience. Some of the most popular plays of the Jewish Theatre were those adapted from the stories of Sholem Aleichem, a leading Yiddish author and playwright later made famous in America by

7   B. Wasserstein, *On the Eve: The Jews of Europe before the Second World War* (London: Profile Books Ltd, 2012), 292

an adaption of one of his plays, *Fiddler on the Roof*. The original, *Tevye the Milkman*, told of the struggles of Tevye and his seven daughters living in a small village in tsarist Russia. It was in those plays that Mikhoels was able to return to his roots and to his own childhood in a small village of the Pale of Settlement, to bring to his audience the familiar atmosphere of Jewish rural life – and the lives that they had left behind.

As the mourners gathered in front of the theatre, they were thinking back to the best roles and plays directed by their favourite actor. Many were also worried about the future of the Jewish theatre. Rumours had been circulating that Mikhoels' death had not been an accident. As Chairman of the Jewish Anti-Fascist Committee, Mikhoels actively supported Stalin and was able to travel around the world to encourage support of the Soviet Union in the war against Nazi Germany. While the war lasted, Stalin saw the practicality of such support, but with the victory came the crackdown on communication between Soviet citizens and their contacts abroad, making Mikhoels' work impossible. The rumours that the Soviet state was behind his killing, conveniently away from the capital, would not be confirmed for many years, and it was only with Stalin's death in 1953 that the government's involvement would become clear.

In fact, Mikhoels' murder paved the way for a state-sponsored persecution of Soviet Jews that would last for several decades. For those who were able to read between the lines, the future did not look promising.

Anna and Malia were unaware of the stories. They came to the theatre to say goodbye to an actor who had opened to them a world of Jewish culture – a culture that they were able to understand thanks to their German classes (and Yiddish is, essentially, a mix of German, Hebrew and Slavic languages) and the snippets of Yiddish that they overheard from their parents. As they walked down the streets of Moscow towards the cemetery where Mikhoels would be buried, they were surrounded by his audience – united to commemorate a closing chapter of their city's experiment with Jewish culture.

For Anna, Mikhoels' passing marked the end of her love affair with the theatre in general. In 1948 she was a young woman of twenty-five, and her life didn't allow her much time for theatrical outings. She would always treasure the memories of the artistic world she had been able to discover in her childhood. Before the start of the Second World War, Anna and Malia had become quite the connoisseurs of the repertoire of Moscow's theatres, and it was the pleasure of being immersed into the stage world that Anna would miss the most in the years of her adulthood. 'It was always a comedy or a light-hearted drama,' my grandmother recounts. 'I never wanted to see anything tragic or depressing. There was enough of that in my own life.'

As I listen to my grandmother I suddenly see her face widen into a huge smile and she breaks into a song:

Голубок и горлица
Никогда не ссорятся,
Дружно живут [8]

I look at her in amazement. I have rarely heard my grandmother sing, and this tercet, performed with so much zeal and after so many years, leaves me speechless. It comes from a play called *The School for Scandal* by Richard Sheridan. A satire on the English aristocracy, its popularity in the Soviet Union kept it running in the theatre for many months. The main characters are a married couple, Sir Peter and Lady Teazle, who are constantly fighting and bickering. During the rehearsals, Olga Androvskaya, who played the leading part of Lady Teazle, pointed out that among the English aristocracy of the eighteenth century it was popular for married couples to perform musical duets. Androvskaya spent the best part of the rehearsal time learning how to play the harp – something she insisted she had to do herself. This led to the creation of this musical duet, the lines from which my grandmother remembers and can still sing on request.

---

8 'The dove and his turtledove
   Never quarrel,
   And live peacefully' (Russian)

These are just some of the reminders of the world that allowed Anna and her friend Malia to escape from reality. To imagine the lives they could have had if they had been born as members of the English aristocracy, as they saw in *The School for Scandal*, or in *Anna Karenina*, if they had lived in nineteenth-century Russia. Escaping from the daily life of food shortages and the tense atmosphere at home where they worried about arrests and crackdowns, Anna and Malia immersed themselves in a whole other world, where life was different and positive emotions were easier to experience.

23

Adolphe and Marcus

Geneva, 1950–Moscow, 1952

Ariane rang the doorbell at Aunt Eva's apartment. It was gone midnight. Despite the stifling heat, she was shaking in her nightdress. She had run there as fast as she could. As she waited for Eva to open the door, she was trying to hold back her tears. She reassured herself that her grandfather would be fine, that this was a minor heart attack, similar to what he had had in the past. But she thought back to his cries for help, and the terrified look on her mother's face when she yelled at her to go and get Eva. She was scared.

Eva didn't wait to hear the full story when she opened the door and saw Ariane's puffy face in front of her. She ran out in her dressing gown, telling Ariane and Anita to stay together and try to get some sleep.

It was going to be a long night. Ariane had already been in bed when she heard voices coming from her grandfather's room next door; then her mother rushed in shouting at her daughter to run to Eva's. Ariane tried to catch a glimpse of Adolphe's room as she passed it; her grandfather lay in bed, his newspaper by his side. The panicked expression on her mother's face stopped Ariane from asking any questions. Fumbling for her shoes, she ran out of the door. She could hear her mother screaming for help in the hallway.

On 6 June 1950 Eva arrived at her parents' building to find her sister panicking on the stairs, waiting for the doctor. Genia's hands nervously gripped the railings as she rambled on about their father feeling unwell after a long train journey, complaining that the gruelling heat had made him very tired. Eva made an effort to concentrate on what her sister was saying as she tried to lead her back into the apartment. In the living room they sat on the sofa. The room was dark, but the lights remained off.

Genia explained that it had been getting late, and her father had asked for a glass of water before going to bed. Genia worried that he looked pale; his shirt clung to his back. She watched him go to his room, wondering whether she had made the right decision not opening the windows during the day; she was trying to protect the air inside from the heat outside. When she returned with a glass of water minutes later, Adolphe looked like he was in pain. Clutching his chest, he was leaning back on the pillows stacked on his bed, breathing heavily. 'I am going to die. I am going to die,' he moaned. 'Call the doctor now!' Her hands shaking, Genia put the glass of water on the bedside table and ran into her daughter's room, telling her to go and get her aunt.

Slowly, Eva got up from the sofa and made her way to her father's room. Genia was still talking but Eva already knew what she was going to find. Her sister was too scared to say it aloud. The room was exactly as he had left it before setting off on a trip to one of his favourite spas in the Swiss Alps. The papers on his big mahogany desk were a reminder of all work he had come back to. The short holiday was never enough. She saw her father on his bed. Genia hadn't moved the newspaper. It was

Adolphe Neuman. Geneva, 1950

still lying open by his side, as if Adolphe had momentarily closed his eyes for a quick nap. But he was pale and immobile. Eva brought her hands to her mouth to stifle a scream; this was not a dream. Her father would not wake up. In tears, Eva rushed downstairs to wait for the doctor.

Adolphe had died from a heart attack at the age of sixty-six.

Heartbroken, Genia and I called Uncle Shura and Aunt Berthe, they in turn called their sons Sam and Henri, because mother was away. She was doing a thermal cure in Loeche les Bains – we couldn't telephone her with such terrible news and Uncle Shura said that he would go and get her with Sam. [...] My poor mother, when she saw Uncle Shura knock on her door at 6am, she told me that he just said one word, 'Adolphe', and she understood. The rest was like a nightmare from which we still haven't recovered.

In Moscow, two years later, Anna would bury her father. Two brothers, who shared a childhood and a home until life took them on very different paths, both died from weak hearts within two years of each other.

'He was a good man and a good father.' The tragedy, Anna tells me, is that her father didn't live to see the death of the Soviet leader. Joseph Stalin, the man who destroyed Marcus' life and was responsible for the deaths and misery of so many others, died in 1953.

Marcus was a broken man, his beliefs shattered by his arrest and exile, from which he never recovered. A man robbed of his daughter's childhood, he grew disillusioned and disappointed over how the country of his dreams turned out. He had hoped for a better life, as the move to Moscow had promised opportunities for him and his family. Instead, he became witness to the persecution and purges of Soviet Jews of all walks of life; artists, writers, academics, scientists and doctors were killed, removed from their jobs and sent into exile. They were denied immigration rights and accused of helping 'American imperialism'. For Marcus, and many like him, who had placed their trust in the Bolshevik leaders and believed that they could build a better way of life, the reality was crushing.

In the end, Anna reflects, he paid the price for his beliefs and commitment, while trying to do his best for his loved ones.

A kind and affectionate man, in his later years Marcus lacked the drive and self-confidence of his brother. Their separation affected him deeply. He questioned the idealism of his youth, which had taken him so far from the life Adolphe was able to enjoy in Western Europe. They were in touch for as long as they could be, their correspondence interrupted by the Soviet repressions and the Second World War. Often communicating via intermediaries to avoid any suspicion of anti-Soviet activity falling on Marcus, they remained in contact.

And yet Marcus died not knowing that his brother had passed away almost two years earlier. Anna tells me that by then the contact between the two families was not frequent and when she learnt of her uncle's passing she was too scared to bring the news to her father. Marcus would have been devastated.

Adolphe and Marcus did not live to see the post-war years of Europe. They died before their daughters and granddaughters were able to stand on their own two feet in a world by then dominated by the Cold War between the Soviet Union and the United States and its allies. For Soviet citizens it became almost impossible to communicate with the outside world, bringing the already sporadic contact between the two branches of the family to an end.

In Geneva, Eva and Genia, and their daughters, Anita and Ariane, tried to find stability after the painful years of the war. They married and re-married, raised their children and enjoyed their day-to-day lives amid family dramas and intrigue. As Western Europe concentrated on regaining its strength after being torn apart by Hitler's hostile ideology, Adolphe's descendants returned to the normality of Swiss life.

In Russia, peace failed to bring stability to Anna and her family. They tried to navigate their lives amid the increasing paranoia of the Soviet regime, which saw enemies among its own people. In moments of greatest despair, Anna continued taking out the family album to look at her cousins – their beautiful smiles and kind words written on the back

Marcus Neyman. Moscow, c 1950

of the photographs. She would think of trying to make contact with them again, to hear their news and maybe look for a way out. She knew that it would be reckless and dangerous to attempt to leave the country. She would think of the arrests and jails, knowing that she would never take the risk.

Part Four

24

A match made in Paris

Paris–Geneva, 1950

'We chose Jacques because he was so funny. He made us laugh,' Anita tells me. 'My aunt was already interested in a certain Lev Ch., an amazing man whom she had met in France, but he wasn't as fun as her lawyer, Jacques. She made them both come to the Alpine resort of Crans-sur-Sierre where we were on holiday, one after another, and she introduced them both to her family. And when they were gone, she told Ariane and me to pick one.'

Lev Ch., a poet, an intellectual and a highly educated man of medicine who would become the first person to introduce the theory of psychosomatic disorders to Switzerland, never stood much of a chance against Anita and Ariane. The cousins, by then sixteen and fourteen years old, didn't think Genia would seriously listen to what they had to say, but their reaction confirmed her own suspicions – she felt she would be much happier to spend the rest of her life with Jacques.

There is, perhaps, another reason why Genia picked Jacques. Both their hearts already belonged to an affable greying cocker spaniel. When telling Genia about his time in Cairo, where he had been stationed with the Free French Forces during the war, it was Digi, his old pooch, he remembered most fondly. When leaving the Middle East, he brought his ageing companion back to France with him. The dog was buried in Jacques' hometown of Rouen several years later, and Jacques often returned to the burial place to remember his friend. Genia was surprised by the story – she used to have a dog called Nigi, she told Jacques. Their names were similar in an uncanny way, but neither were prepared for the conclusion they were about to draw. When Jacques showed Genia a picture of Digi, in it she recognised her own cocker spaniel, Nigi. She had had to leave him with the British Forces in Cairo when it was time for her and Ariane to return to Europe. Nigi had been with them for many years, and Ariane had been particularly attached and wanted to take him to Geneva with her.

If Genia still had any doubts over her upcoming marriage, she would later claim that this remarkable coincidence settled all her uncertainties once and for all.

Together, Jacques and Genia spent their time exploring the French capital in its post-war revival. The food shortages had subsided and cultural life was coming back to the city in full swing. They enjoyed the opera and ballet, and attended fashionable soirees with their friends. Jacques' life story mirrored Genia's own, and he shared Genia's experiences of the Middle East. He was happy to be back in Europe where he could enjoy the comforts of life and a stable job. In Paris, Jacques headed a legal office, which was where he first met Genia when she came to him seeking his help in her separation from Kurt. A tall, good-looking man with a long straight nose, an enigmatic smile and black hair, receding slightly, Jacques had been a long-time bachelor.

Their bond over their wartime pet, as well as the humorous approval of Ariane and Anita, decided Jacques' and Genia's future. They married in a civil ceremony in Paris. Eva and Marie attended the wedding along with Jacques' mother and siblings. Anita and Ariane were not invited. They were furious at being excluded from a wedding that they believed only came about because of their matchmaking, and sent Genia an angry telegram, voicing their disapproval. 'We were very naughty and probably shouldn't have done it, but we were cross!' Ariane tells me.

The wedding was modest and tasteful, marked by the post-war atmosphere of Europe and the recent death of Adolphe. This was the first decision Genia made without her father's advice and opinion, and although she didn't need his approval, she often wondered what he would have thought of her new husband. She tried to look at him through her father's eyes, noting that he came from a good Jewish family and had a successful career, and was able to provide for himself and secure his lifestyle. She knew that Adolphe would have appreciated Jacques' professional achievements – a self-made man himself, he valued employment and commitment and would have been pleased to know that he would not need to support his daughter in her new marriage.

Ironically, once Genia and Jacques were married, they moved to Geneva, but across the border, Jacques would not be able to practise law. Qualified in France, his credentials needed to be confirmed in Switzerland, and so the newly married couple began their life together without the promise of a stable income. The move to Geneva to be closer to the rest of the family would eventually bring about the demise of their marriage, but the newlyweds settled in the family apartment on Avenue Bertrand and tried to make it their new home.

Marie had moved to a smaller place after her husband's death. After five years with her grandparents, Ariane suddenly found herself living with her mother again, a new stepfather, and soon, two more siblings.

Jacques introduced Ariane to jazz and football, allowing her to do things that her mother would have never permitted. She felt she was becoming an adult, learning about life and savouring new experiences.

Genia and Jacques Meyer-Morton on their wedding day. Paris, 1950

On Saturdays, Jacques would take Ariane and Anita to a football match. In the evenings the girls listened to popular music that was gaining ground across the Atlantic.

Ariane noticed that Jacques made a huge effort to get along with her, but she was not sure that his relationship was as smooth with her mother. Several arguments overheard from her bedroom suggested that things were not going well at the watch factory. Etna Watch, run successfully by Eva since the death of Adolphe, had recently been entrusted to Jacques, who knew nothing about the industry and was not the best man for the role.

The decision was hard for Eva. She knew that her sister was making a mistake. It was not a man's world, as Genia had claimed, and it was not necessary to have a man at the head of the family business to ensure its success. Putting Jacques in charge of a company he knew nothing about and demoting Eva to the job of secretary, the job she had held for her father ever since her return from Belgium during the war, meant that the factory's prosperous future was no longer assured. Despite her disagreement, Eva found it difficult to argue with her sister, who was more dominant and wanted to ensure a job for her husband. For the sake of Etna Watch, Eva buried her pride and stayed involved in the operations. She tried to advise Jacques as much as she could, capitalising on her knowledge and experience of the industry. But it was Jacques who now had to undertake the yearly trips to the United States in search of new clients, and there was nothing Eva could do to ensure his success across the Atlantic.

The family drama took place during some of the most important years for the Swiss watch industry. For Adolphe, the period during the Second World War had been relatively successful. He had been able to maintain contact with his American clients, for whom he continued to supply Swiss watches and watch parts. The imports replaced the domestic US industry, which had been largely diverted to help the war effort. In the 1950s, after the war, the market changed again, and watchmakers in Switzerland once again had to find new tactics to survive. The US market was growing and expanding, and with added competition from Asia, investment and innovation were needed to stay ahead of the game. The industry was on the verge of what would become known as the quartz crisis. Electronic watches and the nascent quartz technology would become the next big thing. The Americans and the Japanese were rushing ahead with the research, but many Swiss factories were wary of the idea. Some bigger Swiss manufacturers were also researching quartz technology, modernising their factories and increasing the skill base of their staff, but the smaller plants were less willing to accept a change to the industry.

Quartz would bring a fundamental change to watchmaking, introducing the accuracy of a mechanical watch to electronics for the first time. It would be the biggest shift since the mechanical clock was invented in the fourteenth century, but it needed a canny industry insider to spot the direction of travel in the research and innovation. Etna Watch was lagging behind, but Jacques was not the only one who missed the need to diversify and invest. Many traditional factories in the Jura region were also reluctant to embrace modernity, and it would cost them dearly.

For Etna Watch, these proved to be the defining years. As his US clients began to dwindle, Jacques struggled to attract new ones. Without investing in quartz, Etna Watch did not have the latest technology to offer its clients, nor the prospect that it would be forthcoming. Without Adolphe's guiding hand, Jacques and Eva found themselves in a predicament that determined the future of the family enterprise in a few short years.

Jacques buried himself in his favourite pastime of denial – bridge. Soon he was spending several afternoons a week playing the game at his club.

For Genia, card playing was a vice. She was as sure about that as she was about the fact that her marriage was on the rocks. Jacques was wounded by his wife's attitude, but he kept his feelings to himself. Genia was busy and exhausted at home. In the last three years she had given birth to two children, Jean-Michel and Anne, and had been renovating the apartment for their expanding family. Jacques was happy to write off his wife's displeasure as long as he could continue coming home to spend time with his children. He was certain that once the renovation was complete and the problems at the factory were somehow brought under control, life would resume as normal.

Eventually the slow demise of Etna Watch became impossible to deny. The card playing added to the tension at home, and Genia frequently found herself arguing with her husband late into the night. Jacques' temperament was a match for hers, and they tried to keep their angry discussions to English to stop the children from understanding. Jean-Michel remembers that it made no difference. A child of any age can sense the emotion in the air, and Jean-Michel could tell that his parents were fighting. He was soon used to their emotional outbursts.

Genia refused to accept the near bankruptcy of the factory. She was convinced that if Jacques had spent more time in the office, he could have learnt more about the business and would have known to invest and innovate to keep it attractive to the US market. Jacques tried to defend himself, but the growing pressure made him retreat into the world of bridge even further.

The marriage came to an abrupt end when Genia discovered that her husband had been unfaithful to her. She refused to let him back into the house. For all their fights and arguments, she would have been happy to tolerate Jacques' flaws for the sake of her family, but finding out about a wealthy lover who lived permanently in one of Geneva's best hotels was the last straw. She felt humiliated and heartbroken. Having been through one divorce with Ariane's father, she had been determined not to break her family apart once again. She ended their relationship once and for all, telling the children Jacques was away for business.

25

A romance rekindled

Geneva, 1952

When Eva said goodbye to Simon days before her wedding in 1933, she was picturing herself with Stanis, her husband-to-be. She wrote to her friend Hélène that she didn't know whether she would be able to be happy. She wondered whether she had picked the right man, and agonised over her future. She couldn't have known then that she would be able to recreate the youthful romance she enjoyed with Simon two decades later. Broken-hearted, Eva blamed herself for not being able to hold onto the man she fell in love with. She was desperate at the thought of never seeing him again.

However, Geneva was a small city. After Eva married, she would often bump into Simon on her return to Switzerland, when visiting her parents.

She would see him while she pushed the pram in Park Bertrand, or he would return her greeting in a restaurant in the centre, and once or twice they would simply pass each other in the street. They were brief, awkward meetings, always punctuated by news of their friends and families, neither of them ever broaching a subject too close to the heart, nor daring to smile a second too long. Eva was always stunned by these encounters. She felt that a small part of her had never let go of the man she had been in love with in her youth.

By the time Eva returned to her hometown, it was wartime, and Simon was far from her mind. She was mourning the loss of her husband, as well their friends the Sternbergs, and her friend Ti in particular. Their arrest as they fled occupied Belgium and attempted to reach the safety of Switzerland, and their subsequent deaths at the Nazi death camp in Auschwitz, came as a huge shock. Knowing that Stanis had discovered the truth about her affair with Ti only days before his death devastated Eva. She had never wanted to hurt her husband, and as she attempted to come to terms with the loss of her loved ones and rebuild her life as a widow, she was overwhelmed with immense sorrow.

The war left a mark on this once adventurous and fun-loving woman. The uncertainty of living in wartime Belgium, followed by the years of waiting for news of her husband, made her stronger and more decisive about her life. When the war was over and she learnt that her husband was dead, she buried herself in her work. Her job at the watch factory, a place of no emotion as dictated by her father, was the perfect setting to block her fears and memories. Adolphe did not want to know of his daughter's suffering, and she hid her feelings. She knew that only time would heal her pain.

During their long years of separation, it was the memory of the brief moments in Eva's company that helped Simon see a brighter future for himself. He was certain that morally he had done the right thing by letting Eva go. His conscience was clear, but with it came a growing awareness that he had missed his chance of being happy, and so he did not look for another opportunity of finding love. He covered his agony with his trademark smile – always happy in the company of his friends, and glad to be entertaining a crowd late into the night. Having hidden his true feelings in such a way, he continued his life in peace, his bachelorhood eventually becoming an accepted fact on the Geneva social scene.

Eva and Simon were different people by the time a random encounter on the street brought them to a local restaurant. They talked of the days long gone, reminiscing about their first meeting and the lightness they felt that could only exist in certain years of one's youth. They remembered the naivety they had felt about the world around them.

They were no longer those people. Their romance seemed a lifetime ago. They were now adults, free to open up to each other, and share the regrets and disappointments of years gone by. For the first time in decades they were free from other commitments, open to follow their hearts. Eva thought back to herself as a young girl, torn between the man she had agreed to marry and the man she unexpectedly fell in love with just weeks before her wedding day. She had been naive, and desperate to do the right thing. Eva's heart grew heavy as, sitting in the cafe looking at Simon

Eva and Simon Chaikhine. Geneva, c 1953

so many years later, she realised how much grief and tragedy separated that young girl from the woman she had become.

Their rendezvous continued. Photos from Eva's albums reveal two people who were happy to find each other again. Eva, by then in her mid-forties, is radiant with her short brown bob arranged neatly in waves behind her head, her expression serene. Simon, half a head taller and twelve years older, looks like a man who finally found the reason to live. He has many lines around his eyes, laughter lines, and altogether looks like a perfect gentleman.

Eva and Simon married on 29 October 1953. Under the beautiful white wedding Chuppa, to mark the Jewish tradition and to symbolise the home that the couple will build together, Eva felt like a young bride again, only this time with her childhood sweetheart.

I was wearing a black dress, a hat with velvet black and white wings. Behind me, Genia, one month away from giving birth to Anne, Simon's mother, our friends the Starobinskys, an amazing buffet, amazing photos and my Simon and I. We left at the end of the afternoon to spend a honeymoon weekend in Montreux.

Eva had rediscovered life. Simon's support was extremely important after the loss of her father, and as she attempted to keep the family business afloat and reverse the damage done by her brother-in-law, Jacques. Together, they would live some of the happiest years of their lives, taking frequent trips to Italy, France and Israel. Simon was her husband, her friend and her confidant.

26

Almost famous

Geneva, 1954

Anita remembers the first time she was recognised on the street. A petite brunette with short hair and a radiant smile, she was studying at the University of Geneva, but it was her other pastime that attracted the attention of some passers-by.

It was 1954 and the Swiss broadcasting corporation was experimenting with a new medium – television. Nineteen-year-old Anita, fresh from completing a year-long journalism degree in Paris, was interested in trying the new form of expression and wrote a letter to the head of the station. She thought that the new format was going to be a great success and didn't hesitate to express her view. 'It was all very outlandish at the time,' she tells me.

The broadcaster was looking for someone who was able to do commentary for films. Anita was invited to an interview. She was told that she had to demonstrate her skill by recording an audio track to pictures. The subject was *l'histoire de l'art*, the history of art. Anita was proud to be able to show off some of what she had learnt about art when she lived in Paris, but when she got to the viewing room she realised that it wouldn't be so simple. She put the reel onto the player, and as she started turning the handle, she was astounded to see images of water. She turned the handle faster and then slower, but nothing changed. She realised that it was a slow moving, wide river. That's when it hit her – *l'histoire de l'Aar* was in fact the subject of the exercise, one of Switzerland's main rivers, the Aar, a tributary of the Rhine. Anita's heart sank. There would be no opportunity to show off her knowledge of the impressionists and modernists that she so admired. It was time that she learnt more about Swiss geography, a subject she confessed to knowing nothing about.

Geography was not the main problem. After several hours at the university library, Anita had gathered enough information for the short film. It was only when she got back to the studio and watched the reel in more detail that she understood the meaning of the sellotape she found lying next to the player. The film, old and worn, kept snapping. To be able to keep watching it in order to write a detailed commentary, Anita spent hours sticking the matt sides of the tape together and praying that it wouldn't snap again as soon as she turned the handle of the player. Inevitably, in her inexperienced hand, it did. She added layers of sellotape over the already existing tears. By the time she had watched it enough times to write her script, time was running out.

Eventually, Anita would master the skill of sticking together bits of film and making sure that she was more careful with the handle to stop old films being butchered so badly. Her history of the River Aar landed her the job of freelance producer; she would be called upon on request and without a contract. She would be paid thirty francs for each job, a huge sum of money for a young woman who still lived at home and relied on her mother for her clothes and daily expenses.

Excited about her new job, Anita continued her studies at the university. Her days were busy with classes and lectures. Whenever the opportunity arose she spent an evening or an afternoon at the television station. For the first time since her return from Paris, Anita didn't feel like coming back had been a bad idea. She was learning that in her hometown she could also be relatively independent and live a life that was separate from her mother, Eva, and her new stepfather, Simon. With her friends she discovered the fashionable cafes of Geneva and attended parties and soirees organised by the university. As her job picked up and she got called more frequently, Anita was learning the skills to build a successful career after university. She was more confident and outgoing. Having mastered the commentary on short films, she soon got the break that would get her recognised on the streets.

As is often the case, Anita's first appearance on television happened when the main presenter was ill and she was asked to replace her. When she arrived in the studio, nervous in anticipation of her first on-air broadcast, she discovered that the pre-recorded programme would concentrate on the latest news from the Tour de France cycling competition. It was July, and most of Europe was gripped by the event. Anita was to summarise the main developments of the day for the evening news, announcing the names of some of the main cyclists and the places they went through – and she had to do it quickly. She was lucky that she could practise, but the cameraman grew angry and frustrated. The time for the broadcast was approaching, and Anita was still stumbling over the names. Eventually, anger and frustration gave way to tears and laughter. Somehow, they managed to finish recording the segment before the news bulletin that evening.

More on-air work followed. Anita interviewed singers, actors, musicians and artists for the culture show and was standing in for the news anchor; she was finally doing what she had trained to do at the journalism school in Paris the year before. Some of the interviews were broadcast live on air. The young television star would summon all her nerves and perform for the audience she knew was watching at home. While she didn't yet know that her television career would not last very long, she was becoming the person I know today – not afraid to say what she thought and express her opinion to anyone who would listen, often leading to unexpected consequences.

The world of freelance contracts is unpredictable and often ungrateful. Anita had lots of ideas. When her bosses were looking for new programmes to be commissioned, she put her thoughts forward. In the process, she told them what didn't work with the current practices and what could be improved. Maybe she was too brazen in her judgements, or not politically correct about the people behind the shows that she criticised and suggested should be replaced. Eventually, the phone calls ceased. Many of her proposals for children's programmes, animated cartoons drawn by kids based on their own stories and other more serious suggestions, would eventually be realised by her former employers. Anita's collaboration with the experimental and constantly growing presence in people's homes came to an abrupt end.

Anita is too much of a positive spirit to worry about this chapter of her life ending so suddenly. Yet there was a time, she tells me, when she did think that she could go on to become a journalist, continuing in her quest to innovate and improve television while it was still in its infancy.

There are no recordings or tapes to go back sixty years to see the early days of Swiss TV and Anita's nascent career. Standard practice didn't dictate for live broadcasts to be recorded, and pre-recorded material wasn't kept for very long. Swiss Television celebrated its sixtieth anniversary with a retrospective on its history, with many of the anchors and presenters from the early days invited to tell their stories, but Anita was not among them – not found in the archives, forgotten as one of the early explorers of the new format.

27

A university romance

Geneva, 1938-58

It was a snowy day in Geneva. Anita, a cute three-year-old toddler, was visiting her grandparents from Antwerp. Adolphe brought his granddaughter to the factory where the little girl could observe the technicians put the watches together. She was fascinated by the tiny red rubies she could see on the work surface of one of the watchmakers. For hours she didn't want to leave, happy to stare at the men meticulously fiddle with the tiny parts of the watch. Eventually, she allowed Adolphe to drag herself away from the atelier.

As they stepped outside, Anita was almost invisible on the snow-covered streets of the city. In her white coat, white hat with rabbit ears and white muff to keep her hands warm, she proudly held her grandfather's hand as they prepared to cross the road and start their walk home. Just at that moment, Adolphe stopped to say hello to the man who was re-painting the hallway of the building. 'She is very cute,' commented the painter, who enquired after Anita's age. He told the proud grandfather that he had a son the same age at home – Alexandre. The two men exchanged pleasantries and continued the conversation for a few minutes.

I wonder whether Adolphe would have remembered the encounter if Anita had come to him almost twenty years later to announce to her grandfather that she was going to marry the painter's son. He had a good memory and might have been able to recall the painter, but he didn't live long enough – and possibly for the best. 'It was a huge scandal! A *goy*,[9] and not only a *goy* but from a working-class family. It couldn't be worse. And he was a student!' Anita exclaims.

She was gossiping with her friends at the eloquently named UniBar when she noticed one of her friends talking to a man she had never seen before. Anita couldn't see him properly, but she heard his rich, deep voice. She loved its tone and the authority it gave to everything he said. As she listened closer, she knew that she had to find a way to join the conversation herself. She walked over just as her friend asked the man for advice on the flu – it sounded like he was a medical student and knew about the virus that had been doing the rounds for the past few weeks. As she listened to the man's explanation, she could feel her heart beating faster. She was nervous as she prepared her words to explain her sudden appearance in the middle of the conversation. She was going to tell him that she couldn't help but overhear the discussion because her mother was very worried about the flu, and she was hoping to learn something new. But she didn't need to say anything. Alexandre was looking straight at her. His smile didn't give anything away. Her friend interrupted with another question. Anita blushed. She couldn't remember the last time she was lost for words. She hoped to find something funny to say the next time there was a break. Before she could get her thoughts together, the

---

9   Gentile, non-Jew (Yiddish)

man was off. He told Anita that it had been nice to meet her, and left to get back to the medical faculty across town for his next lecture.

Anita was disappointed that she didn't get to learn the man's name and that he hadn't asked for hers, but she had a plan. She went to the concierge – a man who had been in his post for decades, and who knew all the ins and outs of university life. The concierge didn't disappoint. Volokhine – he proudly delivered the answer she was waiting for. But when she asked for the student's first name, he admitted defeat. Anita didn't give up. She had been helping organise the celebrations of the anniversary of the university, and had access to the student archive. There, she found the name of the young man who had made such a strong impression on her.

Marcel Alexandre Volokhine. Born on 1 April 1936. He was several months younger than her, Anita noted. He was Swiss, and a medical student at the university.

When she was left the building at the end of her day, the concierge smiled at her. 'You'll never guess,' he told her. 'Volokhine came back to ask me if I knew you. "You don't know, by any chance, who was that giggly brunette?" he said.' The concierge had given Volokhine her name, and told him that she could often be found at the secretariat helping with the preparations for the university's celebration.

Anita pauses for effect, and announces that she is going to make a cup of tea. I think back to the interviews I've done with my Moscow-born grandmother, who is almost Anita's contemporary. The accounts they give me could not be more different. My grandmother tells me facts, key moments and dates through a prism of such negativity that it can be difficult to continue. I feel her judging events past and present as she talks about them, concentrating on those she thinks need to be told. With Anita, there is laughter, as she remembers anecdotes and gossip, though she becomes serious at times and asks me not to put certain comments in the book. I am the one who is struggling – in Geneva for four days only, I am nursing a bad cold and dream of spending the afternoon in bed. But the energy of my eighty-year-old cousin keeps me going.

The day after their first meeting, Anita came to the bar on her coffee break to find Alexandre waiting for her. One coffee led to another, and then another, and the next day – another coffee. Alexandre had just come back from six months of military service – compulsory in Switzerland at the time. He had to concentrate on his studies. Students were not given time off from their studies, and he was expected to catch up with the syllabus before exams came. Yet he always found time to see Anita, meeting her for coffee or going to the cinema. Alexandre was passionate about cooking. Soon she was spending almost every evening at his apartment, where he wooed her with elaborate renditions of Swiss and Italian specialities.

After dinner Alexandre walked Anita home. 'We talked about everything. Our future, his studies, we made plans. We didn't notice the time pass.' It would be almost midnight by the time they said goodbye. Sometimes Anita would accompany Alexandre back to his apartment, only for him to then turn back and walk with her again. 'After three months we were inseparable. There was only one thing we could do. I was worried that we'd only known each other for a few months, and maybe it was too soon to talk about marriage, but we decided to get engaged and wait with the wedding until Alexandre got his medical certificate.'

Anita and Alexandre might have decided to wait for a year, but it was not that simple. 'My mother and aunt obviously convoked him to find out, as they said, what his intentions were. "And your father?" they said to him. "He is a worker."' Alexandre explained to Genia and Eva that he came from an Old Russian noble family of military aristocracy – the Voloshins. Family legend had it that Alexandre's great-grandfather, Count Voloshin in Russia, had a village with two thousand souls to his name and a regiment in the tsar's army. When the Great War began he was told by the tsar to stay where he was and save himself. As it happened, the count was in Geneva, where he stayed with his family. The son of Count Voloshin, Alexandre's grandfather, ran off to Paris, leaving his wife and young son quite a bit of money for the family.

I am not sure Genia and Eva bought the far-fetched account. Even if they did, if some of the details passed down the family tree generation after generation were indeed true, they didn't diminish the fact that

Adolphe's granddaughter was planning to marry a son of a socialist worker, of dubious Russian origin.

Anita's already difficult relationship with her mother was put under significant strain by Eva's opposition to the marriage. Alexandre didn't have a penny to his name, and Eva knew that both Anita and Alexandre would have to work to support themselves. More importantly, in the closely knit Jewish world the Neuman family had inhabited since their move to Geneva, Eva thought that her daughter could have married any Jewish boy she wanted. She begged her to think again about her decision. In her mind, any boy would have been a better match than Alexandre. Anita disagreed.

The wedding took place on 20 November 1958 at the elegant Eaux-Vives town hall built in the traditional Swiss chalet style. As the registrar read through the official part of the ceremony, Anita could hear her mother mumbling under her breath. She closed her eyes and concentrated on the future ahead of her. Her hand tightly held by Alexandre, there was no doubt in Anita's mind about the man she had chosen to marry. Her mother and her prejudices would have to become a thing of the past, as Anita was determined to live the life that she wanted and choose for herself.

The family animosity didn't spoil the party. The bride, elegant in her blue dress, was surrounded by relatives and friends. She looked radiant as she stared into the eyes of her husband. Alexandre was a dapper and tall young man with dark hair. Together they made a striking couple.

Anita's marriage marked a turning point in her life. After the wedding she distanced herself from her family and the rest of the community as she built a life with Alexandre. She would still live next door to her mother on Route de Florissant, and would be only metres away from Avenue Bertrand where her Aunt Genia continued living with Jean-Michel and Anne, but Anita would spend less time visiting her relatives. With a job and a stable income, soon matched by Alexandre's earnings as a doctor, the couple could afford to try new neighbourhood restaurants and dine out with their friends. They were young and excited to have found each other. They revelled in their independence and made the most of the freedom that for so long Anita had thought unattainable.

Anita and Alexandre Volokhine on their wedding day. Geneva, 1958

By the time Anita became a mother to a baby boy, three years after her wedding, the Volokhine family were living in the suburbs of the city. Anita and Eva tried to reconcile their differences and attempted to spend time together. Monthly dinners organised at the Route de Florissant, or in the suburbs, gave the impression of a family idyll, but mother and daughter knew that their relationship had suffered damage that would be difficult to repair.

28

A summer dream

Tel Aviv, 1960

Ariane watched the once again familiar streets of Tel Aviv float past her from the window. As her taxi made its way to the port where she would begin her journey back to Europe, she thought back to the day she had left Geneva almost three months earlier, exhausted and worn out by a difficult year of nursing studies. She had been looking forward to spending time with her father and his family, hoping that the Mediterranean climate and Israeli cuisine would cure her of the gloomy thoughts and self-reflective moods she had become prone to in Europe. She hadn't been back to the country of her birth since her departure in 1945, some fifteen years earlier, and she was looking forward to rediscovering her hometown as an adult.

By the time Ariane disembarked in Tel Aviv after a week-long journey on the glamorous *SS Constitution*, her radiant smile was back illuminating her face and the spark had returned to her eyes. Even the absence of her father, who was meant to be meeting her at the port, didn't ruin her mood – for she was in love.

She smiled as she thought of Maurice. Still in her daydream, Ariane watched as her taxi pulled into the port. Just there, three months ago, was the spot where she had said goodbye to her beloved and waited for her father to pick her up. Arriving in Tel Aviv after all these years, she had been nervous that her father would spot the excitement in her, forcing her to reveal her secret maritime romance to him ahead of time.

In the end, that didn't prove to be a problem. Her father left almost as soon as she arrived. He had volunteered for the Israeli Medical mission to the Democratic Republic of Congo, which was setting off in two days' time. A raging civil war, which followed after the country declared its independence from Belgium, meant that doctors and nurses were urgently needed. Israel was among the first in the international community to offer help. David didn't think twice.

Ariane was only slightly disappointed in her father. She was proud and relieved that she would be able to spend time with her fiancé without David's supervision.

For hers was not just a youthful infatuation, but a romance that was born on board the ship that brought her to the Holy Land. The man of her dreams was a tall, blonde young man from England. Maurice had declared his undying love and proposed to the enigmatic young woman, who at first appeared uninterested, but eventually couldn't resist his charm, his enthusiasm and deep voice. His passion for his chosen career, psychiatry, as well as stories of his adventures and travels in his mother's native South Africa, helped him sweep Ariane off her feet before her summer holidays even began.

Ariane imagined transferring her nursing studies to one of London's schools to be closer to Maurice. She hadn't yet announced her plans to her mother. As the moment of her return to Geneva approached, she knew it would not be easy to convince Genia to let her go. But they were engaged. She would have to find a way of joining him. Her handsome fiancé had returned to England several weeks earlier, but not a day went by without a letter bringing news of life in London and his hopes of seeing her in the near future.

Ariane thought back to the beginning of that summer. On board the *SS Constitution*, she had spent the first day furious at her mother for buying her a first-class ticket. In her early twenties, she felt bored amid the lacquered panels of her luxurious cabin, too far from the young people she knew were having fun two decks below. She could hear the music, summoning her to join the festivities, but first she had a dinner to attend with her fellow wealthy travellers – most of them three times her age. The thought of their conversations bored her. She was momentarily overwhelmed to find Yitzhak Ben-Zvi, the president of Israel, travelling in one of the cabins, but the novelty of the famous neighbour soon wore off, and Ariane went back to quietly sulking in her bedroom. It was typical of her mother, she thought to herself, to buy her a first-class ticket when cabin class would have sufficed, and she would have even been happy in third. Of course, Genia would have heard none of it. She was a true daughter of her father, and if luxury could be bought she would spend the money.

After dinner, set in a bright spacious room decorated with white tablecloths and a table setting fit for a royal wedding, Ariane made her escape. On the promenade deck she stopped to breathe in the warm June air, letting the calm sea breeze blow her short strawberry blonde hair in her face. Freedom, she thought. She watched couples, dressed in elegant evening wear, promenade and admire the stars. They were younger than her first-class companions, whom she had just left in the dining area, but a certain aura of European snobbery hung around them, Ariane thought, as she squeezed past a woman with fur draped over her shoulders on her way downstairs.

She noticed him immediately, and not because of the blonde hair and striking blue eyes that she would soon find irresistible. It was the crowd of giggling girls that surrounded him that drew her attention to the tall man at the bar. Ariane found an acquaintance from Geneva, and was talking to her about the adventure of the week ahead when she looked up to see him distance himself from his admirers and head in her direction.

A whirlwind romance that could have been an inspiration for an Audrey Hepburn film began that evening and swept Ariane off her feet.

The taxi driver's voice woke her from her reverie. They had arrived at the port, and he was already unloading her bags onto the pavement. Ariane rummaged through her handbag and handed over the money. She was still in her dream, but the bustle and noise of the port snapped her back to reality. She needed to hurry if she wanted to make it aboard her ship she realised, as she nervously looked at her watch. Several minutes later she was following a porter who had loaded her suitcases onto a trolley and was navigating his way towards the docks, masterfully avoiding the pigeons and the children who, it seemed, were doing everything they could to get run over by the rushing men and their heavy loads. Ariane followed swiftly behind.

Aboard the ship reality hit. Ariane was back in another first-class cabin, but this time she was not itching to go and explore. Her surroundings reminded her of her other world, the one she had managed to ignore over the summer, pretending to herself that serious decisions could wait a little bit longer. Now she knew that in only seven days' time she would be back in Geneva, where she would have to explain herself to her mother. She didn't imagine the conversation would be easy. In her last letter, Genia sounded concerned at Ariane's extended absence from the city and her daughter's choice of pastime while her father was away. She hadn't heard about Maurice yet, but the fact that Ariane had got herself a job as a radio presenter while she was in Israel didn't impress her mother.

It was so simple, Ariane thought to herself with a smile, turning up at the Kol Israel radio station in Jerusalem and telling the man in charge of French-speaking radio that he should hire her. She would never have imagined that she would have the audacity to do something so, well, audacious, and brave. But it had worked. The man was taken aback, and after making Ariane audition with the other candidates – all men, since the station was searching for a male announcer – they settled on the young girl from Geneva. Her exquisite French accent and youthful voice encouraged them to take a chance on her. Her slightly flirtatious nature and shy coquettish smile also helped. The grating voice of the French announcer on radio had bothered her so much that she had decided that it was her duty to do something about it. Now that she had, she also had a fun way to pass her time while Maurice was doing his internship.

Ariane also realised that the new adventure had been just that – a summer holiday. Life at the radio studios was new and exciting, but it didn't give her the sense of belonging and satisfaction she had felt with her nursing training. With Maurice gone as the end of the summer approached, she was impatient to attempt a move to London herself. Her mother's letters were urging her to return to Europe.

Ariane in Kol Israel. Jerusalem, 1960

237

Ariane is calm as she tells me that in the end she wasn't able to join Maurice in England. I already know that she didn't end up marrying him, but the softness of her voice tells me that she has enjoyed reminiscing about her summer romance, remembering herself as a young woman in her twenties. The rejection from the London schools, which found her Geneva curriculum too different, was a serious blow to her self-confidence. I have no doubt that Genia had to fight very hard to keep her daughter at her nursing college, when all Ariane wanted to do was to be reunited with her fiancé. A compromise was reached when Ariane was promised a trip to London for Christmas. She would see her fiancé again for the first time in almost four months.

Frequent phone calls and letters could not have prepared them for the awkward airport reunion. Ariane hesitated as she saw the tall figure waiting for her. He seemed different. Away from the sunny climate of the Mediterranean his hair was less blonde, his eyes less sparkly. She was not sure whether she had misremembered their attraction to each other. Panic overwhelmed her, and by the time she had approached her beloved to give him a kiss and a hug, she was no longer sure that she was doing the right thing by spending her Christmas holiday in his company.

Maurice hadn't noticed. He seemed happy to be welcoming her to his city. Ariane told herself to take a deep breath. It must be normal to feel nervous after so many months of separation. She felt her stomach tighten; a gradual feeling of sickness crept up unannounced. She recognised the first symptoms of stress. She longed for her home in Geneva and the comfort of her own room. She was fine, she told herself. The anxiety would go away and she would be able to relive her summer romance, which with the approach of Christmas would have a similar festive sensation as she had experienced upon their first meeting on *SS Constitution*.

Several days later Ariane was still trying to convince herself that her intuition was wrong. Maurice was a wonderful man and had all the qualities she would have wanted in her husband. They were just struggling to connect after a long separation, she reasoned.

She could tell that soon he was feeling it too. He too was convinced that they could not let this new strangeness eclipse the wonderful time they had enjoyed together in the summer. They reminisced about their romantic walks along the Tel Aviv coastline and dinners in beach cafes where they held hands and watched the sunset night after night. Something had to be done to bring back the emotion of their first meeting, the passion and the freedom they had felt for their love.

In London, Maurice was feeling the pressure. His efforts at recreating the romance fell flat. Ariane found him indecisive and hesitant in his attempts. Having seen in Maurice a confident young man over the summer, she was surprised to discover the less secure side to her fiancé, one that needed constant reassurance and guidance. Not being able to recreate the man of her summer dreams, Ariane felt that there could be no future for them together.

Everything fell apart at Victoria Station. The train station, the place of thousands of happy reunions and dramatic separations of millions of couples, was scene to another prosaic moment in two people's lives. As they were about to board the train to Manchester where his family waited to meet the girl he had not stopped talking about for the last six months, Ariane knew she couldn't go through with it. She tried to buy time; she talked about the past – but the words didn't come. When Maurice got on the train, she pulled away at the final whistle. The outstretched hand of her fiancé dropped as he realised that the train was on the move and Ariane was slowly becoming a small dot on the platform. Her eyes filled with tears but her heart felt slightly lighter at the realisation that she had made the right decision about the man she thought she loved.

29

Ariane and Moutz

Geneva, 1962

Ariane stood in the middle of the sunlit living room. Clutching the telephone, she wiped away her tears and looked for an escape route. Despite the open windows the room suddenly felt hot and airless. But she was trapped. Ariane knew she had to stand as still as she could while the seamstress meticulously added the finishing touches to her wedding dress.

Tears streaming down her face, she replayed the conversation with Jacky in her head. Hearing his voice for the first time in many months had brought back the memories she thought she had buried deep at the bottom of her heart. Hearing him tell her that he had always been planning to propose to her once her exams were over made her shoulders shake uncontrollably. How did she get herself into this mess? How was it possible that Jacky did not read the letter she sent him weeks ago, and chose today of all days to call her? Of course, he knew that she was about to get married. She had invited him to the ceremony herself. He had no doubt seen the announcement in the paper. But calling her like this, out of the blue, to explain his silence and tell her that he was shocked to hear about her engagement when he returned from a lengthy trip to the United States – this Ariane hadn't expected. Now she needed to pull herself together and work out what to do next.

She thought of her husband-to-be waiting for her at the synagogue. Wasn't Moutz everything she had always wanted in a man? He was charismatic, decisive, caring and strikingly good-looking, Ariane thought to herself. It had only been four months since they first met, but it took him two weeks to propose to her. She had let herself get carried away by the romance. She was convinced that she had made the right decision. From the very first time she saw him as she walked out of her front door to find a striking Studebaker driving past her, she had been intrigued. One of the most stylish American cars of the time, in metallic grey – you couldn't not notice and admire it. Behind the wheel was an extraordinary-looking man. His tanned face was strikingly handsome, his greying hair adding an aura of maturity to his otherwise boyish face with dark features. Ariane was stricken as she followed the disappearing car with her eyes.

At dinner with a family friend that evening she was introduced to Moutz – or Dr Isidore Bonstein. Ariane studied her new acquaintance. Away from the sunlight of that morning, Moutz didn't seem as confident and assured as the man she had glimpsed behind the wheel of his car. He seemed tense, almost shaken. He watched his words as he spoke to Ariane, as if trying to restrain himself. Such was her effect on him, she would later learn. He was significantly older than her – eighteen years older in fact. Despite the conscious effort to stay calm and focused, he had the energy of a young man. He talked to Ariane and looked at her as she replied to his questions, hungrily swallowing every word she said. She did not discourage Moutz's interest in her. At twenty-four years old, she had already been engaged once and had thought herself in love more than a handful of times. With Moutz, she continued to enjoy a light flirtation, not expecting it to lead to anything serious.

And yet, Ariane was flattered to hear Moutz's voice at the end of the phone line two days later. She hadn't given him her number, but Geneva was a small place. It would have been easy to find her. At dinner later that evening she learnt that he was born into a Jewish family in Lausanne, but came to Geneva as a student and concentrated on his career as an obstetrician and gynaecologist. He preferred not to talk further about himself, asking Ariane questions about her life and paying her one compliment after another. Moutz's age and life experience attracted her, despite – or maybe because of – the fact that he was old enough to be her father.

They talked late into the night. Ariane at first tried to impress her date with stories of her studies and recent travels, although soon she felt that she was falling for his charm. The conversation flowed as they discussed their lives. Moutz's relaxed and insouciant manner and his sense of humour made her feel safe and comfortable. It was his confidence that she appreciated the most, a feature rarely found in the indecisive young men of her age. With Moutz, Ariane wanted to explore what the world had to offer. Under his protection and guidance, she was ready to embrace life.

It took Moutz another week to propose. When he heard that Ariane was planning to go to Israel and work at the Hadassa hospital once her exams were over, he didn't try to convince her to change her mind and stay in Geneva.

'You should marry me instead,' he told her.

Ariane was stunned. They barely knew each other, but something told her that in Moutz she had found not only a fun and adventurous companion, but a caring and thoughtful husband.

She said yes.

As for Jacky… Ariane had thought of him, of course. A childhood friend so important and dear to her, who over the years had been a constant infatuation as other men came and went, Jacky had also been a bit of a mystery. Their tender and caring relationship had never developed into anything resembling a romance. Secretly in love with him as a young girl, who later exchanged hidden glances in hope of a confirmation of her feelings, Ariane had been sure that one day they would tie their lives together. But the passion she discovered with Moutz, the whirlwind romance that made her forget all her friends and rendered it almost impossible to study for her final exams, was like nothing she had ever known. At the back of her mind she kept meaning to write to Jacky, but the thought stayed with her as days passed. Only when her engagement had been confirmed, and she knew that her life was about to change forever, did she wish to see him again. She wanted to find out whether she had been wrong for so many years, whether he thought of her as a sister more than a friend, or a future bride – to give her heart the freedom to move on and be happy.

In a long and emotional letter she told him of her feelings and asked for forgiveness. There was not much to say without going into details; she tried to be gentle. She hoped that he would realise that she had made up her mind, but that he would always have a way to her heart, that it was not too late for him to make her adolescent dream of marrying him come true.

She sealed the letter and put it under her pillow. She expected a sleepless night full of worry and anxiety about the choice she had made. But having finally expressed her thoughts and explained herself to the man whose opinion had once been the most important of all, she slept soundly.

Ariane hoped her confession might prompt Jacky to act. She was expecting him to turn up on her doorstep and beg her not to marry Moutz. Or maybe he would give up and admit that he should have acted sooner. What happened – or did not happen – in the next few weeks took Ariane by complete surprise. Jacky did not reply.

His response, when it did come on the morning of her wedding three months later, brought with it heartbreak that would not heal for many months. The revelation that Jacky had simply been waiting for a suitable moment before discussing their future confirmed to Ariane what she had known in her heart all along – she had not been wrong. The bond that tied them together was real, and her imagination just ahead of its time. But the words that she had been longing to hear, of love and passion that she had heard spoken by other men and which she herself had shared with Moutz, did not come. Even in his attempt to stop her from marrying another, Jacky didn't dare tell her how he felt.

It was a crushing realisation for Ariane, and one that almost came too late. As she composed herself and walked over to her bedroom where she would finish putting on her make-up before leaving the house to face her now almost-husband, she knew that it was Jacky's indecisiveness that had ruined any prospect of them being together. With Moutz, she had found the love and commitment she had been looking for.

30

Third time's the charm

Geneva, 1970s

As Ariane settled into married life, it was her mother's turn to find happiness. Genia was in her fifties when she met her soulmate. Simon Meyer came into her life when she didn't expect another relationship, and least of all one that would last for the next fifty years. It was with Moun, as he was known to friends and family, that she would reinvent herself, discovering a comfortable existence she would have struggled to imagine in her younger and more turbulent years.

Moun was unlike any man Genia had known. A French Jew from Algeria, which he had fled when the country was in the throes of the war of independence, she found his Sephardic background unusual and exotic. She was introduced to a new culture with a different view of the world and its own culinary preferences. Couscous soon replaced gefilte fish, and stuffed peppers baked in the oven won over chicken soup. If the variety of spices at first seemed overwhelming, Genia soon adopted many as her own, creating dishes that were a fusion of her mother's cooking, rooted in the Ashkenazi traditions of the Polish shtetl, and Moun's experience of the Jewish custom from the Maghreb.

Cooking became a favourite pastime. In a small French city, away from their friends and family, Genia and Moun built a simple life for themselves. A beautiful medieval town on the Saone River in eastern France, Mâcon became their refuge. The pharmacy that Moun ran in the town centre became a beacon of their stability. For the duration of the week they could forget their past as well as the present. Their complicated lives in Geneva were left behind when they set off for the week early on Monday morning. On Friday evening Moun headed back to Geneva to spend the weekend with his two children and his estranged wife. He would never dare to ask her for a divorce but his marriage had long been a formality, sustained by his love for the children and the fear of what an official separation would mean for their relationship. Genia returned to her apartment on Avenue Bertrand. It had been a difficult time for her children, Jean-Michel and Anne, who in their adolescent years often rebelled against their mother and chose to live with their father, Jacques, around the corner. They were old enough to decide for themselves, and Genia tolerated their choices because of her own frequent absences, and because she hoped that it would make them happy.

By Monday morning, both Moun and Genia were ready to leave Switzerland and return to the stability of their lives in Mâcon. At the pharmacy, Genia found her true calling. While Moun was in the back of the shop preparing prescriptions for his clients, she ruled at the front. Giving advice to many patients who often popped by just to talk to her, she was careful not to dispense any medical information – after all she had no medical education, other than having been previously married to a doctor for ten years. Her ability to lend an ear established her reputation as the local agony aunt, and she thrived in the environment.

In their apartment above the shop, Genia and Moun talked about the events of the day. They felt accepted in the community, with many locals becoming their friends and often coming for dinner to sample the couple's innovative cooking. Her life fulfilled and complete with her new job, Genia felt that the hectic years of her youth were very far away.

The couple's idyll continued for two and a half decades. It was only when Moun was in his late seventies and it was time for him to retire that they moved back to Geneva. With trepidation Genia waited to see where Moun would go. His continuing marriage was a source of frequent friction between the couple, and Moun had never lived with Genia in Geneva before their arrangement in Mâcon became official. Even after so many years together, Genia was worried that he would feel pressured into moving back in with his family. Genia was too proud and stubborn to ask her companion directly of his plans. In the same way, she had never been able to admit to herself that she was bothered by his marital status and would have preferred to be married to her partner of so many years. With a huge sigh of relief she watched him take his suitcases to her apartment.

Genia and Simon Meyer in 2001

Surrounded by friends and family, Genia and Moun adjusted to their new lifestyle. Both now retired, they filled their days with social events and walks in the park. Moun disappeared for hours with his dog, seeking the solitude he had enjoyed at the back of his pharmacy, and giving Genia the time and space she needed to reconnect with her thoughts. The transition to retirement was far from idyllic. With so much time to spend together, bickering and arguments became more frequent. The onset of old age didn't help, and Genia became easily irritated by Moun's imperfections. Now that they were living together in her home, the dynamic of their relationship also seemed to have shifted. But Ariane, a frequent visitor to her mother's house, noticed that Genia was also more jovial and relaxed. The rituals of Friday night dinners and the Jewish day of rest reappeared in her home, and Genia relished the time spent with her family and friends.

31

A journey of self-discovery

Geneva, 1980s–1990s

How do people age?

Some, with grace. Surrounded by their friends and family, they continue an active lifestyle and enjoy the hobbies they wish they had had more time for while they were in work. For others, retirement becomes a ticking time bomb. With nothing to do and no one to see, people tend to get older faster. Lamenting the lack of a social circle they failed to build in their more active years, they have little to look forward to and their recovery from any ailment is less likely to be successful.

Ariane was in her mid-thirties when she made these observations. She was working at the newly opened geriatrics hospital near her home in Geneva, an experience that set her on a career path that became her passion. Could she help someone prepare for old age? How difficult would it be to convince a career man or woman that plans needed to be made for when they were old and not working every minute of every day? Hobbies and social activities extend and enrich lives, but how could you make someone look into their future and plan for the kind of life they would want to lead?

With two children at home and a husband who would have preferred she look after the house, Ariane was determined to help others. Having always been fascinated by psychology Ariane realised that it was the perfect connection between the body and the mind. How could you influence and exploit that interaction to improve someone's life? Was it possible that the mind was so strong that it could determine the speed of the physical recovery of a patient when there was something to look forward to? And was it possible for anyone to transform their experience through psychotherapy to ensure a happier and longer life?

The answer to the last question came only after Ariane herself had to undergo psychotherapeutic treatment. A need for a hysterectomy at a relatively young age left her unable to have more than the two children she already had, something that she was finding difficult to accept and move on from. After many months of struggling to get her life back together, Ariane started seeing a psychotherapist, whom she would credit with saving her life at a time when she didn't think she could turn it around. Hours of self-analysis and a need to look more deeply into her past proved painful, and at times revealed thoughts she would have rather suppressed. Her relationship with both her parents, and their relationship with each other, often came to the fore, reminding her of the many issues she had been forced to deal with when growing up and watching Genia's and David's marriage disintegrate. Eventually, Ariane was also able to see how her life had made her into the person she had become. She concentrated on refocusing her mind on her family and getting back on her feet. When her treatment was almost complete, Ariane no longer had any doubts. If she was able to deal with her issues in such an effective manner, then psychotherapy was the path she was going to pursue to help others put their mind above their bodies to ensure a long and happy life.

Ariane chose to follow in the footsteps of Richard Erskine, one of the global visionaries in the field. His method of integrative psychotherapy, which incorporates different schools and elements of analysis, was a relatively new approach at the time. Since it was not taught in Switzerland, Ariane would spend the next ten years travelling to England, France and America to pursue her studies. When she began in 1978, she was forty-one years old. She was not deterred by the late start. Her two daughters, who were born in the early years of her marriage to Moutz, were by then young adults. They were capable of looking after themselves while their mother was away attending lectures, seminars and practice courses to fulfil her dream of helping others.

It would take Ariane almost two decades to become a fully qualified professional. With the encouragement of Richard Erskine himself, she persevered. While in Geneva, Ariane had continued working to be able to support herself for the duration of her training. One of the more fulfilling experiences came from her work with a local centre for troubled teenagers. It was there that she set up an anti-tobacco training programme she had completed in Israel under the guidance of her father, who by then was a health official who had been implementing the method in his country. While people in Geneva were aware that tobacco was bad for your health, the official response was restrained. For the young people Ariane was working with, her clinic provided a lifeline for the future and a psychological incentive to stay out of trouble.

Ariane finally qualified as a psychotherapist the week of her sixtieth birthday. Today she receives patients in the practice she set up in the spare room of her apartment on Avenue Bertrand, and she has no plans to stop working in the near future. As she had hoped when she was just starting out, her work became her hobby. She has recently reduced her hours to spend more time with her grandchildren and extended family. When she looks back on her life, she knows that there are many things that she could have done differently. But the result would have always had to be

Ariane with her husband Isidore 'Moutz' Bonstein and
daughter Carole in 1972

the same. Helping others get past their problems and refocus their lives has been her mission in life. As she approaches her eightieth birthday, she is confident that her thirty-year-old self would have been proud had she had had an opportunity to get a sneak preview of the future and see herself ageing.

32

Eva and Anita, mother and daughter

Geneva, 1975–2002

Simon knew that the doctors had almost no chance of saving his life. He thought that by protecting Eva from what the doctor had told him, he would make his wife's life easier and save her from the terrible suffering. He was mistaken.

> *After the day for the surgery was confirmed, we had a couple of days together at home. Then one day at the hospital and five minutes after the operation when he could sense my relief. He smiled at me, caressed my face. At home, before the operation, he had been talking, writing letters. He sat at the table without eating, he went to sleep holding my hand all*

night long, and didn't tell me anything. He was on his own in his despair, alone, without any communication with anyone.

Eva mourned the loss of her husband for the remaining twenty-seven years of her life. She dedicated hundreds of pages of her diaries to her beloved Simon, telling him about her daily life and reminiscing about the moments they were able to enjoy during their two decades together. If her memory was sometimes not enough, she had hundreds of photos that helped her evoke the old days.

A photo in her diary, from a holiday to Venice in 1975, was taken on the last trip Eva and Simon took together. It is one of the final shots of the husband and wife posing for the camera, blissfully unaware of what was to come. Standing by one of the canals, they are smiling only slightly, and appear happy and relaxed. Eva's coat protects her from the chilly spring winds coming from the water, but the weather does not bother the seasoned travellers. They would spend several weeks in Venice; Eva would remember every detail, re-visiting the cathedrals and the piazzas in her head. Her memories filled pages of her diary in her silent conversation with Simon, addressing him as if he was just around the corner, popped out to get the morning paper.

The sincerity of some of the passages is moving. The postcards and letters stuck to the pages of the journal are a glimpse into her life with Simon, and how happy they both were to have found each other again at a time when neither was burdened by a commitment to someone else. Their experience was made more poignant by the tragedy Eva had lived through during the war.

A year after Simon's death, Eva wrote this:

I am watching the days go past. A year ago, my beloved was alive. His hand was warm, and it was tight in mine. We were so together, nothing could separate us. A mirage – and death separated us forever. But there is no moment in the day or at night when I don't feel that you are around me and that you are supporting me.

Eva sold their favourite house in Crans-sur-Céligny, in beautiful Geneva countryside. Now on her own, she didn't want to return to the retreat where she had spent some of the happiest days of her life. She thought of Simon looking after the garden and reading books under the shade of his favourite fir tree, while she pottered around, preparing the house for weekend guests. Visits from family and friends brought joy to the reclusive couple who would often not return to Geneva for months at a time.

There was another reason why the house was so precious to Eva. Bought with the money Eva had left after the sale of her father's watch factory, it was the last link she had to the past. When the time came in the 1960s and it became obvious that the factory would not survive the transition into the modern world of watchmaking, Eva and Genia made the decision to sell the family business. Cutting the cord to something that had been so precious to their father, and something they had both grown up with, was one of the most difficult decisions of their lives. But the risk of bankruptcy was too high. After deliberating for months and trying to find another solution, the sisters knew there was only one decision they could make. They had to accept that moving on would be the best option for their family, but also for the factory itself. They hoped it would thrive under new owners, continuing their father's legacy into the future.

The weight of responsibility lifted off her shoulders, Eva had felt free once the sale had gone through. She mourned the loss of her 'little watch factory', her father's dream, but also her own place of work of many years, where she had been able to prove to Adolphe that she was capable of hard work and commitment. With both the factory and the holiday home gone, Eva was acutely aware that a long chapter in the history of her family was now closed.

At her top-floor apartment on Route de Florissant, where she had by then lived almost half her life, Eva's passion for writing her journal helped her cope with suddenly finding herself alone. Most of the entries in her diary were dedicated to her late husband, but she also remembered Stanis. Anita's father had never been fortunate enough to earn her love, but she credited him with being a good husband and a perfect father for her little girl.

Eva lamented her relationship with her daughter and wished she could see her more often. She refused to accept any responsibility for how things with Anita had deteriorated so quickly and what steps she could have taken to fix it.

There are two sides to every story, as Anita points out to me one afternoon. Her mother wrote the diary to be read. As she frequently mentioned herself on the pages beautifully written in black or blue ink, she was addressing her grandchildren and their children, often trying to find excuses for things that happened in the past, asking them not to judge her. I've wondered whether the main audience for the diary has been Anita herself. As a child and then a young adult, Anita found it hard to forgive her mother's betrayal of her father, and in the years after Stanis' loss, seeing her mother first grieve but then move on with her life left Anita alienated and heartbroken. She resented her mother for being able to replace Stanis and move on, while she would never have another father and would only have the memories of the first few years of her life to hold onto.

Anita first fled to Paris, and then moved away from central Geneva soon after she had her first child. A bigger apartment in a quieter suburban neighbourhood of the city suited her and Alexandre better as a family; Anita didn't miss the busy streets of Geneva. Having left town amid a series of arguments with her mother, she had also lost contact with other members of her family. Ariane would continue seeing her cousin at occasional family gatherings, but the friendship the two girls shared from a young age was suspended until Anita's life presented her with the shock of Alexandre's death and she came back to the streets where she grew up.

Anita was sixty-two years old and had spent the best part of her life looking after the house and raising her two sons. Alexandre's death was unexpected. It is a subject still too painful to discuss after almost twenty years and Anita often diverts the conversation to the happier memories of her life. She tells me about the classical music concerts at the beautiful Victoria Hall in downtown Geneva she attended with her husband,

and the museums and exhibitions she visited with her friends while the children were at school. Out of her love for art and music she volunteered at the Museum of the Petit Palais, where for many years she organised concerts and evening shows to promote the museum's reopening after years of renovation. Being surrounded by artists and musicians of the city reminded Anita of her days as a young TV journalist, interviewing many of the same people as part of her job.

It was only when her children were older that Anita went back to work. Finding a job at an insurance company, Anita regained some independence and discovered a world that became her second home. As a salesperson, Anita came into her own. With her gift of the gab well known to her family and friends – but which she herself often finds surprising – she discovered that the job came naturally to her. People listened to her once she had their attention. When she started telling them about the latest insurance promotions her company had on offer, she was more likely to reach a successful sale than many of her colleagues. She discovered a world where she could talk to people from different walks of life, and her conversations with her clients often strayed beyond her professional responsibilities. She was similar in character to her Aunt Genia; Anita thrived on social contact. When the time for retirement came, she was almost sad to return to the life of a housewife that had become so familiar and often dull so many years before.

Now in her eighties, Anita is happily settled in her childhood neighbourhood of Champel. Around the corner from Avenue Bertrand, which she still associates with the happy memories of her grandparents, Adolphe and Marie, her life follows a pleasant course of social activities with her friends, dinners with her children and frequent family gatherings. When Alexandre died and Anita was forced to confront her past, she decided to move back to the streets of her childhood. She was seeking peace and solitude, as well as an opportunity to rebuild the ties she once had with her family.

Eva and Anita, mother and daughter who lived through the horrors of the war and shared so much together, reconciled in the later years of

Eva's life. Living minutes away from each other, and with Eva soon moving to a care home, they tried to remain patient with each other and spent hours discussing radio programmes and events that were taking place in the world. Eva took great care to follow news from the Middle East; she was concerned about spikes in anti-Semitism in Europe and worried that the horrors of the Holocaust, of which she was a direct witness, would be forgotten. She engaged with political theory and analysed how attitudes changed to Lenin, Trotsky and Communism. She could remember her father Adolphe's leftist leanings from when she was a child; pictures of Soviet revolutionaries could be found in their home. She was particularly proud of her father's philanthropic efforts. With each year's award of the Prix Adolphe Neuman – which still exists today – to the students of the University of Geneva who excel in the studies of aesthetics and morality, as well as Judaica, she studied the recipients and celebrated their success. In her tiny room in the care home, furnished with the wooden furniture she inherited from her parents, she spent many hours writing down her thoughts.

Anita often sat by her mother's bedside, as Eva recounted stories of the war. She wondered what would have happened if her mother had been brave enough to stand up to her father and cancel the wedding that she didn't want. Their lives would have been very different, but it was not a prospect either of them felt ready to discuss.

Eva was ninety-six years old when she died in 2002. A disabled woman from birth, Eva campaigned for disability rights by writing letters to supermarkets and shopping centres that had no step-free access. She knew that most people in Geneva didn't understand what it was like to be suffering from a disability. She wanted to make a difference. Having struggled since she was a little girl, she had gone from trying to pretend that she was able to play tennis and hike to Geneva's Salève Mountain in the presence of her father, to comfortably accepting life in a wheelchair in her later years. An old Peugeot bought after the war gave her a new lease of life. She would become inseparable from the car, driving it on holiday and even shipping it as far as Israel – for she couldn't imagine life without it.

Eva's life spanned almost the whole of the twentieth century. She lived through some of the darkest days of European history. In her later years, she tried to make up for those days with a life of leisure and holidays, making sure that happiness found her in the end.

For Anita, the loss of her mother came five years after she buried her husband. A sense of closure came with it, knowing that they had been able to reconcile their differences and spend Eva's last days together.

Part Five

33

Love in the USSR

Moscow, 1952

In Moscow, Anna felt trapped. Life in a small communal apartment, in a room that she shared with her husband and his parents, had become unbearable. Every sound, every squeak made was heard by the people she had to share her space with. It was true that the room was large. A dining table was its centrepiece, with four chairs to accommodate the whole family on the rare occasions they ate a meal together. On either side of the table, curtains marked an attempt at privacy, protecting the makeshift bedrooms from the eyes of those who would not usually see into the private space of a husband and wife. Plenty of light got in every morning as the sunshine woke the inhabitants of this unhappy place.

Anna preferred to sleep in as everyone got ready to start their day. This was her respite. She was working at a local university where she taught German to evening students. The mornings in belonged to her alone, and she treasured the time of solitude. Only once everyone had left the room for the day did she open her eyes. Through the opening in the curtain left by her husband, she observed the usual mess from the night before – the unwashed dishes piling high on one corner of the table, books and yesterday's newspapers on the other. In a moment, she would get up and start tidying to make sure that the room was clean again before she left in the afternoon, but she always tried to enjoy the last few minutes in her warm bed, untroubled by the day ahead of her.

Anna thought back to the last seven years. She had only been twenty-two years old when she married Matvei Nepomnyaschi – or 'the first man who proposed', as she puts it. The years had gone by and a once temporary solution seemed to have become permanent; they were still living with his parents, unable to find a place of their own and get on with their lives.

Matvei was the cousin of one of her mother's friends, and he had made a positive impression on Anna. Fresh from the war, where he had served in aviation and suffered a serious head injury, which sent him to hospital for several months, Matvei seemed determined to get on with life and forget his wartime experiences. His mother, Revekka, a Jewish woman from the Ukrainian city of Konotop, was like family to Anna. Her manners and demeanour were familiar, and she felt like she could instinctively under-stand this woman, who tried her best to make her new daughter-in-law feel welcome. But despite the warmth of her feelings towards Revekka and her second husband, living with them was never Anna's plan.

There were no men around in 1946. They had all either died at the front or returned home to a life of poverty and psychological distress. Anna tells me that she was young and stupid to marry Matvei. There is a certain fatality to the way she recounts the stories that surround her first marriage. At the time she felt that if she had waited any longer, she would remain on her own for the rest of her life.

Anna and Matvei registered their marriage at the local ZAGS – a registry office. In modern-day Russia, a ZAGS ceremony often resembles a wedding factory, with up to four marriages being registered every hour. Brides and grooms, as well as their guests, often have to wait in the hall along with other wedding parties for their turn to be called into the main room, especially if the registry is running behind schedule. Once inside, they are greeted by a quartet performing the wedding march on an almost non-stop loop. Outside the venue, elderly ladies are on standby to sweep the confetti and flowers away and clear the way for the next party.

In my grandmother's days, there was no confetti. No white wedding dress for the bride or a convertible waiting to whisk the newlyweds away for a tour of the city. In the hungry post-war years, even flowers were a luxury. Anna made do with five red carnations from the local market.

Anna and Matvei didn't know each other well when they decided to tie their lives together. Back from the front, Matvei was looking forward to stability. For Anna, getting married was the natural thing to do. Yet once committed to a life together, the signs of post-traumatic stress disorder became visible. Matvei shut himself away for days at a time. The flashbacks of his time at war came in the middle of the night, leaving him exhausted and unable to communicate with his family or lead a normal life. He was one of thousands of men living quietly with the pain without getting any help. Stressed and on edge, his behaviour scared Anna. She had no experience of helping someone with mental health problems. She had to learn to read her husband's mood and accept that his outbreaks of anger and frequent nightmares were not something he could control. Without professional help, however, Matvei's condition put a huge burden on his young wife and their nascent marriage.

Anna lost count of the number of times she wanted to leave him. Something always stopped her. The fear of upsetting her mother. And her father. The status of a divorced woman, not uncommon in the Soviet Union, but not welcomed in society. The feeling of guilt for leaving behind a man who could have been a better husband had he not been unwell.

Anna and Matvei Nepomnyaschi on holiday in 1949

For seven years Anna spent her evenings at work, enjoying the sense of freedom it gave her. In the classroom, she was her own boss. She chose the materials and the syllabus, and the interaction with her students encouraged her to keep up with the developments in their lives as well. During the day, she had time to think about her life. While Matvei was at work running a fabrics shop in a prestigious arcade in central Moscow, Anna roamed the streets, wondering what had happened to her dreams of starting a family and living a happy life.

Anna dreamt of having a child, but Matvei's ailing health always stopped her. Wondering whether she was going to leave her husband or stick around, Anna postponed the decision for many years, using abortion as a method of contraception. The most common means of birth control in the Soviet Union, abortions were illegal under Stalin – and my grandmother was not only endangering her health but also breaking the law by resorting to such drastic methods. Like many Soviet women, she was also not aware of the dangers of this procedure for her future fertility.

As the years went by, the longing for a baby intensified. She knew that she could be a mother if only she wanted to. The emotional agony of every termination became more pronounced. The next time she fell pregnant, she already knew that she would be keeping the baby.

In 1952 Anna was almost thirty years old and expecting her first child. She lay awake at night wondering how to tell her husband that this time it was different. She knew that the days ahead would not be easy. Matvei's health was deteriorating. He seemed less interested in what was going on around him and concentrated on getting through the days. The untreated psychological problems had given way to physical torments caused by the wartime head injury. Anna watched her husband stoically attempt to get on with his life.

I find a photo taken a month after their daughter, Marina, was born. Matvei's arms are wrapped around the baby and he is smiling for the camera. He has aged a lot in a few years, his hair greying and dishevelled. There is a sense of the exhaustion that he had been trying to fight to be able to get to know his daughter. Matvei perhaps already knew that he would not live long enough to see his child grow up.

Marina would not remember her father. She was not even a year old when Anna's premonition became reality. Anna's world collapsed around her when one evening her husband was taken to hospital with stroke-like symptoms. With her baby daughter in her arms, Anna was told that her husband had suffered a brain haemorrhage and was in intensive care. The prognosis was bleak. Having spent nearly a decade with a man she believed she didn't love, she now found herself hoping for his recovery. In the waiting room at the end of the corridor she stared blankly at the yellow walls. Her daughter was now her responsibility, and she would be a single mother. Her life would never be the same again. She watched the doctors come in and out of the room where her husband was being treated. There was little time left. She was told to come back the next day, and for the whole of the next week she patiently sat next to Matvei's bed, gathering her thoughts. His limp body, stricken by a coma that would bring an end to his life, lay in front of her. The tubes connected him to the machines and their humming provided a subtle accompaniment to her thoughts. When the doctor finally told her that it was time to say goodbye, she was ready.

At the age of thirty, Anna became a widow with a baby in her arms, and she moved back in with her mother. It had been more than a year since Marcus passed away, and Zina welcomed her daughter back to their home off Sretensky Boulevard. The familiar rooms where Anna had spent her own childhood brought comfort and stability as she tried to keep herself busy and get used to her new life. They made changes to the apartment. Zina kept her bedroom, where she continued to work on dress patterns in front of her old mirror, but Anna curtained off a larger section of the living room to make space for herself and her daughter. She picked the spot by the window, where her Nanny Lousha used to sleep on her old chest. She hoped the sunny corner of the house would be good for Marina, who at almost a year old was already an active toddler trying to get on her feet.

Anna with her daughter Marina. Moscow, 1952

Anna had a roof over her head. Very soon she was back at work at the university, but the sense of loneliness and despair remained. At home during the day, Anna helped her mother around the house and played with her daughter. But if the familiar walls of her childhood home had once been a reassuring presence, she soon began to see them as an oppressive reminder of the failure of her life. She would have done anything to get out.

Anna couldn't tell when one day ended and the next one began. Zina's clients streamed through the door, complementing Anna on the dark-haired toddler who welcomed everyone with a wide smile as she learnt to walk, holding onto chairs as she went. There were few visitors for Anna. Her friends worked during the day. The sense of disconnect from the social life she used to have was wearing her down. A respite from her gloomy thoughts came with an unexpected visitor.

Konstantin Ragozhin had been Marcus' friend from his days in exile working at the factory in Gorky. Anna remembered the tall and charismatic man from her school years. He would visit her father and make sure that he had a present to give to Anna as well, often bringing hard-to-obtain sweets and foreign-bought chocolate that he purchased during his trips abroad. Anna would look forward to his visits, flattered that a man fourteen years her senior would be so interested in hearing her news.

Back in Moscow after completing a posting in Czechoslovakia, Konstantin started visiting the family again. His gifts included baby clothes for Marina. Anna didn't know how to express her gratitude. It was his company that brought her the most joy. She was happy to welcome home a friend of the family she had known all her life. Konstantin's return to Moscow would be life-changing for Anna.

The man whose surname I carry, but memories of whom my grandmother has buried at the bottom of her heart, was a simple man from a village on the Volga River. In the few photos I have of him, my grandfather has a determined look, his deep-set eyes staring straight at the camera, his black hair ruffled slightly to one side. With high cheekbones and a raised hairline, he is a good-looking man. In a different photo, he sits at his desk at the Ministry of Foreign Trade. He is older, with the same ruffled hair and the unwavering look of a man who knows what he wants in life.

Konstantin was an ambitious man. From very humble beginnings, he joined the Komsomol – the communist youth organisation – and quickly rose through the party to the top. During the Second World War he served as a *PolitRuk* in Siberia. A *politicheski rukovoditel*, or a political commissar, was a supervisory political role attached to the armed forces, dealing with the ideological education of the military. The role was hated by most men in uniform. One of the duties of my grandfather was to snoop for any sign of opposition or dissent within his units. Aged thirty-two by the time the war broke out, he was a trusted member of the party. After the war, Konstantin was rewarded with a job at the Foreign Trade Ministry, which included travel abroad – a rare privilege for a Soviet citizen. From Czechoslovakia, where he often lived for months at a time, he brought back Czech glassware and many tomes of Russian literature – published in Prague in Russian. Books were easier to buy abroad than within the Soviet Union.

Konstantin Ragozhin in his office at the Ministry of Foreign Trade. Moscow, 1950s

Anna's voice betrays no emotion when she talks about her second husband. She is grateful for his support in the years of her father's exile, but today her memories are overshadowed by the years of their life together and the moment that marked its end.

Anna's sister, Lyucia, first suggested that Anna should consider marrying Konstantin. He had been visiting the wooden house off Sretensky Boulevard for months. It was obvious to everyone that his feelings for Anna had grown as he got to know the young woman. Anna felt that she had nothing to lose. Alone with a baby in her arms, she conceded.

I can hear the regret in my grandmother's voice. 'He was a man with an incredibly difficult personality. He was stubborn, used to getting his own way and likely to explode in anger. But he was clever and entrepreneurial,' she adds. He had studied at an elite academy and had a privileged job. She thought that he would be a good husband to her, making her life a little easier.

Anna and her daughter moved in with Konstantin. In his two small rooms in a shared apartment they would try to build their life together. It was another *kommunalka*, the reality of which was all Anna had ever known. Yet unlike her previous experience of life with Matvei, here she shared a room with her husband, and Marina slept next door – a huge privilege for their newly created family. Anna and Konstantin didn't celebrate. They didn't even register their marriage straight away, choosing to live in what was known in Russia as a civil union. A common-law marriage didn't have the same legal status as a registered union, but it carried no stigma. They eventually signed the formal wedding agreement several years later when another foreign posting appeared in sight for Konstantin.

Finland, where they were going to live, was on the other side of the Iron Curtain. Although Konstantin was looking forward to exploring a different part of the world, the move didn't happen. Anna was pregnant, as she discovered during routine medical tests required by her husband's employer. The foreign posting was cancelled. Soviet citizens should be born on Soviet soil and not abroad, the thinking went, and the family had to abandon their plans.

Anna's second daughter, my mother, Elena, was born on 14 October 1957.

34

'*Kvartirni vopros*'

Moscow, 1958

Kvartirni vopros – or 'the apartment question', literally – was one of the existential issues of the Soviet Union. Memorably observed by Bulgakov's mysterious professor, Woland, in the novel *The Master and Margarita*, *Kvartirni vopros* brought out the worst in the Muscovites. The expression has since had television programmes named after it and has been quoted in many jokes. But for most people of my mother's and grandmother's generations, it was no laughing matter. Living arrangements were a constant worry for the families who were trying to improve or expand their accommodation as their households grew. In the Soviet Union, apartments were allocated by the authorities; a special department was in charge. The system was not simple. Every member of a family had to be registered. As space diminished with every marriage and every newborn baby, it was time to think about solving the *Kvartirni vopros* – how to get a bigger apartment.

Soon after giving birth to her second daughter, Elena, Anna learnt that her childhood home was up for demolition. To combat chronic house shortages and to move the capital into modernity, the central streets of Moscow were being re-planned and new apartment blocks built for the masses. They were to become known as Khrushchevkas, after the Soviet leader Nikita Khrushchev who orchestrated the industrialisation of house building. A first attempt at pre-fabricated accommodation, the four- and five-storey concrete-panelled apartment blocks would become home to hundreds of thousands of Muscovites.

Anna was happy at the prospect of having her own apartment. She was still registered in the *kommunalka* off Sretensky Boulevard, along with her two daughters and her mother. Because the building was being knocked down, they could expect to be given a two-bedroom apartment for four people. Remaining registered in the old apartment, despite not residing there, was a strategic decision; she was allowed to live elsewhere as long as she maintained a contact with the old property. Since rumours about the demolition of the old neighbourhoods had been circulating for a while, Anna thought it wise to maintain her connection to her childhood home to be able to get a bigger apartment when they were eventually relocated.

Anna was getting worried that soon the workers would come to start taking apart her mother's home, and there was still no sign of a decision from the authorities. When the verdict did eventually come, Anna was left angry and dismayed. The family were being offered a one-bedroom apartment on the outskirts of Moscow. Today, the VDNKh district, a mouthful of an acronym that describes the general purpose trade show complex built in the 1930s to showcase the achievements of the national economy, would be considered a fairly central location in the metropolis. But in the 1950s the city was still growing, and the area was not well located. For Anna, the bigger problem was that the authorities were undermining their own regulations by trying to move a family of four people into a smaller space than should be allocated to them. She was prepared to fight.

At the MosSoviet, the authorities dealing with the allocation of apartments, she was bluntly told that if she was not happy with what she was being given, she could have two bedrooms in a *kommunalka* instead. Anna was devastated. The dream of owning an apartment that wouldn't be shared with anyone else was crumbling before her. She persevered. Hoping to intimidate the staff at the allocation office, she returned the next day with her brother, Salya. An imposing man of significant height, he was on leave from the Navy and was wearing his full uniform. Anna was sure that he would make a good impression on the women at the office. Yet they had seen it all before. Salya and Anna left empty-handed.

Anna was lost in the world of bureaucracy. She went to visit the one-bedroom apartment she was being offered and tried to imagine living there with her two children and her mother. Zina joked that she would not sleep on the kitchen floor. Anna knew that it was time to ask for help.

I stop my grandmother here. A two-bedroom apartment is better than the one-bedroom she was being offered, but why would her mother have to sleep on the floor? She wasn't planning to live there for the moment, since she was living with her two daughters and Konstantin in his shared apartment. 'You never know what could happen,' is the philosophical answer of my grandmother. She might have been aware that her marriage to Konstantin would not last, and she was trying to plan for the future. 'It was better to plan ahead a little and make sure you would still have a roof over your head if things went wrong. If I'd settled for the smaller apartment, our chance for a two-bedroom apartment would have been gone forever.' A lesson learnt in the uncertain Soviet reality.

Anna's determination paid off in the end. What counts is who you know and not what you know. Through a contact at the MosSoviet, Anna was able to finally claim what was rightfully hers. One of her students, a certain Mr Selivanov, listened patiently to the problem. A middle-aged bureaucrat with a receding hairline and thick glasses, he had enough power to help with this relatively mundane predicament. He picked up the once-white receiver of the old phone and spun the dial. The digits were long worn out. Anna wouldn't have been able to make out the numbers even if she tried. She nervously looked around. Her quickened heartbeat almost faded out Selivanov's conversation with the allocation office. Minutes later, she became aware of his smile. A brief conversation was enough to make sure Anna received the apartment appropriate to the size of her family.

'I had a two-bedroom apartment in Sokol. I was so happy!' Almost sixty years later, Anna beams at the memory. It was that simple. She didn't need to bring her brother in uniform with her to influence the decision, or her husband. One contact in the right place was enough to help. She couldn't believe her luck.

In Russian, *sokol* means 'falcon'. Leningradsky Prospekt, a large avenue, dominated the district, making it a bustling place in the growing city. In the courtyards hidden within the newly built apartment blocks, the peaceful and quiet squares provided a getaway for the residents. At Leningradsky Prospekt number 78, in a Khrushchevka of a later design, Zina's new apartment was on the sixth floor of a nine-storey building.

Two days later, Zina moved into her new home. The two bedrooms of the apartment were adjoining, and you could go round in a circle – from the hall to the living room, continuing to the first bedroom and then into the second, and ending up back in the hall. The unpractical feature was very popular with Anna's daughters, who chased each other around the apartment when they came to visit their grandmother.

Zina brought her belongings with her, the most important of which was the mirror that had been torn out of the wardrobe in defiance of the authorities some forty years earlier. She looked for the best spot for it in the apartment, finally fixing it on the wall next to the doorframe and opposite her new wardrobe. She could tell natural light and occasional sunshine would reflect in the glass and make her room brighter. Only once she was satisfied with the arrangement could she feel truly at home.

Zina quickly adjusted to living on her own. For the first time since the condensation policy began, Zina was able to live in a home that she didn't share with strangers. For the first time in her life she was living alone. Her three children were grown-up. Zina enjoyed the freedom of her apartment. She had retired from her job at the atelier and was now only working with private clients who came to see her. With most of her mornings free, she explored her new neighbourhood and quickly made friends with some of her neighbours. Zina didn't know that her solitude would not last long. Within half a year Anna would be back on her doorstep, this time with two children in tow, her marriage to Konstantin having finally broken down.

If the worst was brought out in Muscovites by the housing issue, then my grandfather seems to have been one of the victims. While Anna was on her feet all day trying to secure her mother's apartment, her husband was dreaming of getting out of his rooms in the *kommunalka* as well. Despite his high position in the Foreign Trade Ministry and his status of a newly married man, the bureaucracy was slow to prioritise him for new accommodation. He was becoming impatient. The only person registered at his apartment, he would at best be looking for a one-bedroom place in a different neighbourhood, but he saw a different solution. He suggested an apartment swap. If they joined forces with Anna's mother, they could swap the newly acquired two-bedroom apartment and their two rooms in the *kommunalka* for a big three-bedroom apartment where everyone could live together. In theory such two- or three-sided swaps were possible – multiple properties were exchanged all the time and as long as all the parties were happy it was a straightforward process. In Anna's case it was not that simple.

Zina had always found her son-in-law difficult. A man with a strong personality and an ego, he liked getting his own way. Now that she was finally able to enjoy the peace and tranquillity of a solitary life, she didn't want to move in with her daughter's family.

Anna found herself in an impossible situation. Her husband was furious. He told his wife that he would never set foot in his mother-in-law's house again. He also forbade Anna from seeing her.

'What do you do!' exclaims my grandmother to me. 'Of course I said no! How was it possible for me not to see my mother again?'

In their two tiny rooms Anna and Konstantin tried to continue their lives together. Marina and Elena provided a distraction to their parents, but they were not speaking to each other. Anna returned from work in the evenings to find the girls asleep. They were watched by a nanny while Konstantin shut himself away in the other room. He barely looked up when Anna entered the bedroom at night. In the morning, she woke up to find him gone for the day. They were leading parallel lives. In a confined space, Anna felt that the loneliness that had led to marrying Konstantin was returning. She did not cope well in emotional isolation. Life was about to change again.

For two silent months, Anna tried to talk to her husband, but her apologies and reassurances about a future together fell on deaf ears. Konstantin refused to communicate. His monosyllabic answers made life impossible for Anna and she could no longer see the ties that once held her marriage together. She imagined the next step of her life. There was a room waiting for her at her mother's apartment in Sokol.

Anna proudly took her children and left her husband. With the nanny in tow, she made her way to her mother's house where she knew she would have to face new challenges as a single mother of two children. At least she wouldn't be ignored and patronised by a man who had disrespected her and allowed his family to fall apart.

Anna couldn't have predicted that the apartment that she had spent so much energy securing for her mother would become the undoing of her relationship. She tells me that six decades later she is still trying to make sense of her husband's behaviour all those years ago. When sleep doesn't come, she blames herself for walking away and not sticking with him. Deep down, she knows that his demands were not realistic. Luck was not on her side, and she should have never married a man who was capable of such behaviour, she tells me.

Anna has had plenty of time to reflect on her life. She wonders whether she should have talked her mother into the swap, sparing everyone a lot of pain and disagreement. Elena was two years old and her sister was

Anna with her husband Konstantin and their two daughters in 1958

seven when they moved in with their grandmother. My mother would grow up with only a vague memory of her father, who would eventually start visiting the girls and help with their upbringing. He officially adopted Marina as his daughter when she started school a year later. For many years, the two sisters had no idea that they had different fathers – a banal fact hidden away in the paperwork that Anna kept secret from the children. Marina didn't know a different dad. After the separation she looked forward to Konstantin's visits, to show off her latest drawing or craft work she had made at school.

Konstantin's ailing health brought about his ultimate separation from his family. Years of liver problems caused by a stressful lifestyle and an inevitable drink developed into a late diagnosed cirrhosis. He was frequently hospitalised. Anna brought their daughters along, often staying only for minutes at a time. Konstantin was in a lot of pain. It was a traumatic experience for the family. Yet at the beginning the doctors were optimistic. He was released and decided to return to work. He was to ease off on the travel and the long hours, but stubbornly he continued. For several years he overcame the pain, convincing himself that he could find distraction in work. As he lay dying in hospital, he embraced his daughters. They had grown up in the years since his separation from Anna, but he recognised the childish features in their faces. In the ten-year-old Elena he saw himself – a strong-minded little girl with a tough character and a sense of determination. She didn't know that her father was dying, and wouldn't remember much of him other than the little anecdotes she would hear from her mother and sister. But her personality would forever link her to the father she could only wish she had had a chance to know.

35

An emotional truth

Moscow, 1950s–1960s

The death of Stalin had been a turning point for the Soviet Union. The political atmosphere changed with the arrival of Nikita Khrushchev. In a striking and unexpected move he denounced Stalin and relaxed some of the repressions. People like Anna and her family would forever be cautious of their surroundings and when expressing their thoughts in front of strangers. But hope was rising. There was new air on the streets, and people were taking micro-breaths to absorb it.

For Anna, the biggest hope for the future came with the return of her uncle Nyoma. After seventeen years in Siberian camps, Zina's brother was released and travelled to Moscow. Anna had been a child when he was arrested and didn't recognise the sullen middle-aged man she met at her Aunt Emilia's house. He was supposed to be a year younger than his sister Zina, but he looked ravaged by his experience. The deep wrinkles on his face reflected the suffering he had endured. Health problems would plague him for the rest of his life, but the emotional trauma was the worst of all – left untreated and undiscussed, for no one dared ask him what he had witnessed and experienced.

Despite Nyoma's return, the family were cautious in their celebrations. Millions of former prisoners came back. Experience told Anna's family not to trust Khrushchev's amnesty. The government could change its mind. No one's safety was guaranteed. For Nyoma, the release was bittersweet. He was allowed to come back on the condition that he would not live in Moscow again. His new residence was to be Podmoskovie – the Moscow region. Close enough to the capital, but not close enough to the family he had not seen for almost two decades.

Nyoma was a tormented man. He had spent the last seventeen years trying to survive in one of the toughest labour camps on earth. He was determined to make the most of the time he had left. That included living with his wife, and not an hour away from the city. As he settled in his family home on Gogolevsky Boulevard, some twenty minutes' walk from the Kremlin, he found it impossible to sleep. He was defying his tormentors by moving almost as close to them as possible. In a typical Moscow *kommunalka*, behind closed doors, his hands would shake every time the doorbell rang. In his nightmares he replayed the scene of his arrest many years ago, anticipating another detention for disobeying the authorities.

Nyoma hid in his room for the rest of his life. Emilia trusted her neighbours and knew that they would not reveal that her husband was back in the city, but he listened closely to the conversations around him and feared that the authorities would turn up to check on his wife, to make sure he had not violated the terms of his release.

They never came. Eventually Anna's uncle regained some physical strength and a shade of his former personality, but he would never tell his family about his experience in the Gulags. Anna didn't know about her uncle's sufferings. It was not until certain facts filtered through that she was able to get a glimpse into the kind of life that Nyoma led while he was in detention.

One Day in the Life of Ivan Denisovich by Alexander Solzhenitsyn sent shockwaves through Moscow's intelligentsia when it was published by *Novy Mir* magazine in 1962. The novel, in which Solzhenitsyn describes conditions at one of the forced labour camps and a typical day in the life of one of the inmates, Ivan Denisovich, was published almost a decade after her uncle's release. The horrors of the Stalinist repressions, never too far back in her mind given the detention of both her father and uncle – as well as her own close call at the factory after the war – took on a more vivid turn. She could not have imagined the extent of the brutality of the Soviet regime, and the fact that her uncle had been able to survive his imprisonment seemed like a miracle.

The publication of the novel and the sale of more than 95,000 copies on its first release was the first public indictment of the Soviet Union on such scale. By then people were beginning to talk among themselves, among their most trusted friends and behind the firmly closed doors of their kitchens. They discussed what was happening in the country and around the world. Many became skilled at reading between the lines. But the reality of daily life did not change for most Soviet citizens. A popular joke – always told in absolute confidence – recounted the story of a man who was about to have a birthday party. He went to the authorities to let them know that he was planning a gathering; he did not want to be accused of anything anti-Soviet. He asked them to send someone along to set the record straight in case there were any questions afterwards. 'Show us the list of your friends who are coming,' he was told. When he produced the list, he was told not to worry. 'Half the people on this list work for us already.'

It is a sad, but realistic, reflection on life.

36

Growing up

Moscow, 1971

Marina looked at her wrist as she lay in bed trying to fall asleep. The previous nights had not been easy. She was not a calm sleeper, often tossing and turning in her bed in the middle of the night. The piece of string attached to her wrist meant that she had to try to stay still, or risk waking up her grandmother, Zina. It had all been Zina's idea. In her late seventies, she was neither ill nor particularly frail, but her imagination told her that death could come at any moment. Scared of what that might mean, she wanted to be able to call for help, and her solution was simple. From Marina's wrist, the piece of string stretched across the room she shared with her sister, Elena, and through the gap under the door to

Zina's room, where after a careful positioning along the bedside table, its other end was tied to Zina's wrist. The unassuming solution meant that with a simple tug of her hand, Zina could summon her granddaughter the minute she felt she needed help.

Of course, Zina's invention created more laughter for her and the girls than any practical help. Trying to determine whether the mechanism would work with all the participants asleep, Zina and her granddaughters experimented day and night, keeping each other entertained and distracting Zina from the thoughts that were behind the invention.

Three months later, Zina died peacefully in her sleep. She had not needed to call for help. The piece of string dangled from her wrist when Marina and Elena discovered their grandmother in bed the following morning.

Elena was fourteen years old when she was confronted with her grandmother's lifeless body. She felt that a ray of sunshine had been extinguished from her life. With Zina's passing the girls would lose the energy and spirit that had filled their two-bedroom apartment at Sokol. Zina had doted on her granddaughters and they, in turn, looked forward to spending their evenings with her, listening to her stories and entertaining episodes from the past.

'Tell us about the woman you worked with at the circus,' Elena would say, looking mischievously at her grandmother. With a playful sparkle in her eyes, Zina would recount the story for a hundredth time, telling the girls about the day she went to the market to buy groceries. The queue for the strawberries – a rarity in the Soviet Union – went around the block. Zina, worried that there would be none left, went straight to the front of the line. To her delight, the seller was one of the women she regularly chatted to during her trips to the market, and she was able to buy some strawberries without the wait. To the shouts of complaint at Zina's preferential treatment, the seller, nonplussed, shouted back, 'We worked at the circus together!'

The punch line would send Elena into fits of giggles. It encapsulated her grandmother's jovial nature and ability to turn a situation to her advantage, thanks to her positive attitude and her ability to get on with people from all walks of life.

Zina. Moscow, 1960s

Elena would always talk fondly of her grandmother, whom she remembered not only for her funny stories but for her attitude to life. Nothing was impossible if you put your mind to it, was her motto. Zina stood out in the greyest Soviet days. With her carefully applied lipstick, shoes dyed in a colour to suit her mood or the fashion of the season, and a dress made decades earlier but re-cut to suit the times, she would be off on her most recent quest. Whether it was to meet with a friend or in search for food, Elena always knew that her grandmother would come back triumphant. It was only when she had been out buying sweets that the girls had to be careful not to upset Zina. No matter how hard she tried, she could never hide them successfully when she returned, always discovering several days later that Marina had been able to track down the latest hiding place and empty out her favourite box of sugar-coated cranberries. Marina, who possessed a tooth as sweet as her grandmother's, usually found the locked box under her grandmother's bed, causing Zina to yell in desperation to her daughter Anna: 'Your children ate my sweets again!'

Confectionary wars aside, the bond between Zina and her granddaughters created a balance in the family. With Zina gone, Marina and Elena discovered a more sombre daily life. They were confronted with the realisation that apart from teaching evening classes most days of the week, Anna had been spending less and less time at the Sokol apartment with her daughters. With Zina around, she had been able to rely on her mother to look after the girls, while she pursued a relationship with the man who would eventually become her third husband. With Zina no longer there, Elena and her older sister became the only permanent occupants of the family apartment.

Vyacheslav Zalensky had already been in her mother's life for more than a decade when Elena, shocked, discovered the truth. She had suspected that there was someone in Anna's life after her marriage to Konstantin ended. Her frequent absences at weekends had not gone completely unnoticed. Elena was no longer a child by the time she lost her grandmother. But since Anna had decided early on that she would not live with Zalensky full-time, it took many years for her family to understand the seriousness of her new relationship.

A professor at the Moscow Automobile and Road Construction State Technical University (MADI), Zalensky was a complicated man, a recent widower, whom Anna met in the early 1960s. They drifted towards each other, seeking out each other's company. Their paths in life were not dissimilar – Anna's separation from Konstantin was fresh in her mind. After the loss of her first husband she understood Zalensky's hesitancy when it came to a new romance. Their work in academia brought them together and provided the necessary common ground.

With Zalensky, Anna also discovered a lifestyle she had not been used to. Parties and birthday celebrations were common in this new world. Students, colleagues and friends often came to his summer house on the outskirts of Moscow where festivities continued late into the night. Anna, quiet and reserved by nature, welcomed the distraction that Zalensky's social gatherings brought to her daily life. She was able to meet new people and enjoy a more light-hearted lifestyle.

Gradually, Elena began to notice changes in her mother as well. Once always stressed and worried about the daily challenges of finding

Anna and Vyacheslav Zalensky in 1970s

food and clothes for her daughters, she seemed more relaxed. Anna had learnt better than anyone that having a man in your life would never guarantee stability for your family. But Elena could tell that her mother had something to look forward to, and she tried her best to understand the reasons behind Anna's wish not to unite her whole family under one roof.

For Elena, life became more difficult with the loss of her grandmother. Anna had not inherited her mother's positivity and bright outlook on life. She found it hard to express her emotions. Elena, as the younger child, struggled to reconcile her mother's coldness with the warmth and tenderness she had become used to with her grandmother. She could also see that Anna's complicated routine of living between two homes was making her increasingly tired. Shopping for food, doing housework in the morning and preparing lunch for her daughter while she was still at school, Anna was exhausted by the time Elena returned home and it was time for her to go to work. A fifteen-minute nap on the sofa before she headed out to teach her evening lessons helped her get through the rest of the day. Elena waited for her mother to come back for dinner before saying goodbye to her as she went to bed and Anna prepared to leave the house again to spend the rest of the evening with Zalensky.

With Marina now a student and often away with her friends, Elena now found herself at home on her own. Yet she was not burdened by solitude. An optimist by nature, with a can-do attitude no doubt inherited from her grandmother, she made the most of her newfound independence. Whether doing homework or catching up with friends over the phone, she enjoyed the time when she was free to imagine a bright and happy future for herself, without the Soviet realities of daily life.

Eventually Elena would learn that her mother's memories of those years were a blurred mix of tiredness and stress. Going back and forth between the two apartments, trying to spend time with both her daughters and Zalensky, she felt overwhelmed by her life.

Anna's thoughts would turn to her cousins in Geneva. While she wondered about their lives and wished she could have news from them, she no longer thought that their lives were easier than hers. Since her trip to the East German city of Dresden in the late 1960s, she had decided that life was not easier in Europe. During the visit she discovered a city that had been catastrophically bombed by the Allies at the end of the Second World War, and witnessed the reconstruction taking place everywhere. Many of the buildings were being rebuilt in a more socialist style – for financial and ideological reasons. During her month-long training at Dresden University, Anna was able to admire some of the gothic and baroque architectural masterpieces, but what she saw most vividly was the poverty of the city and its struggle to prosper following the end of the war.

Anna was privileged to have been able to leave the Soviet Union for a trip abroad. For the duration of her stay she was accompanied by the German professor who was hosting the Soviet party in the city – and making sure that there were no irregularities in their behaviour. Defections from the Soviet Union had become popular, and both governments wanted to avoid any embarrassing situations. Anna thought of her children and wished she could have been able to afford to buy them presents. With the little money she had, she went from shop to shop trying to find something for the girls, hoping that there would be a gift that she could take home with her. What she noticed were the food shortages affecting the German population. Long queues for necessities were familiar to her, but she was surprised that even abroad, the situation was similar. Dresden, of course, was in the socialist East Germany, and unlike West Germany didn't participate in the Marshall Plan, which saw the US give more than $12 billion in economic assistance to help rebuild Western Europe after the end of the Second World War. East Germany was not part of the German economic miracle, and what Anna saw on her visit was a reflection of that.

The last day of the trip made a lifelong impression on Anna, one that would define her view of foreign countries for many years to come. The German host invited the Soviet group for a farewell gathering at his house. Anna and her colleagues were told to expect tea and cake, but as per Russian custom they arrived laden with gifts of Russian vodka and boxes of chocolates that they had brought with them for just such an occasion. When they sat at the table for tea, Anna was shocked to discover that the afternoon's meal would only consist of tea and cake – just as they had been promised. 'It was such a contrast; we had brought many things for them, and all we got was a little piece of cake, and a cup of tea. I was so shocked. It was stingy. It was in the post-war period, but we were guests. The Russians were so welcoming; when people came to your home you opened the fridge.'

Anna's first – and only – trip to Germany reaffirmed her belief that life was difficult and full of challenges that needed to be overcome, whether you lived in the Soviet Union or abroad. She was certainly influenced by the environment she had come from and cultural misunderstandings, but Germany, which had once felt so familiar, started to seem a lot more distant.

Anna was careful not to share her disappointment with her daughters. However, Elena could tell that her mother had returned from her trip without the excitement and enthusiasm she had been expecting. Elena associated 'abroad' with one particular thing she remembered from her childhood – the Czech crayons her father had brought back for her from one of his trips when she was younger. He gave them to her when she had to spend two weeks in hospital during a dysentery outbreak at her school. The crayons, with their foreign smell and exotic colours, were the best present she had ever been given. She spent every day drawing pictures, while also trying to be careful not to waste the crayons, wishing they would last forever. When she later became an engineering student at university and spent many hours doing technical drafts and drawings, she would try to conjure up the smell of the crayons from her childhood. But all she could picture were the crayons themselves, left in a pile of children's toys after she was allowed to leave the isolation ward, but forced to leave her precious gift behind.

Elena did not understand how her mother could not have enjoyed her first experience of foreign travel. To go to another country seemed like an unattainable dream to the girl who would grow up to travel the world, but who, as a child, appreciated even the simpler things that life had to offer.

Anna's relationship with Zalensky would distance her from her daughters. Elena in particular drifted further away as she got older. As a teenager, she was strong, stubborn and decisive. She had inherited these traits from her father, whom she barely remembered, but also from her grandmother, Zina, whose influence on Elena's life would be long-lasting and fulfilling. As a young woman, Elena would be able to better understand the struggles her mother had to overcome to provide for her and her sister, but the difference in their personalities and attitudes to life would mark their relationship for many years to come.

37

A Soviet way of life

Moscow, 1980s

In Russia we often refer back to the time when the trees were tall: a time of nostalgia and childhood memories, the naivety of the past and a wish to return to days long gone. Coming back to the streets of my Moscow childhood after a fifteen-year absence, I was struck by how tall the trees actually were. They were much taller, greener and fuller than I remembered them. The roads seemed smaller, the cars more numerous, and only the fourteen-storey blue and white high-rise still stood high and proud, overlooking the old courtyard and the rest of the neighbourhood.

The trees had indeed been smaller when I was growing up, and were barely strong enough to survive when my parents had moved to the neighbourhood in the mid-1980s. The high-rise, one of the many tile-covered new apartment blocks being erected in Moscow's suburban neighbourhoods, was their dream come true: a place of their own to call home. After many years of sharing an apartment with her sister, Marina, and eventually with Marina's new husband and baby son, Elena moved into her own apartment.

In the post-Stalin Soviet Union there were two ways of obtaining a new apartment. One was to queue up with the local authorities – the Rayispolkom – *Rayonni Ispolnitelni Komitet*, or the so-called Neighbourhood Implementing Committee. The queues were long, and proof was required of residence in extremely cramped conditions of about five square metres per person. For Anna, Elena and Marina, as well as Marina's new husband and son who were all registered at the two-bedroom Sokol apartment, this was still not the case.

Elena pursued the other option: she joined a cooperative. The organisation was created by the authorities to run within state companies in order to allocate housing for the population. Spaces there were also limited. She still had to prove that she had a problem with her living arrangements, but the criteria were not so strict.

I am sitting through my father's very tedious and detailed explanation of the system because my knowledge of Soviet bureaucracy is not extensive enough to understand its complexity. The bottom line is that my mother's employer's cooperative was short of people, and she was allowed to join. She then had to find a way to pay for the apartment she would eventually be allocated, which only became possible with Anna's savings. For many years she had been saving the sum she had received from the sale of Konstantin's car after his death. It was 1983, and a Volga sold fifteen years earlier was worth about the same as a small apartment through the cooperative. After completing all the hurdles of the bureaucracy, my mother was about to become the proud owner of a small two-bedroom apartment.

As the final preparations were being made and Elena was finalising a small detail, she was told that there had been a problem with the allocation and her request had been denied. The apartment on the eleventh floor of a high-rise near the Babushkinskaya metro station in the northeast of Moscow, which had become hers as a result of a draw only five days earlier, would now go to someone else.

No explanation was given, no reassurances that anyone was going to look into the matter or come up with an alternative solution. Just like her mother nearly three decades earlier, Elena knew that she would have to achieve the impossible to claim back what had already been allocated to her. She would not accept that someone higher up the pecking order probably needed to be allocated an apartment and that she became a victim who would have to make alternative arrangements for her future. Once again, Anna's teaching contacts were useful, and through one of her students she was able to find help at the MosSoviet. After weeks of discussions and customary visits to the office with boxes of chocolates and bottles of vodka to help seal the deal, Elena's ownership of the apartment was finally confirmed.

The makeshift table, created with the help of a big wooden door and a couple of boxes, was bursting with drinks and pickles as Elena and her friends celebrated her luck and fortune. The *Kvartirni vopros* was one of the realities of Soviet life. Few people would have been able to avoid the struggles involved in buying, swapping, exchanging or getting allocated an apartment. They came together to help Elena move her boxes and furniture into the apartment and to raise a glass to her future in her new home. It was that day that most of Elena's friends became aware of Anatoly, Elena's future husband.

While the men did the heavy lifting, my father found his natural role in delegating to others and suggesting where things should be placed in the apartment. 'Don't worry about him,' with a smile Elena waved away questions from her friends, 'we will move things around later.' She didn't know that her wedding to the quiet and serious Anatoly Landsman would take place later that same year.

Elena, a young woman with an endless amount of energy, was in her mid-twenties. Since graduating with a mechanical engineering degree with honours from Moscow's MADI University (where her stepfather was a professor), her social life had brought her some of the most exciting and fun-filled years of her life. Her university friends and colleagues from the research institute where she was developing roadworks machinery didn't dwell on the complexities of their lives. They celebrated each other's achievements and would for many years treasure the memories of the kayaking trips to the lakes of the Caucasus and skiing trips in the Carpathians, not forgetting the parties held in Moscow and quick trips to the Russian dachas belonging to one of her friends' families or her stepfather Vyacheslav Zalensky. Elena was one of the driving forces of the circle. Her optimism and positivity were contagious.

Elena and Anatoly met at work. Born in the city of Perm near the Ural Mountains where the European part of Russia ends and Asia begins, Anatoly had come to Moscow for his studies. Six years older than his future wife, he studied hard and concentrated on his career. He wasn't a natural socialiser, preferring quiet evenings on his own to the parties and adventures favoured by my mother. But soon he was learning how to ski and following Elena on hiking expeditions in Russia's less explored parts.

My parents, Elena Ragozhina and Anatoly Landsman in 1983

Her pitch-black hair tied in a ponytail, and her face rarely bearing more than a trace of make-up, Elena knew that despite the shortcomings of the Soviet system and the constant challenges that she would have to overcome, she could be happy anywhere. She often thought of her relatives in the exotic country called Switzerland and imagined the happy life her cousins led amid the green hills and mountains of central Europe, but she didn't think that she herself would ever want a different life. Even in the late 1980s, when Jewish emigration from the Soviet Union picked up and people around her started making plans to go to the United States and Israel, the thought didn't cross her mind.

In the early 1990s, Elena and her husband, Anatoly, watched the tanks as they rolled towards the Russian White House, which housed the Russian parliament. Amid the chaotic scenes they tried to follow the negotiations that were taking place behind closed doors. They hoped for stability and democracy, knowing that before that became possible they would face a very uncertain future. The attempted coup d'état against the Soviet leader Mikhail Gorbachev would make way for the creation of an independent Russia. It was with the notions of *glasnost* and *perestroika*, which had been declared in 1985, that most people in the West became aware of the changes that were going to bring an end to the Cold War and destroy the country the United States saw as the biggest threat to the world's stability.

Every night they turned on the television in the kitchen of the apartment that Anatoly had so attentively helped to decorate seven years earlier. My parents were hoping that whatever came next would be different from what they and their parents had lived through. They didn't want their children to be scared of repressions and labour camps. They hoped my sister and I would not live at the mercy of the authorities and would have more opportunities in life than they themselves had been able to enjoy. They had no idea what life in the new country would be like; their biggest challenge of all would be to adjust their lives to survive in a new environment.

Elena re-qualified as an accountant. After a sudden realisation that engineering was not going to be a career of the future, at least not in

Russia, she worked from home and managed the books for many of the newly created companies. My father's foray into the world of finance proved to be the right decision at the right time, providing a future for him and his family.

The creation of the new Russia became the liberation of many people. The freedom to travel abroad, to own property and make independent choices allowed my parents to lead lives that started to resemble those of the people in Western Europe. For Elena, one of her first trips to the West was a holiday to Switzerland. She would always remember the colours – the brightly painted buildings and the vivid palette of the Swiss Alps. The delicious taste of pizza eaten for the first time and the discovery of more variety of cheeses than she ever imagined existed. Leaving Russia in the mid-1990s, she felt like the world had opened up in front of her, and in this parallel universe the possibilities were endless.

My mother always maintained that she was not an immigrant by nature, but the draw of the West, with its opportunities and unexplored promises, was too strong. The move to London came two days into the twenty-first century, changing the course of our family history. It brought together the descendants of Adolphe and Marcus, one hundred years after their journeys first began.

38

Family

Geneva, 2013

Genia looked around the beautifully decorated events room of her retirement home. The faces of her son and daughters, grandchildren, great-grandchildren, her niece and cousins, as well as cousins once and twice removed – all were seated around the big square table. She examined their familiar features, their eyes, noses, hair. In many of them she could see traces of her parents, Adolphe and Marie. In others, it's the facial expressions that brought back memories of days long gone and forgotten. The youngest children tried to be patient as they waited for the birthday meal to be served, disciplined by their parents to be on their best behaviour for this momentous occasion. For Genia, the smiles brightened up what had already been an intensely emotional day. There would be more tears before lunch was over.

Family had been everything to her, she told us when everyone had finally settled and lunch was about to begin. In sadness and in happiness, she would rather be surrounded by her loved ones, than mourn on her own. That's why, despite only learning news of her partner Moun's death that morning, she had decided to celebrate her 100th birthday, and Moun's life, in our company. Her voice slow but steady, Genia didn't allow the room to fall silent. Her hand shaking only slightly, she raised her glass and proposed a toast to her family.

If Genia had not had time to process Moun's passing in her head, she didn't show it. Having been suffering from the late stage of Alzheimer's, his death at the age of ninety-eight did not come as a total surprise. Choosing to go ahead with her birthday lunch and celebrate the life of her partner of fifty years at the same time was Genia's way of paying tribute to the man who had made her happy for half of her life.

Genia's attitude symbolises her spirit and attitude to life. At the age of 100, at the height of her wisdom, she wanted life to be celebrated.

That afternoon we laughed and dried our tears at her memories. We had travelled from at least four different countries to express our love, admiration and respect to the woman who for many years had been an example of strength and resilience for four generations of her descendants.

This was the last time Genia would see her entire family together. As I sat down next to her later in the afternoon to enjoy a few minutes of her undivided attention, she told me about her childhood and the postcards she used to write to her uncle in Russia. She always told him that she was happy to hear that he and his family were in good health.

She was grateful that my mother, Elena, and I had found them on the internet, that the two families were able to connect again and that eventually she met her first cousin Anna. As a child she would have never imagined that the recipients of her postcards would turn out to be real people, and that the small dark-haired girl in the photographs that arrived from the Soviet Union would one day travel to Geneva to introduce her to her own family.

In the twenty-first century, the two sides of our family have come full circle. Between London and Geneva, we speak French and English to each other, read the same books and watch the same films, often calling each other to discuss our experiences.

The two brothers, who had left their mother's home in Warsaw and travelled to the opposite ends of Europe, were seeking a better life. They had hopes for the future; they sought stability and prosperity, but ended up worlds apart. They never saw each other again, and their decisions affected the lives of their daughters. But their families were eventually reunited to share their stories. Having lived through separation and the political upheavals of the twentieth century, they couldn't believe their luck.

Genia and Anna. Geneva, 2010

Epilogue

London, 2020

On a quiet afternoon I visit my mum. Her resting place under a tree at a west London cemetery is serene. I don't come as often as I would like, but not a day goes by when I don't think about her. Today I've come to thank her. I've dedicated this book to her, and it was her I often thought about when I struggled with the story or the narrative.

My mother was fascinated with our family history and a line of women who lived as long as the century itself. She always believed that she had the same genes and would live to see her grandchildren, but her fate was decided otherwise.

She taught me that anything was possible if I set my mind to it. She always told me that I could do more, that I could do it better and that I had to dream big. A woman of many talents, she reinvented herself again and again, adjusting to the twists and turns that life threw her way. She taught me to make the most of every day and to enjoy every moment in life. I want to thank her for that, and I hope that I will be able to pass her message on to my daughters.

I also thank her for inspiring me to look for Adolphe's descendants, which, in turn, led to the writing of this book. Finding my Swiss family has been one of the most enriching experiences of my life. I feel a deep connection to my cousins in Switzerland, France and Israel, and knowing the shared history of our family has brought us closer together still.

The story of our family is not uncommon. Tragically, families are still being separated around the world. Political ideologies interfere in people's lives, making them flee towards greener horizons. Once there, they lose the connection to their native land and to their loved ones. They struggle to survive and sometimes they succumb to the injuries – physical and otherwise – inflicted on them by their oppressors and persecutors.

But it is by remembering events of centuries gone by that we can hopefully avoid making the same mistakes. It is by writing about the experiences of our ancestors that we keep their memories alive, and their lives remembered.

Acknowledgements

The book you hold in your hands would not have been possible without the publishing team at SilverWood Books. Helen Hart and Enya Holland have been incredibly patient in guiding me through the publishing process, and Eleanor Hardiman designed the most beautiful cover.

The meticulous work of my editor Anna Paterson transformed my writing.

The invaluable assistance of the historians and researchers who helped pull together the facts for this book must not go unnoticed. Jacques Davier at Archives de la Ville de Genève; Catherine Fischer at History Museum in Grenchen; Olivier Hottois at Musée Juif de Belgique;

Mikhail Katin-Yartsev, a Russian historian and genealogist who helped penetrate the Soviet archives; Salome Moser at Stadtarchiv Grenchen; Lawrence Paterson, whose infinite knowledge of WWII facts is second to none, and Anna Przybyszewska Drozd at The Emanuel Ringelblum Jewish Historical Institute in Warsaw – thank you for your help and enthusiasm for my family's history and for sharing your expertise to help me find out the truth about their journeys.

Anna Leader generously allowed me to use her translation of 'Die Lorelei', by Heinrich Heine.

I am forever indebted to all my friends who encouraged me to work on this book, and who later read drafts, asked difficult questions, spotted mistakes and offered solutions when I was at my wits' end. Alastair Elphick, Roland Hughes, Simon Kantor, Yan Leder, Daria Plakhova and Nabeelah Shabbir – you helped in more ways than you can imagine.

To my family: I am immensely grateful to have you in my life. My grandmother, Anna Nepomnyaschaya; Anita Volokhine; Youri Volokhine; Jean-Michel and Luisa Meyer; Yoni Yarom; and Herbert and Maryse Bonstein – thank you so much for answering my endless questions, sitting through hours of discussions, and not giving up on this project. It is with your help that I was able to put everything together and tell this story.

My aunt, Marina Neyman, added detail to my grandmother's stories where memory failed and helped me see Anna's life in perspective. She would have been excited to read more of her family history; it's a tragedy that she left us too soon. My sister, Katya Ragozhina, and Mark Sabah, you were immensely helpful whenever I tested your patience with questions and pleas for assistance, whether it was day or night. My father, Anatoly Landsman, talked me through life in the USSR when he felt I was losing my grasp of Soviet reality and made sure I didn't get lost in my own imagination.

It was a privilege and an honour to have met the matriarch of the Neuman/Neyman clan, Genia – my grandmother's first cousin. Her resolve and wisdom will stay with me for the rest of my life, and I am forever grateful to have been able to spend time with her. Her cousin, Maurice Dumtschin, the son of Marie's sister Berthe, was a real gentleman from a time gone by, and it was fascinating to hear his childhood stories of interactions with the Neuman household.

A special thank you to my (third) cousin Carole Bonstein, for her tireless efforts to unearth information about our family buried deep in the Swiss archives, and for her help navigating the family politics. Travelling together to Grenchen and Solothurn to see where Adolphe's journey began was an emotional experience for both of us. Thanks to her, this book was easier to write; and the past, easier to understand. It was also a lot of fun.

Ariane Bonstein has been an inspiration. My second cousin once removed, but this feels too distant a term to describe our bond. She has been my confidante and I can barely imagine a time when we didn't know each other. She let me into her life and that is the biggest treasure on earth.

My husband, Bård Aune – my (sometimes brutally) honest and vocal critic from the outset – he read too many drafts to count, spotted historical blunders, encouraged me to go on when I floundered, and listened to me endlessly read chapters and paragraphs aloud. He made me a better writer by questioning my assumptions and urging me to let go of the BBC journalist inside. Thank you for always being there, ready to discuss, brainstorm and imagine.

And most importantly, this book would not have happened at all without my mother, Elena. When, after our first visit to Geneva, I first said that a book should be written about our family, she told me that I would be the one to write it. I didn't believe her. Mum, I very rarely acknowledged that you were right, but you were right about this. I wish you could read it.

To contact the author, find out more about Nadia's journey to trace her roots, or check out an extended photo gallery of the Neuman and Neyman families, visit nadiaragozhina.com

Lightning Source UK Ltd.
Milton Keynes UK
UKHW010129211120
373782UK00003B/1117